IN SCIENCE'S
SHADOW

IN SCIENCE'S SHADOW

Literary

Constructions

of

Late Victorian

Women

PATRICIA MURPHY

University of Missouri Press
Columbia and London

Library of Congress Cataloging-in-Publication Data

Murphy, Patricia, 1951–
    In science's shadow : literary constructions of late Victorian women / Patricia Murphy.
        p. cm.
    Summary: "Through close analysis of noncanonical Victorian-era literature by
Thomas Hardy, Wilkie Collins, Charles Reade, Constance Naden, and Marianne North,
Murphy reveals how women were often marginalized, constricted, and defined as intellectually inferior as a result of the interplay of sociohistorical trends driven by scientific
curiosity and the 'Woman Question' "—Provided by publisher.
    Includes bibliographical references and index.
    ISBN-13: 978-0-8262-1682-3 (hard cover : alk. paper)
    ISBN-10: 0-8262-1682-X (hard cover : alk. paper)
    1. English literature—19th century—History and criticism. 2. Literature and
science—Great Britain—History—19th century. 3. Sexism in science—Great Britain—
History—19th century. 4. Women in science. 5. Women in literature. 6. Sexism in
literature. 7. Prejudices in literature. 8. Marginality, Social, in literature. I. Title.
    PR468.S34M87 2006
    820.9'356—dc22   2006028281

♾ This paper meets the requirements of the
American National Standard for Permanence of Paper
for Printed Library Materials, Z39.48, 1984.

Designer: *foleydesign*
Typesetter: Bookcomp, Inc.
Printer and binder: Thomson-Shore, Inc.
Typefaces: Bauer Bodoni, Castellar, and Minion

In Memory of
My Wonderful Parents,
Sue and James Murphy

Contents

Acknowledgments

I will be forever grateful to my extraordinary parents, Sue and James B. Murphy, whose unfailing love, encouragement, kindness, and wisdom have been so important in my life. Though my parents are gone now, their influence will always be with me and everyone else whose lives they touched, especially those less fortunate. I wish my parents could have seen this book, which they were so supportive of, be published.

There are many others to whom I owe a debt of gratitude. Heidi Johnson Carrier has, as always, been a true friend and invaluable colleague. Her astute commentary and suggestions throughout this project are greatly appreciated. I also wish to thank Kris Swenson for her sound advice as this book moved toward publication. The anonymous readers of my manuscript provided many helpful suggestions for revision, and I appreciate the time and energy they gave. I am grateful as well to *Victorian Poetry* for permission to publish in this book a modified version of my article on Constance Naden's poetry.

Thanks also go to my sister and brother, Sue Roche and Jim Murphy, for their unflagging interest and support in this project. Finally, I wish to thank K. Schoenbrod for sage advice that has made such a difference in my life.

IN SCIENCE'S
SHADOW

1

Introduction

The Gendered Context of Victorian Science

Statements that Victorians were intrigued by science and preoccupied with the Woman Question are certainly not extraordinary pronouncements, since both nonfictional and fictional texts of the period amply display the significance these concerns held. As numerous nineteenth-century essays and treatises composed by biologists, physicians, anthropologists, psychologists, and other scientists disclose, the two issues were often overtly interwoven, with "objective" findings ostensibly providing conclusive evidence that long-standing cultural perceptions of an innate female inferiority were correct. Literature, too, brought the Victorian engrossment with science and gender to the fore, albeit often in a highly subtle manner, to posit or interrogate a causal relationship between them. Though interest in gendered science was reflected in literature throughout the Victorian period, some of the most complex and compelling texts to scrutinize the topic appeared in the late decades of the century. Perhaps the 1871 publication of Charles Darwin's *Descent of Man, and Selection in Relation to Sex* acted as a kind of cultural trigger for stimulating literary interest in the subject through the treatise's gender-charged scientific assertions and the prominence of its controversial author. Among the most instructive and fascinating of post-*Descent* literary offerings providing valuable insights into gendered science are those featuring a woman directly affected by science. Such writings placed the multifarious gender configurations of Victorian scientific thought in sharp focus through the intense attention given women's close encounters with the scientific world. In the chapters that follow, I explore several of these illuminating literary texts—produced by a poet, a memoirist, and three novelists—that intertwine science and gender in utterly engrossing ways. By foregrounding science as a major thematic element and centering on women whose lives are so dramatically shaped by it, these texts provide especially significant revelations about gendered science that underlay other contemporaneous literary works as well.

My goal in this study is not to provide an exhaustive analysis of late Victorian literature featuring women linked to science but to delve microscopically into a sampling of texts, all noncanonical, that illustrate the telling ways in which scientific discourse could be manipulated to define, marginalize, and exclude women. Though previous literature had at times presented women characters with connections to science, primarily in the sometimes controversial figure of a nurse, late Victorian writings were inclined to probe the topic more broadly and intensively. Whether reifying or refuting presumed verities about gender and science, the texts performed important cultural work through their participation in the debate over the disquieting Woman Question.

Aside from the influence of scientific texts such as *The Descent of Man,* literary speculation on gendered science can be attributed to the cultural turmoil of the late century. With pressures to broaden women's educational opportunities, expand occupational horizons, address inequities in marriage laws, interrogate sexual mores, consider the New Woman's agenda, and alleviate dissatisfaction in sundry other matters affecting women, it is no surprise that gender-related anxieties would intensify. Nor is it astonishing that scientific speculations would be marshaled both to validate and to undermine long-standing presumptions that women were inherently and immutably inferior to men. Science served as a powerful weapon that could be deployed to stifle or stimulate social change directed at enabling women to loosen some of the constraints associated with their domestic universe.

Despite the fact that much of Darwin's *Descent* emphasized the animal kingdom and human development in general, pertinent passages reinforced both long-standing and contemporaneous suppositions of male superiority that carried important ramifications for Victorian society. Darwin commented, for example, that "[m]an is more powerful in body and mind than woman," and he displays "greater intellectual vigor and power of invention." In an unflattering comparison between women and children, Darwin surmised that the latter "resemble the mature female much more closely than the mature male." Darwin additionally pointed to certain traits women supposedly evidenced far more than did men—"powers of intuition, of rapid perception, and perhaps of imitation"—which, at least to some extent, he deemed "characteristic of the lower races, and therefore of a past and lower state of civilization."[1]

Darwin summarized the matter in no uncertain terms with this oft-cited comment:

> The chief distinction in the intellectual powers of the two sexes is shown by man's attaining to a higher eminence, in whatever he takes up, than can woman—whether requiring deep thought, reason, or imagination, or merely the use of the senses and hands. If two lists were made of the most eminent men and women in poetry, painting, sculpture, music (inclusive both of composition and performance), history, science, and philosophy, with half a dozen names under each subject, the two lists would not bear comparison. We may also infer, . . . that if men are capable of a decided pre-eminence over women in many subjects, the average of mental power in man must be above that of woman.[2]

Literature penned after *Descent*'s publication reveals a familiarity not only with Darwin's precepts, however, but with an array of gendered scientific suppositions circulating in the culture at large. Dissemination of purportedly objective scientific findings was not limited to the pages of professional journals or comprehensive tomes; it extended into general-interest publications, provided by social observers as well as scientists, and these writings were avidly consumed by a lay audience, as recent

1. Charles Darwin, *The Descent of Man, and Selection in Relation to Sex*, 620, 628, 580, 587.
2. Darwin, *Descent*, 587.

scholarship has shown.[3] Like the nonfiction essays and treatises, the literary treatments of scientific topics were at times skewed and confused, even more so as literature compounded error through misinterpretation of prevalent conclusions or reprisal of discarded theories.

Though an overt interrelationship between science and gender may have received less literary attention before *Descent,* the culture's enormous interest in and familiarity with scientific topics themselves, fueled especially by Darwin's monumental 1859 *On the Origin of Species,* were certainly tapped by diverse and widely read writers. The opening paragraph of Charles Dickens's 1853 *Bleak House,* for example, reminds readers of geological discoveries that pushed back the age of the earth to a startlingly distant time in musing that the sodden London streets appeared "as if the waters had but newly retired from the face of the earth, and it would not be wonderful to meet a Megalosaurus, forty feet long or so, waddling like an elephantine lizard up Holburn Hill." The novel's preface includes Dickens's well-known defense of his belief in spontaneous combustion, stating that he had taken "pains to investigate the subject" and referring to "the recorded opinions and experiences of distinguished medical professors." Earlier, the 1836 *Pickwick Papers* also began with scientific references by mentioning "the unwearied researches of Samuel Pickwick" and pondering "the inestimable benefits which must inevitably result from carrying the speculations of that learned man into a wider field." Assuming that a reader would recognize the humor, the first chapter identifies Pickwick as "the man who had traced to their source the mighty ponds of Hampstead, and agitated the scientific world with his Theory of Tittlebats," and the chapter additionally refers to the Pickwick Club's "proceedings of great men" in a phrase reminiscent of the weighty deliberations of scientific bodies.[4]

Other influential texts of the high Victorian period also reflected a

3. Modern scholarly work has also been immensely valuable in unearthing and providing anthologies of important scientific writings. I wish to express my gratitude to the compilers of such work for pointing toward many important primary sources addressed in my study, especially the following anthologies: Katharina Rowold, ed., *Gender and Science: Late Nineteenth-Century Debates on the Female Mind and Body;* Jenny Bourne Taylor and Sally Shuttleworth, eds., *Embodied Selves: An Anthology of Psychological Texts, 1830–1890;* Barbara T. Gates, ed., *In Nature's Name: An Anthology of Women's Writing and Illustration, 1780–1930;* and Regina Barreca, ed., *Desire and Imagination: Classic Essays in Sexuality.*

4. Charles Dickens, *Bleak House,* 49, 42; Dickens, *The Pickwick Papers,* 67–69.

cultural absorption in scientific issues. Tennyson's lengthy 1850 "In Memoriam," for one, conveyed a comfortable familiarity with scientific developments through its references to such matters as the earth's formation, humanity's beginnings, and evolutionary progression. Like other contemporaneous novels, both *Jane Eyre* and *Wuthering Heights* featured among their arrays of characters the minor figure of a physician, whose profession would receive greater focus many years later in *Middlemarch.*[5] The psychology of madness captured the popular imagination, manifested in sensation novels of the 1860s, and in an obvious confluence of science and gender in pre-*Descent* literature, rapt attention to female madness was apparent in the characterization of Lady Audley, and more than a decade earlier, Bertha Mason. Charles Kingsley's 1863 *Water Babies,* a fantasy spawned directly from evolutionary ideas, revealed the profound influence of Darwin's *Origin.*

In our own time, of course, critical commentary has probed the workings of Victorian science in literature, often specifically within a Darwinian framework. George Levine, for instance, investigates Dickens's oeuvre in particular, tracing scientific resonances in such novels as *Little Dorrit, Martin Chuzzlewit,* and *Our Mutual Friend,* as well as *Bleak House* and *The Pickwick Papers.* Scientific elements wending their way through the fiction of George Eliot, Anthony Trollope, and Thomas Hardy, as Levine discusses, display the culture's interest in Darwinian discourse, both directly and indirectly. Gillian Beer's detailed study of the Darwinian shaping of the narratives of Eliot and Hardy further attests to the vital role scientific precepts played in Victorian fiction. Other scholarship cites numerous texts spanning the century that exhibit varied scientific influences, including many noncanonical writings such as Elizabeth Gaskell's 1848 *Mary Barton,* Benjamin Disraeli's 1847 *Tancred,* Kingsley's 1850 *Alton Locke,* and the late-century evolutionary writings of Samuel Butler.[6]

5. I am using the term *physician* broadly here rather than indicating a specific form of practitioner such as an apothecary or surgeon.

6. George Levine, *Darwin and the Novelists: Patterns of Science in Victorian Fiction;* Gillian Beer, *Darwin's Plots.* See also, for example, J. A. V. Chapple, *Science and Literature in the Nineteenth Century,* Janis McLarren Caldwell, *Literature and Medicine in Nineteenth-Century Britain: From Mary Shelley to George Eliot,* Lilian R. Furst, ed., *Medical Progress and Social Reality: A Reader in Nineteenth-Century Medicine and Literature,* and Kristine Swenson, *Medical Women and Victorian Fiction.*

It is instructive at this point to look more closely at a handful of literary texts appearing almost at the same moment as *Descent*. Though they addressed scientific issues, they did not do so in elaborate gender configurations, perhaps because *Descent* had not yet had sufficient opportunity to influence these early writings. Most obvious in this short catalog is the 1871–1872 *Middlemarch*, with its extensive treatment of medical debates and advances occurring earlier in the century presented through the characterization of the ill-fated Lydgate and his clashes with fellow medical practitioners. Despite being "fired with the possibility that he might . . . make a link in the chain of discovery," Lydgate, of course, fails in his desire to meld the "pursuit of a great idea which was to be a twin object with assiduous practice of his profession."[7] The argument could be proffered that the novel is making a statement about science and gender simply through a male physician's being a central character and the machinations of his frivolous wife to draw him from serious scientific pursuits to a more lucrative practice; yet the presence of a male physician is certainly not an extraordinary occurrence in Victorian fiction, nor are the gender inflections of Lydgate's situation developed to any extensive degree. Similarly, Hardy's 1873 *A Pair of Blue Eyes* could be interpreted as quietly interrogating the masculine nature of science; the novel's signature and frequently cited scene presents a kind of evolutionary timeline as barrister Henry Knight, fascinated by geological matters, struggles to maintain his hold on a dangerous cliff from which he is ultimately rescued by the novel's female protagonist. Yet again, an in-depth examination of gender and science is not present. It is later in the decade that literature tends to address the gender implications of scientific conclusions more prominently.

Perhaps the most obvious example of such attention is Eliot's 1876 *Daniel Deronda*. As Gillian Beer has demonstrated, the novel displays the workings of sexual selection on a human scale, reversing the customary practice found among animal species in that men rather than women wielded the power of selection. Beer comments on Eliot's recognition that sexual selection served the agenda of a male-dominated society, observing that women's function as reproductive vessels came under increased scrutiny as well. Also indicative of *Descent*'s preoccupations is

7. George Eliot, *Middlemarch*, 146, 147.

George Meredith's 1879 *The Egoist* with its overt references to sexual selection. Clara's choice of the title character is described in Darwinian terms by the narrator, who muses that "[w]e now scientifically know that in this department of the universal struggle, success is awarded to the bettermost." Sounding as if it was taken from the pages of *Descent,* the narrative continues, "You spread a handsomer tail than your fellows, you dress a finer top-knot, you pipe a newer note, have a longer stride; she reviews you in competition, and selects you." Despite the intriguing revelations of these novels, neither can offer the unique gender perspectives that late Victorian texts featuring women with a more direct relationship to science can provide.[8]

A suggestion that this specific focus appears primarily in noncanonical writings may seem at first glance an odd one, but these texts occupy a rather unique place in literary history; in effect, a kind of canonical vacuum existed. By 1871, Dickens was dead, as were Charlotte and Emily Brontë. Tennyson had turned his attention to Arthurian legend and other thematic preoccupations, and the prolific Pre-Raphaelite poets were entranced with nonscientific concerns. In the years following publication of *Descent* and other nonfictional writings that helped to stimulate literature's yoking of science and gender, few well-known authors were focusing upon the subject in general, much less more specifically on a woman's interactions with the scientific world.

In the chapters that follow, I examine provocative noncanonical writings through highly detailed readings so as to consider not only the relatively apparent connections between gender and science, but also the myriad shadings of language that are so immensely instructive in revealing crucial nuances.[9] Science in these writings participates in the delin-

8. Beer, *Darwin's Plots,* 211, 220; George Meredith, *The Egoist,* 37. Leo J. Henkin also makes this point about sexual selection in his discussion of the quote I cite. The main character "congratulates himself that Clara, who has money and health, beauty and breeding, has chosen him as mate above the many others who have been competing for her hand" (205). Henkin states, "There need be no doubt that George Meredith completely espoused the Darwinian principle of sexual selection, as he expressed it in *The Egoist*" (*Darwinism in the English Novel, 1860–1910: The Impact of Evolution on Victorian Fiction,* 205–6).

9. I wish to clarify a point about my own use of language as well. Though certainly recognizing the heterogeneity of Victorian women, scientific thought, and social concerns, I use such terms as *woman, womanhood, scientific discourse, culture,* and *Victorian mind* to underscore the homogeneous assumptions that typified much nineteenth-century thought.

eation of feminine and masculine domains with clear boundaries, and the texts labor to reinforce, question, or elide those divisions. Though recent scholarship has suggested that the concept of separate spheres did, in reality, offer more space for female agency and self-determination than previously assumed in cultural study, the texts I investigate tend to assume a sharp demarcation between private and public realms. Informing my hermeneutic objective are the early theorizations of Luce Irigaray, Julia Kristeva, Hélène Cixous, and Judith Butler, which are especially appropriate in briefly establishing a helpful perspective for analysis.

Rather than progressing chronologically in the subsequent chapters, or grouping texts according to male or female authorship, I believe that a thematic approach works most effectively in revealing the various strategies by which science could be perceived to participate in the marginalization of Victorian women. In brief, the chapter progression traces the following maneuvers in the late-century texts I explore: first, a bleak recognition that scientific discourse indeed establishes itself as a gendered space providing little play for female agency; second, a determined effort to reinforce and protect such a gendered binary; third, a vituperative textual response to a transgressive female character who dares violate the binary and indulge in scientific study; fourth, a narrative strategy of denial whereby a female voice attempts to neutralize and transcend the gender implications of science; and finally, a seemingly positive and hopeful portrayal of a woman scientist that instead underscores the disturbing essentialist preconceptions of the discipline. With this brief encapsulation of the thematic approach in mind, let me turn more fully to the particular focus of each chapter.

I begin my study with the 1880s poetry of Constance Naden, a natural-sciences enthusiast whose numerous verses carefully demonstrate that women are excluded from and by the scientific realm. The verses' formal elements participate significantly in this objective and thus are worthy of lengthy discussion, I believe, in that poetic conventions are both adopted and manipulated through sophisticated techniques to convey with striking emphasis the unsettling messages relayed by thematic content. Throughout Naden's oeuvre a distinctly pessimistic tone persists as female characters are refused access to or diminished by the masculinized scientific domain.

Chapter 3 points to the disturbing textual approval rather than disapprobation of women's marginalization by and from science with Thomas Hardy's 1882 *Two on a Tower*. Though generally deemed a "minor" novel in Hardy's oeuvre, the narrative represents a highly complex treatment of gendered science. *Two on a Tower* compulsively attempts to demarcate and protect science as an exclusionary masculine arena by constructing a tight and seemingly inviolable binarism. Nevertheless, female intrusion constantly threatens, often even as the novel is busily at work buttressing science's gender-delineated boundaries. The novel reveals an overwhelming apprehension of female encroachment into this male-defined space and the sense that an accompanying contamination, disruption, and subversion poses a continual menace.

Next, I examine one of Wilkie Collins's later novels, the 1883 *Heart and Science,* which also is frequently categorized as a minor novel but, like *Two on a Tower,* is an important text for assessing the gendered aspects of science. *Heart and Science* moves alarmingly beyond the anxieties presented in *Two on a Tower* by vituperatively denouncing a woman captivated by science. Her absorption in this avocation is blamed directly for her abhorrent behavior as a wife and mother. Incessantly assailed for her shortcomings as a Victorian woman, she is presented as a figure of both condemnation and ridicule. Her deviation from the feminine ideal is brought into acute relief through a comparison to the conventional niece whom she nearly succeeds in destroying. The point is insistently made that a woman is intended to be a passive object of science, not an active agent.

In Chapter 5, I move to nonfictional writing in assessing the autobiographical travel accounts of painter and botanist Marianne North, which pursue a rather unexpected strategy to respond to the gender ramifications of science. North's narrative voice seeks to neutralize such gendered elements by proceeding as if they can simply be bracketed off. The lengthy memoir attempts to establish an ungendered space from which North can speak with authority, indirectly responding to scientific pronouncements of female inferiority by endeavoring to establish rhetorical distance from prevalent essentializing perceptions. In effect, the narrator seeks a kind of disembodiment to further this project of gender neutralization.

Chapter 6 focuses on the fictional plight of a scientifically oriented woman who struggles for acceptance as a physician in Charles Reade's

1877 *A Woman-Hater.* Her choice of profession seemingly would cast her as a transgressive figure, yet the novel expresses much sympathy. That apparently progressive stance is problematized, however, by *A Woman-Hater*'s adherence to troubling essentialist presumptions; the novel contends that women are temperamentally more suited than men to become physicians and believes that women will eventually evolve toward the higher mental capacity traditionally attributed to men. *A Woman-Hater* casts its female physician as a kind of evolutionary pioneer who will help shape future generations of "womanly" medical practitioners. Yet the novel's own female doctor is regarded as a masculinized anomaly.

Before investigating these absorbing literary texts, however, it is helpful to review prevalent scientific conclusions so as to provide an appropriate interpretive framework. My intent here is not to break new archival ground but to summarize the dominant strains of scientific thought that functioned to marginalize women, along with the occasional dissent, shortly before and subsequent to Darwin's declarations on the issue. To provide a full picture, I include references to materials published even after the literary texts I will be addressing in subsequent chapters. Those later scientific materials would, of course, have been influenced by discourses circulating the culture in previous decades.

Despite Victorian presumptions that science was an objective field, proceeding disinterestedly from hypotheses to conclusions, in actuality the process was infused with cultural prejudices and subjective preconceptions. As W. B. Carpenter surmised in an 1872 presidential address to the British Association for the Advancement of Science, the "surest" assessments "are those dictated by what we term 'Common Sense.'" Nowhere was cultural bias more evident than in the "common sense" pronouncements on women, particularly in regard to mental ability.[10] The scientific judgments on the female mind tended to follow several

10. W. B. Carpenter, "Man the Interpreter of Nature," 422. As Susan Sleeth Mosedale relates, scientists "provided rationales and prescriptions based *outside* of science for maintaining the female status quo." She adds that the scientists rarely "evaluate[d] hypotheses distinct from social consequences" ("Science Corrupted: Victorian Biologists Consider 'The Woman Question,'" 3). See also Cynthia Eagle Russett, *Sexual Science: The Victorian Construction of Womanhood,* and Rachel Malane, *Sex in Mind: The Gendered Brain in Nineteenth-Century Literature and Mental Sciences.* Because I learned of Malane's new book late in the production of my own, I am limited to footnote references of similar interests.

prominent yet intersecting paths. Though these strands of opinion resist individual analysis because of their interdependence, efforts to unpack these concepts nevertheless prove fruitful for understanding their nature, scope, and acceptance. As the extensive quotations show, Victorian scientific observers pursued an array of rhetorical strategies to gain credence for their often outlandish contentions.

EMOTIONALITY VERSUS RATIONALITY

Although Darwin's *Descent* helped to establish the parameters of late-century scientific discourses on the female mind, the issue itself was by no means revolutionary. The traditional supposition that men were the more rational and intellectual sex, whereas women were the more emotional and intuitive sex, had long prevailed. In the nineteenth century, this cultural verity simply gained additional force through scientific pronouncements that purported to bring irrefutable evidence of a biologically determined and physiologically immutable difference. Shortly before *Descent* appeared, the presumably sex-based distinction between emotionality and rationality was smugly summarized by anthropologist J. McGrigor Allan in an 1869 essay confidently titled, "On the Real Differences in the Minds of Men and Women." As Allan characterized the distinction, "man's realm is the intellect—woman's the affections." One of Allan's contemporaries, fellow anthropologist Luke Owen Pike, similarly observed in 1872 that "[i]f man's highest prerogative is to think, woman's noblest function is to love." Claiming biological grounding for his contentions, Pike agreed with the generally accepted belief that women "possess . . . more emotional characters." To underscore his point, Pike asserted that "it will hardly be denied that in all ages and in all climates women are and have been more prone to the display of emotion than pure reason." Even earlier, T. H. Huxley wrote in 1865 that "[w]omen are, by nature, more excitable than men—prone to be swept by tides of emotion, proceeding from hidden and inward, as well as from obvious and external causes."[11]

More than a decade later, Allan continued to press the matter. In an

11. J. McGrigor Allan, "On the Real Differences in the Minds of Men and Women," cci; Luke Owen Pike, "Woman and Political Power," 86, 84, 85; Thomas H. Huxley, *Science and Education Essays*, 71.

1881 essay in *Knowledge,* Allan reiterated that "[m]an is a being of the intellect; woman of instinct and emotion." Therefore, "[m]an reasons and reflects; woman perceives and feels." In stressing that "[t]o man belongs the kingdom of the head; to woman the empire of the heart," Allan approvingly quoted an assertion that "[w]oman has a cell less in the head, a fibre more in the heart." In case any obtuse reader missed his point, Allan reiterated that a woman "is less guided by intellect than by feeling and impulse." Even feminist Antoinette Brown Blackwell, who argued that women were by no means mentally inferior to men, made such essentialist statements. "Women's thoughts are impelled by their feelings," Blackwell wrote.[12]

Prominent psychologist George Romanes echoed Allan's opinions a few years later, maintaining that a woman's emotions "are almost always less under control of the will" than those of a man, which makes her "more apt to break away . . . from the restraint of reason." In his 1887 essay, Romanes proceeded to catalog the presumably "meritorious qualities" in which women excel, seamlessly reinforcing the cultural view of the appropriate characteristics of a proper woman: "affection, sympathy, devotion, self-denial, modesty; long-suffering, . . . reverence, veneration, religious feeling, and general morality." Two years later, the highly influential *Evolution of Sex* by Patrick Geddes and J. Arthur Thomson followed the premise that males were "katabolic," or more active, than the "anabolic" females. Among the traits the scientists assigned on the basis of this distinction were that women, "especially as mothers, have indubitably a larger and more habitual share of the altruistic emotions." Women "excel in constancy of affection and in sympathy," one of the "facts" the scientists identified as "consistent with the general theory of sex and verifiable in common experience." In sum, "[m]an thinks more, wom[a]n feels more."[13]

Even the final decade of the century saw such opinions being mouthed. Psychological specialist Harry Campbell advised in 1891 not

12. J. McGrigor Allan, "Influence of Sex on Mind: Cranial Contour," 78; Antoinette Brown Blackwell, *The Sexes throughout Nature,* 131.
13. George J. Romanes, "Mental Differences between Men and Women," 657, 658; Patrick Geddes and J. Arthur Thomson, *The Evolution of Sex,* 270–71. In a less complimentary mode than his above utterances, Romanes cited Francis Galton's studies of sex-based differences, which supposedly " 'begin to assert themselves even in the nursery, where all children are treated alike' " (662). The female, Galton noted, " 'is capricious and coy, and has less straightforwardness.' "

only that women were "less intellectual" but that the "emotional and intellectual portions" of females and males exist "somewhat in inverse ratio." Resembling children, Campbell added, women are "inclined to be weak-willed, acting upon the impulse of the moment" with their "very emotional" natures. The same year, the positivist Frederic Harrison postulated that women proceed "rather through sympathy than through action," through a function "equally intellectual as that of men, but acting more through the imagination, and less through logic." He concluded that "[t]he heart of the matter is the greater power of affection in Woman, or, it is better to say, the greater degree in which the nature of Woman is stimulated and controlled by affection." Harrison identified her "true function" as educating children and men to achieve "a higher civilization." Like Romanes, Harrison reinforced the Victorian ideal of womanhood in claiming that a female would achieve this educational goal by "diffusing the spirit of affection, of self-restraint, self-sacrifice, fidelity, and purity." To Harrison, "[t]he spontaneous and inexhaustible fountain of love, the secret springs whereof are the mystery of womanhood, this is indeed the grand and central difference between the sexes." Women's intellect, he stated, was "[p]lainly" marked by greater delicacy, emotionality, and sensitivity than men's but "less capable of prolonged tension, of intense abstraction, of wide range, and of extraordinary complication."[14]

Indirectly, suppositions about male rationality and female emotionality helped support the cultural verity that the sexes were meant to be complementary, not competitive. The concept of complementarity occasionally threaded through scientific and popular discourse as a means of bolstering perceived sexually specific mental qualities. Physician Henry Maudsley, for instance, argued in an infamous 1874 essay that, though complementary, the sexes were decidedly not equal. "[T]he female qualities of mind . . . adapt her . . . to be the helpmate and companion of man," Maudsley contended. The belief that "[m]an and woman do complement one another's being" was "no less true of mind than it is of body," he insisted. Many observers averred that the sexes did not necessarily display a relationship of inferiority and supe-

14. Harry Campbell, *Differences in the Nervous Organisation of Man and Woman: Physiological and Pathological*, 84, 162; Frederic Harrison, "The Emancipation of Women," 442, 444–46.

riority, but instead one of difference; nevertheless, they made clear in describing the sexes' mental traits that males were indeed superior. Anthropologist Pike, for example, though claiming "there is neither superiority nor inferiority" in the sexes, immediately protested that "it does not therefore follow, as has been hastily assumed, that there is equality." He opined that "women, on the average, prefer millinery to geology, and men, on the average, applaud the preference." Anonymous articles in the *Saturday Review* and *Westminster Review* also heralded the presumed complementarity of the sexes, with the former noting in 1871 that "the advance of our race has been marked by an increasing diversity between men and women, which makes one, not the contradiction, but the complement of the other." In an essay nervously titled "Female Poaching on Male Preserves," the *Westminster Review* maintained in 1888 that "[f]rom the starting-point of history, and all along its path, woman figures as the complement of man"; in fact, "[s]he has ever followed his evolution, albeit in the rear." Underlying the theory of complementarity was the often-stated notion that other female traits helped women to compensate for their lesser intellectuality.[15]

THE SEXED MIND

With such assertions on a sex-based link between emotionality and rationality, the slippage into more critical differences between female and male minds would seem to Victorian scientists a logical extension of their ideas. Ultimately, the varied and sexually specific traits the scientists would assign to mental ability enabled many to argue that men were more intelligent, based on physiological laws, and were destined to remain unequivocally superior to women in this regard. The premise that the sexes' mental capacities differed in kind as well as degree was so widely accepted that not until the later years of the century did serious resistance emerge, in large part due to the enviable achievements women had displayed in the newly opened university programs and occasionally in professional venues. Darwin helped set the tenor of the early discussion by arguing in *Descent* that "[w]oman seems to differ from man

15. Henry Maudsley, "Sex in Mind and in Education," 472; Pike, "Woman and Political Power," 82–84; "The Probable Retrogression of Women," 11; "Female Poaching on Male Preserves," 290.

in mental disposition," as well as by noting that "[m]an is more coura-geous, pugnacious, and energetic than woman, and has a more inventive genius."[16]

In the same vein, Herbert Spencer disputed the concept that the sexes were "mentally alike," asserting that such a contention was "as untrue" as if the sexes were "alike bodily." To Spencer, "[t]he representative fac-ulty in women deals quickly and clearly with the personal, the special, and the immediate," while she "less rapidly grasps the general and the impersonal." He blamed a woman's "vivid imagination of simple di-rect consequences" for this perceived shortcoming, which "mostly shuts out from her mind the imagination of consequences that are complex and indirect." To women, Spencer had assigned "the ability to distin-guish quickly the passing feelings of those around," a characteristic so frequently demonstrated that it represented "a feminine faculty." Dif-ferences in reproductive responsibilities led to the sexes' varied mental traits, he argued, as did numerous other Victorian scientists.[17]

Anthropologist J. McGrigor Allan also weighed in on the issue. In his 1869 essay, the frequently vitriolic Allan exclaimed stridently that "*there must be radical, natural, permanent distinctions*" in the sexes' mental abil-ities. Allan's often outrageous and acerbic commentary is particularly appropriate for extensive quotation, not only because his words mirror and anticipate prevalent sentiments but because they reveal the inten-sity with which the scientific community approached the question of female mental ability. "In reflective power," he avowed, "woman is ut-terly unable to compete with man." He maintained that "[a] woman will (by a power similar to that sort of semi-reason by which animals avoid what is hurtful, and seek what is necessary to their existence) ar-rive instantaneously at a correct opinion on a subject to which a man cannot attain, save by a long and complicated process of reasoning." The female's physiological constitution fails to "lead her in the purely intellectual direction," he scoffed. Indeed, a woman "is content, in most instances, to let others think for her" and "discover[s] the most proper person to do so."[18]

16. Darwin, *Descent,* 586, 580. For background on this issue, see Joan N. Burstyn, "Education and Sex: The Medical Case against Higher Education for Women in England, 1870–1900."

17. Herbert Spencer, "Psychology of the Sexes," 31, 36, 33.

18. Allan, "On the Real Differences," cxcvi, cxcvii, cci.

Not even education, Allan believed, could elevate a woman's intellect to the level of a man's. A woman educated "to the utmost of her capacity" will still be unable to compete with an uneducated male, whose conclusions will reveal a "more profound, broad, and luminous" cognitive faculty. Allan considered such attempts at intellectual parity to be not only fruitless but dangerous. "Any encroachment of one sex on the physical and mental characteristics of the other, is unnatural and repulsive to all well-constituted minds of men and women," he said. "A woman with a masculine mind, is as anomalous a creature, as a woman with a man's breasts, a man's pelvis, a man's muscular leg, or a man's beard."[19]

Biology, Allan prophesied, would unfailingly prevail: "[I]n intellectual power, woman will always fall far short of man, owing to the important distinction in physical organisation between the sexes," which predisposes men for intellectual and women for reproductive work. "In man we have a being formed expressly for undergoing long-sustained mental and physical labour," he explained, whereas "[i]n woman, nature has produced a being whose principal functions are evidently intended to be love, leading to gestation, parturition, and nutrition."[20]

If biology did not convince skeptics, Allan apparently believed his conception of cultural and historical evidence would. As proof, Allan noted that "[t]he inventing, discovering, creating, cogitating mind is pre-eminently masculine," so much so that "the history of humanity is conclusive as to the mental supremacy of the male sex." He elaborated:

> Men carry on the business of the world in the two great departments—*thought* and *action;* the ideas on which depend all the marvellous acts of human intelligence. . . . So little demand is there for the direct assistance of women in the mental departments which are the special province of man, that could all the male intellect in the world be suddenly paralysed or annihilated, there is not sufficient development of the abstract principles of justice, morality, truth, or of causality and inventive power in the female sex, to hold the mechanism of society together for one week.

Allan returned to this point in an 1882 *Knowledge* essay, pontificating that "[t]he ideas on which depend all the marvellous acts of human

19. Ibid., cxcvii, ccii.
20. Ibid., ccvi.

intelligence, scientific discoveries, jurisprudence, political, civil, military institutions, [and] maintaining the social structure, are elaborated by men." Moreover, "[i]n the domain of pure intellect it is doubtful if women have contributed one profound original idea of any permanent value." Instead, "almost every woman is steered through life by the reflecting brain, strong will, and protecting arm of a husband, father, brother, or son."[21]

Other anthropological enthusiasts also expressed their views on mental ability. The remarks of Emma Wallington at an 1874 anthropological society meeting departed from the misogynistic utterances of a J. Mc-Grigor Allan or a Luke Owen Pike in adamantly arguing that male and female minds were not innately dissimilar. Presenting a catalog of distinguished women scientists, Wallington asserted that "the weight of the evidence goes to show that the intellectual capacity of woman does not differ from man's more than that of men differs among themselves; in other words, the differences are not so much of *sex* as of *individuals*." The prevalent bias against "learned" women, Wallington added, "has generally conveyed the sting of reproach instead of the sweet balm of commendation," with the result that "our wonder is—not that women have accomplished so much entitling them to enter the highest intellectual ranks—but that they should have done anything at all." Wallington urged, "[L]et us cast off the mischievous dogma that encourages a faith in *man's* power to elevate himself, while it denies the possession of this power to *woman,* and meets her attempts at emancipation from intellectual thraldom with covert sneers and chilling depreciation."[22]

Not unexpectedly, Wallington's remarks were received poorly by her male audience. In a discussion following Wallington's paper, several participants dismissed her conclusions in following the well-trodden rhetorical avenues disputing women's cognitive equality. "I find an argument essentially feminine, both in its line of reasoning and deductions," sniffed one respondent. He proceeded to claim that "[w]omen can compete successfully with man in following out a beaten path" but lack "the grasp of intellect and the vigour and the boldness" that males display. "[I]n the divine scheme of creation," he added in a standard reactionary

---

21. Ibid., ccx; Allan, "Influence of Sex on Mind: III. Historical Evidence," 230, 231.
22. Emma Wallington, "The Physical and Intellectual Capacities of Woman Equal to Those of Man," 559, 560.

comment, "women are born inferior to man, both in body and mind." Another meeting participant reiterated the cultural principle that "[t]he proper sphere for woman was to excel as a daughter, a sister, a wife, and a mother" who would "guid[e] and prepar[e] the young for important stages of life." The organization's president, though conceding "that women are, to a great extent, kept back," nevertheless reasserted "the general rule, viz., that intellectually women are inferior to men" and pointed to the tiresome argument that "[w]omen have never attained the summit of any art or science."[23]

Although scientific utterances attesting to a marked difference in male and female intellects composed the dominant thread of discourse on the issue, Wallington was not alone in registering disagreement. Among the dissenters was Antoinette Brown Blackwell, who wrote in 1870 that "I find nothing in physiology which indicates that the woman's intellect is organically inferior to the man's intellect." Even earlier, botanist Lydia Becker responded to long-standing cultural and quasi-scientific views by stating that "the attribute of sex does not extend to mind"; there is "no distinction between the intellects of men and women," she stressed. Moreover, there is no greater difference between men and women in intellectual ability "than may be found between two men or two women."[24]

Like John Stuart Mill, several writers blamed circumstances rather than innate abilities for a perceived difference between male and female mental ability. Writing a year before Mill's 1869 *Subjection of Women*, Becker argued that "women have been pent in a small corner." Their supposed mental inferiority stemmed from "the influence of the different circumstances under which they pass their lives," not inherent qualities. "[E]very botanist [is] aware that female plants are quite as strong and big as male ones of the same species," she emphasized. Blackwell's 1870 essay asserted that it would be "impossible to judge of the relative ability of the sexes from an impartial historical basis," for "outside limitations have always been unequal—so unequal that the feminine intellect has been virtually checkmated from the beginning." Blackwell further noted that "external influences . . . are certainly more than sufficient to account for

23. Ibid. ("Discussion"), 560, 561, 563.
24. Antoinette Brown Blackwell, "Comparative Mental Power Physiologically Considered," 413; Lydia E. Becker, "Is There Any Specific Distinction between Male and Female Intellect?" 484, 489.

every form of shortcoming" identified in the female. In her 1875 book, Blackwell insisted: "That [a woman] is not [a man's] peer in all intellectual and moral capabilities, cannot at least be very well proved until she is allowed an equally untrammelled opportunity to test her own strength." Wallington also contended that "opinions and usages have repressed to a much greater extent the natural growth of [a woman's] faculties."[25]

The ensuing decades saw similar views being voiced. In an 1887 letter to *Popular Science Monthly,* Helen Gardener wrote that presumed differences between the brain structures of the sexes arose from women's lesser opportunities. Similarly, Edith Simcox's 1887 essay commented that it is not "altogether unscientific to hold our judgment in suspense as to what feminine brains may do, should circumstances ever become propitious to their productiveness." David G. Ritchie's 1889 *Darwinism and Politics* also pointed to circumstances as the causal agent for women's supposed mental inferiority:

> [O]ne may fairly retain the suspicion that this alleged difference is not a fact, and that the greater average eminence (in the past) of men than of women in intellectual pursuits is *entirely* due . . . to the effect of institutions and customs and ideas operating within the lifetime of the individual and not to differences physically inherited.

He added that "if, on the average, men *show* more intellectual ability than women, this must be due to the way in which the two sexes are respectively treated." Feminist Eliza Burt Gamble made the equally forceful contention that male self-interest led to erroneous suppositions, stressing in 1894 that "[t]he ability . . . to collect facts, and the power to generalize and draw conclusions from them, avail little, when brought into direct opposition to deeply rooted prejudices."[26]

Even some scientists who claimed female mental inferiority, however, conceded that nurture, not simply nature, might be at least partially responsible. Harry Campbell, for instance, admitted that "different envi-

25. Becker, "Is There Any Specific Distinction?" 483–85; Blackwell, "Comparative Mental Power," 406, 413; Blackwell, *Sexes,* 134–35; Wallington, "Physical and Intellectual Capacities," 559.
26. Helen Gardener, "Sex in Brain-Weight," 266; Edith Simcox, "The Capacity of Woman," 395; David G. Ritchie, *Darwinism and Politics,* 82, 83; Eliza Burt Gamble, *The Evolution of Woman: An Inquiry into the Dogma of Her Inferiority to Man,* viii.

ronments to which the two sexes are exposed are capable of producing . . . many of the sexual peculiarities (psychic or otherwise) usually
regarded as innate." In fact, "many of the little weaknesses which are regarded as peculiarly feminine, belong essentially no more to the woman
than to the man" but are "the result of her restricted field of mental
action." More commonly, though, scientists ignored environmental influences. As reactionary physician Henry Maudsley asserted, "the qualities of [women's] minds" are not "the artificial results of the position of
subjection and dependence" but instead are due to innate differences in
the sexes. Maudsley shrugged off the opponents' position in saying that
"those who take this view do not appear to have considered the matter as
deeply as they should." Instead, "they have attributed to circumstances
much of what unquestionably lies deeper than circumstances," which he
identified as "being inherent in the fundamental character of sex." In a
subsequent assault on Mill's *Subjection of Women*, Maudsley turned to
science to bolster his case that nature, not nurture, destined women for
their lesser intellectual role. "Taking into adequate account the physiology of the female organization," Maudsley huffed, Mill's arguments
"strike one with positive amazement." Along those lines, George Romanes claimed that women's "disabilities" in "education, social opinion,
and so forth, have certainly not been sufficient to explain" what he saw
as a "general dearth . . . of the products of creative genius." Similarly,
Darwin stated in his autobiography that he favored Francis Galton's notion "that education and environment produce only a small effect on the
mind of any one, and that most of our qualities are innate."[27]

Many scientists attributed the sexes' presumed mental distinctions to
differences in development of their nervous systems, with males displaying superior progress in this regard. Spencer helped lay the groundwork
of this idea in the 1850s by surmising that "those having well-developed
nervous systems will display . . . a greater tendency to suspense of judgments and an easier modification of judgments that have been formed,"
while "[t]hose having nervous systems less developed . . . will be prone
to premature conclusions that are difficult to change." He added that
"mental evolution" could be determined through "the degree of remote-

27. Campbell, *Differences in the Nervous Organisation*, 93–94; Maudsley, "Sex in
Mind," 472–73, 480; Romanes, "Mental Differences," 656; Darwin, *The Autobiography
of Charles Darwin, 1809–1882*, 43.

ness from primitive reflex action"; drawing "sudden, irreversible conclusions on the slenderest evidence, is less distant from reflex action than is the formation of deliberate and modifiable conclusions after much evidence has been collected." Twenty years later, Maudsley expostulated that with women's "nerve-centres being in a state of greater instability," females became "the more easily and the more seriously deranged." In the final decade of the century, Campbell argued that a man's nervous system was "more vigorous and stable," whereas a "high degree of emotional development conduces to nervous instability." Allowing no ambiguity to enter into the issue, Campbell confidently stated that "woman has a far more unstable nervous system." In contrast, Blackwell, though working from the premise that the sexes were "true equivalents," believed that a woman's nervous system, "the primary organ of mind," evidenced a greater degree of development. The female's "nervous system has become the more complex," Blackwell said in reversing the terms of assumed superiority.[28]

Part of the rationale for the claim that women were mentally inferior stemmed from comparisons of brain size. As Cynthia Eagle Russett has observed, craniologists such as Paul Broca and Carl Vogt reported that men's brains were considerably heavier and larger than women's, and this finding was seized as evidence for the presumption that men were more intelligent. Broca stated, for example, that " 'there is a remarkable relationship between the development of intelligence and the volume of the brain.' " To Vogt, anthropologist Allan explained, the "female skull approaches in many respects that of the infant, and still more that of the lower races," which coincided with the widespread and damning opinion that women resembled such ostensibly earlier evolutionary forms far more than did men. As Russett points out, most nineteenth-century scientists professed that a definite relationship existed between intellect and brain size, and the view continued even into the next century.[29]

References to brain size are sprinkled throughout Victorian scientific writings. Darwin's *Descent,* for instance, noted that the male brain "is absolutely larger" immediately after asserting that males have greater

28. Herbert Spencer, *The Principles of Psychology,* 581, 584; Maudsley, "Sex in Mind," 473; Campbell, *Differences in the Nervous Organisation,* 84, 91; Blackwell, *Sexes,* 11, 123, 130.
29. Russett, *Sexual Science,* 33–35; Allan, "On the Real Differences," cciv.

power of invention. Anthropologist W. L. Distant blithely remarked in 1874 that "it is generally allowed that material growth of the brain is correlative to mental capacity, and these facts therefore go to prove that at present the aptitude for mental achievements is decidedly possessed by the males." The widely read *Popular Science Monthly* included commentaries in the early 1880s that spread the message on brain size, with one essay claiming that not only sexual difference but class difference was discernible, and another piece avowing that "[w]e have as much external evidence of the superior quality of the masculine brain as of the superior breathing power of the masculine lungs." Romanes called attention to the fact that the "average brain-weight of women is about five ounces less than that of men," which seemingly demonstrated "on merely anatomical grounds . . . a marked inferiority of intellectual power." Dissenters, however, disagreed that brain size held a causal relationship to intelligence. Blackwell, for one, contended that "[p]sychical action" cannot be "fairly measured or estimated in its mode of activity by the size and action of the brain alone." She further noted, "How incredibly singular, blind, and perverse, then, is the dogmatism which has insisted that man's larger brain . . . must necessarily prove his mental superiority to Woman."[30]

INTUITION AND PERCEPTION

One frequently identified distinction during the nineteenth century was the belief that males excelled in complex abstractions, judgment, and originality, whereas females evidenced greater sensory ability, perception, and rapid thought. In an 1879 essay, zoologist W. K. Brooks averred that one should "expect certain profound and fundamental psychological differences" between the sexes and then concluded that "we should expect men to excel in judgment." As Brooks presented the matter, "[t]he originating or progressive power of the male mind is shown in its highest forms by the ability to pursue original trains of abstract thought, to reach the great generalizations of science, and to give rise to the new creations of poetry and art." Like other scientists, Brooks complacently said

30. Darwin, *Descent,* 580; W. L. Distant, "On the Mental Differences between the Sexes," 79; G. Delauney, "Equality and Inequality in Sex," 191; Miss M. A. Hardaker, "Science and the Woman Question," 578; Romanes, "Mental Differences," 654–55; Blackwell, *Sexes,* 129, 177.

that "history shows that [such an ability] is almost exclusively confined to men." In a subsequent issue of *Popular Science Monthly*, Brooks further advised that "[w]omen are intellectually more desultory and volatile than men."[31]

In part, Brooks based his viewpoints on a theory that resembled the Geddes and Thomson version that would appear ten years later, designating males as the active and females as the conservative types of organisms. To Geddes and Thomson, "a deep difference in constitution expresses itself in the distinctions between male and female, whether these be physical or mental." Among those differences were a "greater cerebral variability and therefore more originality" in men. They noted, "The masculine activity lends a greater power of maximum effort, of scientific insight, or cerebral experiment with impressions," along with "a stronger grasp of generalities." Conversely, "feminine passivity" is associated with such factors as "more rapid intuition." To Brooks, "the female mind is a storehouse filled with the instincts, habits, intuitions, and laws of conduct which have been gained by past experience"; in contrast, "the male organism" is "the originating element" with "the power of extending experience over new fields." Women "judge rather by intuitive perception than by deliberate reasoning," he approvingly quoted.[32]

Other scientists, including Darwin, made mention of the feminine trait of intuition as opposed to the masculine trait of origination. In *Descent*, as I mentioned earlier, Darwin saw "the powers of intuition, of rapid perception, and perhaps of imitation" as "more strongly marked" in women, conferring a decidedly damning judgment on such abilities. For Spencer, women's greater sensitivity to others' emotions "ends simply in intuitions formed without assignable reasons." Blackwell, though challenging any assessments of superiority or inferiority, nonetheless identified "a special directness in feminine perception" that accounted for women's "rapid intuition." As characteristic of women's intuition, Blackwell commented, was "[t]he indirect method of acquiring truth by reasoning" typical of men's thought processes.[33]

More than a decade later, psychologist Romanes declared that women's mental deficiency "displays itself most conspicuously in a compar-

31. W. K. Brooks, "The Condition of Women from a Zoological Point of View I," 154, 155; Brooks, "The Condition of Women from a Zoological Point of View II," 353.

32. Geddes and Thomson, *Evolution of Sex*, 267, 271; Brooks, "Condition of Women I," 154; Brooks, "Condition of Women II," 353.

33. Darwin, *Descent*, 587; Spencer, "Psychology," 33; Blackwell, *Sexes*, 119, 120.

ative absence of originality, . . . especially in the higher levels of intellectual work." With the sole exception of fiction, Romanes insisted that "in
no one department of creative thought can women be said to have at all
approached men." In terms of judgment, Romanes sputtered that there
was "no real question that the female mind stands considerably below
the male"; a woman's inferior capacity of judgment "has been a matter of
universal recognition from the earliest times." Consequently, "man has
always been regarded as the rightful lord of the woman, to whom she
is by nature subject, as both mentally and physically the weaker vessel."
Like his contemporaries, Romanes attributed to women not only intuitive strength but a higher development of the sense organs and quicker
perception to compensate for being "a loser in the intellectual race as
regards acquisition, origination, and judgment." He referred to another
observer, "who paid special attention to the acquirement of rapidity in
acts of complex perception" and had "known ladies who, while seeing
another lady 'pass at full speed in a carriage, could analyse her toilette
from her bonnet to her shoes, and be able to describe not only the fashion and the quality of the stuffs, but also to say if the lace were real or only
machine made.'" For Romanes, the issue was simply put: "the feminine
type" of mental qualities derives from "weakness," whereas the masculine variety is "born of strength."[34]

Contemporary psychologists William James and Harry Campbell also
expounded on the perceptive and intuitive capacities of women. Females, James stated, tended to display "intuitive promptitude," but "intuitions, so fine in the sphere of personal relations, are seldom first-rate
in the way of mechanic." In a Darwinian mode, Campbell diminished
the value of the supposed female qualities by affirming that the "rapidity
of the feminine perception . . . harmonises with the inferior intellectual
power commonly attributed to her." Campbell noted that women have
"quick perceptions" and made the uncomplimentary statement that females exhibited "feebleness of attention" and "incapacity for abstract
thought." Indeed, he even argued, "[a]cuteness and rapidity of perception are proverbial in the savage"; however, when "culture advances,
the individual becomes more reflective" with "a parallel decrease in the
range of perception." Negative contentions about female mental ability

34. Romanes, "Mental Differences," 655–56, 660.

were disputed in Eliza Burt Gamble's 1894 *The Evolution of Woman*. Though Gamble also made an essentialist argument about "the distinctive characters belonging to the female organization, viz., perception and intuition," she associated them not with inferiority but with "undeveloped genius."[35]

AN ARREST OF DEVELOPMENT

As occasional references above have suggested, scientists tended to compare women's mental capacities to those of children as well as "lower civilizations" or "savages." Underlying such comparisons was the supposition that men held the highest position in evolutionary development, with women invariably positioned below. Because children and "savages" occupied the lowest levels, a woman's supposed similarities to these groups served as evidence of her inferior evolutionary progress. We have already seen Darwin's comparison of women to supposedly inferior civilizations, along with his view that children "resemble the mature female much more closely than the mature male." Anthropologist Distant made a similar claim a few years later in maintaining that "women hold an intermediate position between the child and the man"; the presumed wisdom of such a view would hold sway for many years.[36]

As Campbell approvingly characterized Darwin's conclusions in the early 1890s, a woman is "an undeveloped man," since "the adult female is more like the young of either sex than the adult male." In fact, Campbell confidently asserted, "the proposition that the woman resembles the child more than does the man is correct (and it is borne out by actual observation)." To women's discredit, the mental characteristics of the child are due "to an inferior grade of mental evolution." For insight on the issue Campbell turned to Schopenhauer, who "insisted" that women closely resembled children. Though conceding that the philosopher's beliefs were "not the result of calm and passionless observation," Campbell immediately affirmed that "no one can doubt that women have, as a rule, more of the child in them than men" do.[37]

35. William James, *The Principles of Psychology*, 2:368; Campbell, *Differences in the Nervous Organisation*, 52, 162, 164, 192; Gamble, *Evolution of Woman*, 65, 67.

36. Darwin, *Descent*, 580; Distant, "On the Mental Differences," 84.

37. Campbell, *Differences in the Nervous Organisation*, 153, 155, 161, 162.

Under a prevalent scientific scenario, females developed more rapidly in their youth than did males, but such precocity signaled not an advantage but a failing; the girl stopped maturing just as the boy was moving to another stage of development. The boy's potential for development was far greater and required more time to occur. Geddes and Thomson blithely summarized the issue as follows: "From the earliest ages philosophers have contended that woman is but an undeveloped man." Proceeding to contemporary commentary, the pair avowed: "Darwin's theory of sexual selection presupposes a superiority and an entail in the male line; for Spencer, the development of woman is early arrested by procreative functions. In short, Darwin's man is as it were an evolved woman, and Spencer's woman an arrested man." As psychologist James explained, by the age of twenty a female's "character is, in fact, finished in its essentials." Though "a boy of twenty" is inferior to her "in all these respects," this apparent shortcoming instead indicated that "[h]is character is still gelatinous." The ramifications were crucial, for "this absence of prompt tendency in his brain to set into particular modes is the very condition which insures that it shall ultimately become so much more efficient than the woman's." He continued to make his case in arguing that "[t]he very lack of preappointed trains of thought is the ground in which general principles and heads of classification grow up," allowing "the masculine brain" to accommodate "new and complex matter." Similarly, Campbell returned to Schopenhauer for guidance, agreeing with the philosopher's claim that a male's slower mental development merely evidenced that a female could "not continue to evolve as far on in life."[38]

In Spencer's estimation, the "earlier arrest of individual evolution" that characterized women was "necessitated by the reservation of vital power to meet the cost of reproduction." The presumption that "fitness for their respective parental functions implies mental differences between the sexes . . . is justified," he added. Many scientists agreed that women's mental development was necessarily limited to be capable of providing energy required for gestation and birth. Pike ominously remarked that "the diversion of woman's vital powers, from the course which they take by nature, is neither more nor less than the abolition of motherhood." Distant propounded in 1874 that "it cannot be deroga-

38. Geddes and Thomson, *Evolution of Sex*, 37; James, *Principles of Psychology*, 2:369; Campbell, *Differences in the Nervous Organisation*, 172.

tory to the true estimation of women to describe as her [*sic*] principal mission the reproduction of the race." To that end, "an arrest of individual development takes place" in a female "while there is yet a considerable margin of nutrition," without which "there could be no offspring." Writing the same year, Maudsley cautioned that with "[t]he energy of a human body being a definite and not inexhaustible quantity," it followed that "[w]hen Nature spends in one direction, she must economise in another direction." For biologist and novelist Grant Allen, the destined roles of the sexes could be succinctly and "confidently" expressed in an 1889 essay. "[T]he males are the race," he expostulated, while "the females are merely the sex told off to recruit and reproduce it." Therefore, "[a]ll that is distinctly human is man," and "all that is truly woman is merely reproductive." Such views of women's primary role of reproduction underlay concerted efforts to warn of the hazards of improved education for Victorian females, a point to which I shall return.[39]

With the widespread assumption that women were arrested in their mental development, it required no dramatic leap of logic to contend, as Allan and Darwin had, that virtually all intellectual advancements through history stemmed from men's initiatives. Years later, Frederic Harrison would comment that "no woman has ever approached Aristotle and Archimedes, Shakespeare and Descartes, Raphael and Mozart, or has ever shown even a kindred sum of powers." This line of thought also had important ramifications for Victorian ideas about genius, which was almost exclusively gendered as male. The common scientific approach was to scan the panorama of history in Darwinian style to "prove" the dearth of female contributions to civilization's progress.[40]

As Campbell insisted, "the intellectual disparity of the two sexes [is] unmistakably revealed" when considering the prevalence of genius. "Genius of the highest order is practically limited to the male sex," he argued, denying that inequitable opportunities could account for the phenomenon. "Opportunity undoubtedly accounts for much," he conceded, "but not for all." Campbell claimed that "we cannot doubt that, had a woman Shakespeare or Beethoven potentially existed, the world would

39. Spencer, "Psychology," 32, 35; Pike, "Woman and Political Power," 87; Distant, "On the Mental Differences," 84; Maudsley, "Sex in Mind," 467; Grant Allen, "Woman's Place in Nature," 263.
40. Harrison, "Emancipation of Women," 446.

have heard of her in spite of unfavouring external circumstances." Anthropologist and criminologist Cesare Lombroso was even more forceful in his unambiguously titled *The Man of Genius,* written the same year as Campbell's 1891 tome. "In the history of genius women have but a small place," Lombroso confidently stated, and women of such intellectual caliber are but "rare exceptions." Indeed, "the few who emerge have, on near examination, something virile about them." Quoting another observer, Lombroso added that "there are no women of genius," for "the women of genius are men." Lombroso also referred to Francis Galton's detailed study, which Lombroso said revealed that "genius is often hereditary" and primarily transmitted through the male. Galton's 1869 *Hereditary Genius,* which covered some four hundred eminent men throughout history but only occasionally referenced a female, had concluded that a woman could pass on masculine traits to male offspring that she was unable to display herself. The fact that many men of genius credited their mothers with a positive influence for their intellectual accomplishments simply meant, Galton maintained, that "[s]uch men are naturally disposed to show extreme filial regard."[41]

PRONOUNCEMENTS ON EDUCATION

The discussion of the sexes' mental abilities became particularly heated when applied to the educational arena, especially regarding the higher education of women. The dominant opinion held that female education needed to be closely monitored to avoid straining a girl's intellectual capacities, which were considered less able to withstand rigorous work than a boy's, in fear of jeopardizing her reproductive abilities, among other dangers. Such conservative presumptions did not go unchallenged, however, with dissenters asseverating that an improved educational program was critical to ensuring female health, both mentally and physically. As Emily Davies, who established Britain's first women's college, held in 1868: "Every effort to improve the education of women" to the level of men's "does something towards lifting them out of the

41. Campbell, *Differences in the Nervous Organisation,* 173; Cesare Lombroso, *The Man of Genius,* 137, 138, 139, 142; Francis Galton, *Hereditary Genius: An Inquiry into Its Laws and Consequences,* 55, 319.

state of listless despair of themselves into which so many fall." The same year, suffragist Millicent Garrett Fawcett said that "a lack of mental training" caused "a deterioration in [women's] intellects," which she noted had been used "to justify the widely-spread opinion that [women] are innately possessed of less powerful minds than men, that they are incapable of the highest mental culture." Like other proponents of improved education, she urged that "everything which education could do should be done to produce in women the highest mental development of which they are capable." John Stuart Mill helped bring the issue under scrutiny in *Subjection of Women* by arguing for "better and more complete" female education. Elevating women's "understanding [of] business, public affairs, and the higher matters of speculation" would lead to "a more beneficial . . . influence upon the general mass of human belief and sentiment."[42]

Interestingly, the specific issue of education in science itself was examined in 1869 by Lydia Becker in a *Contemporary Review* essay. Claiming that "[m]ost of the inducements for pursuing scientific studies are common to men and women," Becker argued that "some considerations" made "such pursuits of greater value to women." Becker cited the "monotonous and colourless lives" women were forced to lead through the influence of custom and opinion, urging that women need "scope for the activity of their minds." She warned, "In default of mental food and exercise, the minds of women get starved out," whereas "[m]any women might be saved from the evil of the life of intellectual vacuity" through scientific training and practice.[43]

The debate over female education escalated particularly in 1874 with the appearance of Maudsley's "Sex in Mind and in Education" essay. Responding to concerted efforts to improve educational opportunities for women, Maudsley remonstrated that such proponents had been "[c]arried away by their zeal into an enthusiasm which borders on or reaches fanaticism," which caused them to "seem positively to ignore the fact that there are significant differences between the sexes, arguing in effect as if it were nothing more than an affair of clothes." Because of

---

42. Emily Davies, *Thoughts on Some Questions Relating to Women, 1860–1908*, 131–32; Millicent Garrett Fawcett, "The Education of Women of the Middle and Upper Classes," 512; John Stuart Mill, *The Subjection of Women*, 83, 84.
43. Lydia E. Becker, "On the Study of Science by Women," 388.

these differences, Maudsley huffed that "it will not be possible to transform a woman into a man." Attempts to do so through increased educational activity in youth would damage the woman's vital reproductive abilities.[44]

Therefore, Maudsley averred, women "cannot choose but to be women; cannot rebel successfully against the tyranny of their organization." The supposition that "sexual difference ought not to have any place in the culture of mind" Maudsley viewed as "a rash statement."

> There is sex in mind as distinctly as there is sex in body; and if the mind is to receive the best culture of which its nature is capable, regard must be had to the mental qualities which correlate differences of sex. To aim, by means of education and pursuits in life, to assimilate the female to the male mind, might well be pronounced as unwise and fruitless a labour as it would be to strive to assimilate the female to the male body by means of the same kind of physical training and by the adoption of the same pursuits. Without doubt there have been some striking instances of extraordinary women who have shown great mental power, and these may fairly be quoted as evidence in support of the right of women to the best mental culture; but it is another matter when they are adduced in support of the assertion that there is no sex in mind, and that a system of female education should be laid down on the same lines, follow the same method, and have the same ends in view, as a system of education for men.

Attempts "to assimilate the female to the male mind," Maudsley warned, would require "undo[ing] the life-history of mankind from its earliest commencement." Maudsley subsequently spelled out the proper educational approach:

> Each sex must develope after its kind; and if education in its fundamental meaning be the external cause to which evolution is the internal answer, if it be the drawing out of the internal qualities of the individual into their highest perfection by the influence of

44. Maudsley, "Sex in Mind," 466. For a helpful resource of many of the primary texts in the education debate that I discuss in this section, particularly the 1874 writings, see Rowold, *Gender and Science*.

the most fitting external conditions, there must be a difference in the method of education of the two sexes answering to differences in their physical and mental natures. . . . There is sex in mind and there should be sex in education.[45]

Turning to the argument that reproductive prospects would be hampered by strenuous intellectual activity—a matter to which I will return—Maudsley warned that "a proper regard to the physical nature of women means attention given, in their training, to their peculiar functions and to their foreordained work as mothers and nurses of children." He continued to make his case by melodramatically describing the inestimable harm that would result if woman's primary reproductive responsibility were to be tampered with by radical educators:

> Whatever aspirations of an intellectual kind [women] may have, they cannot be relieved from the performance of those offices so long as it is thought necessary that mankind should continue on earth. . . . For it would be an ill thing, if it should so happen, that we got the advantages of a quantity of female intellectual work at the price of a puny, enfeebled, and sickly race. In this relation, it must be allowed that women do not and cannot stand on the same level as men.

Maudsley underscored the scientific underpinnings of his conservative educational views, pointing to similar claims by "physicians of high professional standing, who speak from their own experience."[46]

Maudsley's comments led to a flurry of essays on the topic. An unsigned 1874 essay appearing in *Blackwood's,* for instance, sided with Maudsley's position in pointing to "the obvious truth that the educational capacities of boys and girls correlate the differences in their sex, and that the actual training both of mind and body must do the same." The *Blackwood's* essay argued:

> The result of Dr. Maudsley's scientific analysis is, that those who seek to improve the education of women must recognise simply what we all knew before,—that it is impossible to transform a

45. Maudsley, "Sex in Mind," 468, 471.
46. Ibid., 471, 473.

> woman into a man; that women cannot have the same aims as men, pursued by the same methods; and that it is injurious to attempt to assimilate the female to the male mind.

Like Maudsley and his adherents, the *Blackwood's* essay warned of the "physical degeneracy" that would result to both the woman and her children by incautious educational ventures.[47]

Such views did not go uncontested, however. Physician Sophia Jex-Blake addressed not the physiological valences of the educational debate but the self-serving motivations of men intent on protecting their own interests, specifically in the medical field. "[N]othing is more curious," Jex-Blake remarked in 1874, than the contentions of those who "constantly assume that no labour is severe except that usually allotted to men, and that it is only when women venture to invade *that* field that they are likely to be overtasked." She pointed to the "absurd inconsistency" of medical arguments cautioning about the dangers to women's health from extended study while ignoring the hazards of more exhaustive work such as midwifery.[48]

In a *Fortnightly Review* reply to Maudsley, physician Elizabeth Garrett Anderson argued that insufficient intellectual work brought harm, not benefit, to the female's physiological health. Garrett Anderson defended the proponents of improved female education in identifying as their "single aim" the desire "to make the best they can of the materials at their disposal." Garrett Anderson called for comparable educational training for girls as for boys, and she maintained that an educational program that "strengthen[s] the best powers of the mind as good food is to strengthen the body" should be available to females, just as "eating beef and bread" would provide to them "as much benefit as men." Maudsley had not proven that such intellectual rigors "would in some way interfere with the special functions of girls."[49]

Though Garrett Anderson championed better educational opportunities for women, she nevertheless shared the dominant view that strenuous intellectual work could bring harm during significant stages of physiological development. Yet she argued that the same logic needed

47. "Sex in Mind and Education: A Commentary," 739, 744, 749.
48. Sophia Jex-Blake, "Sex in Education," 457.
49. Elizabeth Garrett Anderson, "Sex in Mind and Education: A Reply," 583, 584.

to be applied to males, who undergo "[a]nalogous changes" and a "period of immature manhood [that] is frequently one of weakness." Judicious educational methods would thus be required for both sexes, she advised.[50]

Garrett Anderson also employed the example of medical training in her discussion of educational issues; female students, she related, were forced to exert far greater intellectual energies than their male counterparts simply to overcome the daunting obstacles placed in their path and the critics "contesting every step of their course." Despite "this heavy additional burden," the female students displayed no "signs of enfeebled health or of inadequate mental power."[51]

In making her overall case about female education, Garrett Anderson summarized the issue as follows:

> Even were the dangers of continuous mental work as great as Dr. Maudsley thinks they are, the dangers of a life adapted to develope only the specially and consciously feminine side of the girl's nature would be much greater. From the purely physiological point of view, it is difficult to believe that study much more serious than that usually pursued by young men would do a girl's health as much harm as a life directly calculated to over-stimulate the emotional and sexual instincts, and to weaken the guiding and controlling forces which these instincts so imperatively need. The stimulus found in novel-reading, in the theatre and ball-room, the excitement which attends a premature entry into society, the competition of vanity and frivolity, these involve far more real dangers to the health of young women than the competition for knowledge, or for scientific or literary honours, ever has done, or is ever likely to do.

The decay of women's health that Maudsley linked to excessive mental activity, Garrett Anderson also remarked, instead "distinctly" resulted from a "want of adequate mental interest and occupation." As a result, Garrett Anderson explained, women "become gradually languid and feeble under the depressing influence of dulness, not only in the special functions of womanhood, but in the entire cycle of the processes of

50. Ibid., 588.
51. Ibid., 589.

nutrition and innervation." Women become "morbid and self-absorbed, or even hysterical," through the dearth of cognitive activity.[52]

An anonymous essay in the *Saturday Review* found Garrett Anderson's comments intriguing and decried "[t]he evils of the present superficial and often most foolish system of education, if it deserves the name." Agreeing with Garrett Anderson, the 1874 essay held that "young women's minds are often so imperfectly developed that they are incapable of taking a rational interest in intellectual work" and "frequently find refuge in mere frivolities, or in unhealthy sources of excitement." The *Saturday Review* also asserted that "[w]omen ought to learn more, and to learn more systematically," without being kept from "any part of a man's education." Though skirting the question of whether women's minds matched men's "in originating power," the essay advanced the opinion that "at least [women] are capable of acquiring all the knowledge which is supposed to be imparted at our Universities." In an allusion to Garrett Anderson's analogy, the *Saturday Review* remarked, "Boys and girls should both eat beef and bread, and should both learn classics and mathematics." Despite its generally positive opinions on female education, however, the *Saturday Review* questioned whether the sexes "should both eat the same food in the same quantities and at the same time." Extreme competition had brought harm in male education, and such negative experiences should be taken into account when devising an educational approach for "the more docile and less vigorous sex"; reformers were admonished not to become "carried away by abstract theories about human equality."[53]

For Spencer, writing in 1876, advanced education for women was disturbing because it was seen as interfering with the evolutionary progression of the family. In *Principles of Sociology,* Spencer argued that "the genesis of the family fulfils the law of evolution," which he connected to intellectual development as well. The progress of civilization, he mused, has shown that women "in the highest societies" have been "restricted to domestic duties and the rearing of children." As a result, "no considerable alteration in the careers of women in general, can be, or should be, so produced." Thus, according to Spencer's logic, "any extensive change in the education of women, made with the view of fitting them for busi-

52. Ibid., 590.
53. "Sex in Education," 585, 586.

nesses and professions, would be mischievous." He added, "If women comprehended all that is contained in the domestic sphere, they would ask no other."[54]

Prominent social observer Frances Power Cobbe would follow a different path in 1878 in suggesting, as did earlier proponents of education reform, that mental health was jeopardized if females were not given adequate intellectual exercise. "We have heard a great deal lately of the danger to women's health . . . over mental strain or intellectual labour," she said. Though agreeing that "danger in this direction" could occur when girls "study too much or too early," Cobbe proceeded to identify the far greater hazards that accrued to inadequate education. "[F]or one woman whose health is injured by excessive study," Cobbe stated, "there are hundreds whose health is deteriorated by *want* of wholesome mental exercise," with "the vacuity in the brains" leading girls to become "dull and spiritless."[55]

The controversy over female education continued with sharp intensity into the 1880s. As the decade opened, physician Alexander Keiller warned of the dangers of "undue educational brain-toil in the young," yet his remarks were particularly aimed at "[y]oung females, and especially those naturally delicate." He reflected, "The object of female education and upbringing is not, or ought not to be, that of the manufacture of 'bluestockings,' nor the perversion of woman's naturally intended powers, to which unduly forced education often proves injurious." Fellow physician T. S. Clouston returned to the well-trodden argument that the human body had a finite supply of energy, and its use must be carefully regulated. In a rather bizarre analogy, Clouston commented, "If you use the force of your steam-engine for generating electricity, you can not have it for sawing your wood." In another curious analogy, Clouston focused on the particular hazards facing females during adolescence, a time of "summer ripening." Clouston mused, "If the grain is poorly matured, it is not good for either eating or sowing." He added, "Such is the . . . physiologist's way of regarding a woman, her development, and her education." When mental exertion occurs too early in a female's maturation process, "wondrous forces and faculties . . . are arrested before they attain completion." Turning to the popular fear that reproduc-

54. Herbert Spencer, *The Principles of Sociology,* 745, 756, 757.
55. Frances Power Cobbe, "The Little Health of Ladies," 290–91.

tion would be jeopardized by excessive intellectual activity, Clouston queried, "Why should we spoil a good mother by making an ordinary grammarian?"[56]

A somewhat more enlightened commentator, physician Benjamin Ward Richardson, wrote the same year on the differences he had experienced in his own lifetime concerning assessments of female mental ability. Though current thought had somewhat changed, Richardson nevertheless noted that "some men, and still more women" retained the belief that females demonstrated inferior mental capacity. To Richardson, however, "women, equally with men, are capable of developing into physical and mental capacity for any kind of skill, invention, strength, or endurance." He warned, though, of "the present strain after extreme learning," noting that most women "are unequal to the strain, and had better remain unequal."[57]

The president of the British Medical Association also brought his weighty credentials to the fore, as a summary of his 1886 presidential address recounts. Focusing on higher education for females, Dr. Withers-Moore ruminated that "it 'indisposes to matrimony, and unfits for maternity.'" The account added that "weighty corrobative testimony" attested to "the injurious functional effects of overpressure in education upon girls." Withers-Moore's pronouncements gained the approval of the always vocal and ever-reactionary Eliza Lynn Linton. His views, Linton said in 1886, should serve as a "guide" on women with the warnings that "'[e]xcessive work . . . is ruinous to health.'" She cautioned, "[I]f we are wise we [will] stop short of such strain as would hurt the health and damage the reproductive energies," since "[a] girl is something more than an individual" as "the potential mother of a race." Linton added, "Let her learn by all means . . . but always with quietness and self-control—always under restrictions bounded by her sex and its future possible function." Linton exhorted that "there is something to be taken note of in the opposition of most medical men to this Higher Education of Women."[58]

Yet the 1880s, like the previous decade, saw occasional resistance to

56. Alexander Keiller, "What May Be the Dangers of Educational Overwork for Both Sexes . . . ," 251; T. S. Clouston, "Female Education from a Medical Point of View," 216, 219, 223, 224.
57. Benjamin Ward Richardson, "Woman's Work in Creation," 608, 609, 617.
58. "The President's Address," 338; Eliza Lynn Linton, "The Higher Education of Woman," 503, 508.

the common view that stringent educational standards would pose egregious dangers to women. In an 1880 issue of *Nature*, S. Tolver Preston interpreted a telling statement in Darwin's *Descent* to argue that male opposition to women's intellectual progress "for countless generations, has enormously injured his own advance—by inheritance." Preston was building upon one of Darwin's more condescending statements that " '[i]t is indeed fortunate that the law of the equal transmission of characters to both sexes prevails with mammals, otherwise it is probable that man would have become as superior in mental endowment to woman as the peacock is in ornamental plumage to the peahen.' " As Preston argued, the widespread belief that women displayed inferior mental ability "so far from being an argument *against* female education, ought, when justly viewed, . . . be regarded as the strongest reason the other way." Near the end of the decade, the *Westminster Review* criticized assumptions about advanced female education and remarked on the "melancholy fact that most of the opposition to this movement comes, not from the uneducated and illiterate, but from the learned and from those who, with more knowledge, ought to know better."[59]

As we have seen, several commentators on female education considered a more strenuous instructional program to pose dire hazards to future generations of humanity by hampering women's reproductive abilities. The conclusion is an important as well as a popular one, deserving of additional discussion here. Conservatives like Maudsley clung to the presumption that future generations would suffer immensely through women's advanced education, as well as their other expressed desires to expand opportunities beyond the domestic sphere and move toward greater independence. To a writer in the 1878 *Quarterly Journal of Science,* for instance, "the 'woman's rights movement' is an attempt to rear, by a process of 'unnatural selection,' a race of monstrosities—hostile alike to men, to normal women, to human society, and to the future development of our race." To a strident contributor in an 1882 number of *Popular Science Monthly,* "[t]he necessary outcome of an absolute intellectual equality of the sexes would be the extinction of the human race."[60]

59. S. Tolver Preston, "Evolution and Female Education," 485, 486; "The Higher Education of Women," 155.
60. Quoted in Lester F. Ward, "Our Better Halves," 267; Hardaker, "Science and the Woman Question," 583.

Eugenicist Karl Pearson would speculate in 1885 that "[w]e have first to settle what is the physical capacity of woman, what would be the effect of her emancipation on her function of race-reproduction, before we can talk about her 'rights.'" The stakes were precariously high, Pearson believed, for "[t]he higher education of women may connote a general intellectual progress for the community, or, on the other hand, a physical degradation of the race, owing to prolonged study having ill effects on woman's child-bearing efficiency." Pearson held fast to the increasingly outmoded view that woman was "naturally man's intellectual inferior," which could conceivably be attributed to "her prerogative function of child-bearing." If that were the case, "we can only accept the inferiority, and allow woman to find compensation for it in other directions." Referring to a *Westminster Review* essay arguing that "in the future the best women will be too highly developed to submit to child-bearing," Pearson concluded that "the continuation of the species will be left to the coarser and less intellectual of its members." Such a prospect, Pearson added, poses "a very serious difficulty, demanding the most thorough investigation."[61]

Equally apprehensive of the effects on reproduction from excessive mental efforts, physician Richardson predicted that maternal duties would be left only "to the weakest mothers, about as bad an evil as could befall the human race." Sexologist Havelock Ellis also pointed to the seriousness of the reproduction issue in arguing that "[t]he chief question that we have to ask when we consider the changing status of women is: How will it affect the reproduction of the race?" After all, Ellis reminded readers, "reproduction is the end and aim of all life everywhere." Biologist Grant Allen voiced a similar concern about a female's reproductive duty, saying in 1889 that women's "emancipation must not be of a sort that interferes in any way with this prime natural necessity" to keep the human species in existence. Women's "training and education," Allen believed, "should fit them above everything else for this their main function in life." He chided that "[a] woman ought to be ashamed to say she has no desire to become a wife and mother." Fearing that equal educational opportunities for women would lead to their becoming "unsexed"—a term frequently employed by reactionary

61. Karl Pearson, *The Ethic of Freethought,* 355, 360, 374.

observers in the final decades of the century—Allen asserted that "many" well-educated women developed "a distaste, an unnatural distaste, for the functions which nature intended them to perform." He warned of the "danger that many of the most cultivated and able families of the English-speaking race will have become extinct, through the prime error of supposing" that a man's education "must necessarily also be good for women."[62]

Physician Arabella Kenealy, though less strident than some commentators, also expressed uneasiness over potential damage to women's reproductive ability from excess education. "[T]he utmost care is needed in the training of women—the possible mothers of the race—" to prevent damage to "their delicate physical sensitiveness" and "special intellectual and moral characteristics" that could otherwise be "distorted and deformed by mental strain," Kenealy remarked. "All I advance is a protest," the physician explained in her 1890 essay, that woman "shall be forgetful of that grave trust the welfare of her children, and, through them, the progress of the race."[63]

Other commentators attempted to refute the dire warnings that advanced education would threaten a woman's reproductive capacities. In an 1887 essay titled "The Lower Education of Women," Helen McKerlie condemned the notion expressed by Eliza Lynn Linton and others that "[a] highly educated woman . . . is incapacitated for her natural functions," which presumably led to "a woman destroyed, a man not made." McKerlie instead claimed that efforts to hinder educational improvement would "reduce women to one dead level of unintellectual pursuit." The anonymous 1888 essay in *Westminster Review,* though following the standard argument that "serious injury to the health of woman" could result from "overexercise of brain," argued that higher education would provide a "beneficial effect" on "the character of the children borne by such cultured women." The same year, Lester F. Ward queried, "Is it really true that the larger part taken by the female in the work of reproduction necessarily impairs her strength, dwarfs her proportions, and renders her a physically inferior and dependent being?" Though agreeing with

62. Richardson, "Woman's Work in Creation," 619; Havelock Ellis, *Women and Marriage: Or, Evolution in Sex,* 12, 15; Grant Allen, "Plain Words on the Woman Question," 450–53, 457.

63. Arabella Kenealy, "The Talent of Motherhood," 457–58.

the reactionary opinion of zoologist W. K. Brooks that women exhibited greater passivity because of a "principle of heredity," Ward nevertheless cautioned that "[w]oman *is* the race, and the race can be raised up only as she is raised up." In a comment that serves as a cogent concluding sentiment to this chapter, Ward said, "True science teaches that the elevation of woman is the only sure road to the evolution of man."[64]

64. Helen McKerlie, "The Lower Education of Women," 112, 119; "Higher Education of Women," 157, 161; Ward, "Our Better Halves," 271, 268, 275.

2

Fated Marginalization

Women and Science in the Poetry of Constance Naden

How can a Victorian woman find a voice within the masculine realm of scientific discourse that judges her an intellectual inferior? More broadly, how can she even position herself within a culture that disdains rigorous cognitive work by women as unnatural and transgressive? Constance Naden grapples with these questions in a series of fascinating poems published in the 1880s, herself wielding the language of science to interrogate the Victorian woman's relationship with intellectuality, rationality, and logicality. Naden's ultimately pessimistic negotiation of these issues, I suggest, reveals a belief that a woman cannot participate unproblematically as an authoritative voice in the rarefied field of scientific endeavor, with its esoteric and complex lexicon, or the wider universe of learning in which the discipline is located. Instead, Naden deems efforts to enter this exclusionary world as thwarted by nineteenth-century perceptions of female subjectivity that valorize acquiescence, silence, morality, sensibility, and passivity for the sex presumed inevitably flawed in its mental capacity. The discourse of science, then, serves as a vehicle of power whereby Victorian women can be delimited and defined as alterity, though resistance is occasionally evident.

Constance Naden's own life history contradicts her culture's patronizing estimations of women's mental abilities. An avid reader and inquisitive student, Naden included among her many interests a fascination with the natural sciences. Her early studies of botany at the Midland Institute in Birmingham were complemented by later work at nearby Mason College where, as one of her professors recalled, she was the school's "most brilliant student" and received "a very thorough drilling in the subject-matter of the sciences of physics, chemistry, botany, zoology, and geology," even winning top honors in the science and art examinations. "[D]istinctly an evolutionist," as William R. Hughes described her in an 1890 memoir, Naden dexterously infused many of her poems with Darwinian and Spencerian language. Her publications included not only volumes of poetry but also essays on philosophical matters, which received enthusiastic approval from both her peers and the press, as comments included in Naden's *Complete Poetical Works* reveal. Naden's devotion to the study of philosophy—which exceeded her interest in what she considered the amusing diversion of poetry, a rather surprising preference in view of her substantial oeuvre—led to her avocation of the creed of "hylo-idealism," under the tutelage of Dr. Robert Lewins, and its presumption that knowledge is relative and subjective. Naden received the approbation of such diverse figures as the admired Spencer, who, as the *St. James's Gazette* reported, "thought her endowed with the exceptional combination of 'receptivity and originality' in an equally great degree," and William Gladstone, who numbered her among the century's finest poets with their "splendid powers."[1]

Yet contemporary assessments of Naden apply rather spurious logic to account for Naden's undeniable intellectual accomplishments by emphasizing her supposedly feminine qualities. Though one of Naden's professors, geologist Charles Lapworth, effused about Naden's intelligence, he was careful to stress that "there was nothing of the sexless 'blue stocking' about her," for Naden evinced "many of the instinctive procliv-

---

1. William A. Tilden, "Part III," 67–68; William R. Hughes, *Constance Naden: A Memoir*, 24; "Some Personal and Press Opinions on the Works of Constance Naden," 11, 35. For a discussion of Naden and her philosophical creed, see James R. Moore, "The Erotics of Evolution: Constance Naden and Hylo-Idealism."

ities, and all the tender sympathies of her sex." Naden "was always womanly," he proclaimed. Biographer Hughes emphasized the same point in observing that, "although a scientist and philosopher . . . her womanly grace and her womanly sympathy were always dominant." He added, "Like George Eliot, she had the intellect of a man, but the heart of the most womanly of women, and though science and literature were much to her, love and friendship were infinitely more."[2]

Nevertheless, Naden's poetic oeuvre reveals an impressive versatility, spanning a broad range of subjects and stylistics. Her published works include *Songs and Sonnets of Springtime* (1881) and *A Modern Apostle, The Elixir of Life, and Other Poems* (1887). Her collected poems were published posthumously in 1894, a lengthy volume of 360 pages that also includes translated works. Along with scientific matters and philosophic musings, the poems cover such disparate topics as the artistic process, both literary and nonliterary; religion and spirituality, touching on Christianity in general and its clergy in particular, as well as pantheism, mysticism, agnosticism, and other concerns; love and its loss; mythological and other legendary figures; and various facets of nature, such as plant life, the heavens, and seasonal elements. In form, Naden's verse is eclectic, manifested in such configurations as the sonnet, dramatic monologue, and the narrative poem, both brief and lengthy. Speakers vary as well, with first-person male and female narrators, omniscient third-person voices, and even a nonhuman perspective. Some of the poems can be viewed as lightly humorous in certain respects, while others explore grave and profound matters in more serious fashion.

Most interestingly, however, Naden's poetry offers an intriguing perspective on a female's relationship with learning and science, especially in view of her own unconventional life experience. In the poems that I examine, we are given a window onto the obstacles a female faced in attempting to project an authoritative voice within a culture that associates a woman with romance rather than knowledge, especially of a scientific cast, and exerts a continual pressure on those iconoclasts who struggle to widen the parameters of female subjectivity. We see in these poems, then, the ways in which Victorian ideology and scientific discourse inform female language, self-image, and choices.

2. Charles Lapworth, introduction to Hughes, *Constance Naden*, xvi; Hughes, *Constance Naden*, 22, 63.

Naden's adoption of scientific discourse in her verse recalls Romantic poet Charlotte Smith's similar strategy in seeking to craft an authoritative voice. Smith's lengthy 1807 "Beachy Head," one of her most celebrated poems, combines the imaginative and the scientific in an interesting double voice, through which the conventionally poetic language of the main text is glossed through a multitude of footnotes detailing botanical and ornithological facts, as well as geographic, cultural, historical, and other practical matters. Common terminology used to identify a particular bird or plant, for example, is systematically accorded the Latin scientific name in the paratext, and obscure references to events, practices, or locales are carefully elaborated upon in extensive notes.[3] The effect is to convey upon the ungendered speaker of the poetic narrative the perspicacity, omniscience, and reliability demonstrated through the breadth of knowledge revealed in the verse's supplemental components.

Although Naden almost entirely eschews the paratextual format, scientific language—particularly with an evolutionary slant—dominates and informs many of her poems.[4] Yet a marked distinction in the frequency, sophistication, and rationale for these references emerges depending on the gender of the speaker. Male or ungendered speakers wield the diction of science assuredly and elaborately, while female speakers display a far more hesitant and limited deployment of this authoritative language. Naden thereby suggests that a female can participate in this discourse only tangentially and equivocally, as distanced from it in a poetic register as in the quotidian realm of Victorian culture.

Yet Naden was not the only late Victorian woman poet who found evolutionary issues compelling. Mathilde Blind, for example, penned the lengthy *Ascent of Man,* which traces human evolution in Darwinian tones and deftly shifts among an array of poetic forms such as the epic and ode. L. S. Bevington weaves an evolutionary strand into "Egoisme à

3. Stuart Curran observes that the references suggest "an alternate Romanticism that seeks not to transcend or to absorb nature but to contemplate and honor its irreducible alterity" (introduction to *The Poems of Charlotte Smith,* xxviii).

4. "Lament of the Cork-Cell" is the only Naden poem featuring the type of gloss used by Charlotte Smith. In "Lament," an explanatory footnote briefly describes the life cycle of the titular organism. The inanimate speaker reflects in its final conscious moments on the progression in its life cycle from vibrant organism to deadened cork, describing the chemical and physiological changes experienced.

Deux," as does A. Mary Robinson more directly in "Darwinism," while May Kendall's "Lay of the Tribolite" and "The Lower Life" bring a humorous element to the topic. Though Kendall's "Woman's Future," like Mary Elizabeth Coleridge's "A Clever Woman," protests the conventional scientific views of the female mind and probes women's relationship to science, it is in Naden's body of work that we find the most elaborate treatment of the subject.

Critical commentary, both contemporary and modern, has tended to remark upon the often-playful tone of Naden's verses, characterizing her manipulation of scientific language in positive terms. In an 1891 essay, for instance, R. W. Dale points to the entertaining aspects of several poems and notes that they "showed a delightful capacity for making fun of her own serious studies" in the natural sciences. In a series of complimentary commentaries affixed to the collected poems, the *Pall Mall Gazette* and her own Mason College magazine approvingly remark on the charm and humor of Naden's writings. More recently, Angela Leighton observes that "[m]any of her verses cheerfully appropriate a scientific vocabulary to the subject of romance," yet Leighton adds that "the difficult choice of love or work, marriage or vocation, is still presented as primarily a female one." In a related vein, J. Jakub Pitha observes, "Although her poetry is rarely overtly feminist, many of the 'love' poems, humorous or not, explore the delicate negotiations of power in female/male relationships." Despite the fact that Naden's poems seem to invite a lighthearted appraisal with their droll infusion of scientific terminology, they do urge us to consider them in far more somber fashion. Underlying the verses' frolicsome tone is a disconcerting realization that the world of science and learning marginalizes women through exclusion and condescension. The poems' formal qualities frequently and persistently compel us to interpret the narrative in an unsettlingly ironic register to provide a dramatically different reading.[5]

As Luce Irigaray and other theorists have amply demonstrated, language is neither gender-neutral nor ideologically innocent but instead is infused with masculinist biases. A woman, Irigaray asserts, "does not

5. R. W. Dale, "Constance Naden," 513; Angela Leighton, "Constance Naden," 559; J. Jakub Pitha, "Constance Naden," 214. For an analysis of Naden's writings as a "true dialogue between science and poetry," see Marion Thain, " 'Scientific Wooing': Constance Naden's Marriage of Science and Poetry," 164.

have access to language, except through recourse to 'masculine' systems of representation," and "[t]he 'feminine' is never to be identified except by and for the masculine." As Irigaray observes, "the feminine finds itself defined as lack, deficiency, or as imitation and negative image of the subject." Women are excluded from full participation in the symbolic order; indeed, women's "nonaccess to the symbolic is what has established the social order." Moreover, Irigaray speaks of mimicry as a customary response for women, a "path" that is "historically assigned to the feminine."[6] Applied to the Victorian period, mimicry of masculine language underscores the limited possibilities for women denied their own voice, and in Naden's poetry mimicry certainly reflects such a lack of power. Women, in these poems, frequently function primarily as attenuated mimics.

Naden's poetry provides a compelling and disturbing illustration of Irigaray's views of language as a masculine realm. Female characters are shaped, confined, and manipulated through masculine language, especially as manifested through the language of science. The poetry serves as a cautionary tale in demonstrating women's vexed relationship with language and limited possibilities for positive change. Not only does the content of the poems reveal the ways in which language structures female subjectivity, but so also do the formal and acoustic components. As we shall see, these elements operate closely in conjunction with the content to reveal on another level the complex and disturbing ways in which language exercises its power over women. Because of the poems' compelling structural frameworks and aural aspects, I explore in detail the intricate maneuvers that work so strikingly to convey the primarily pessimistic message of Naden's scientific verse.

Despite the negative trajectory of these poems, glimmers of disruption, resistance, and subversion do occasionally appear, both in form and content. Julia Kristeva's theorization of poetic language provides a valuable perspective here, in that the rebellious energy of the semiotic exerts a forceful pressure on the symbolic and offers the possibility of substantive change on a social as well as linguistic plane. As Kristeva notes, "social organization [is] always already symbolic," and the dialectic interworkings of the semiotic and symbolic enable the latter to be altered. "[W]hat remodels the symbolic order is always the influx of the semiotic," Kristeva

6. Luce Irigaray, *This Sex Which Is Not One*, 85, 78, 189, 76.

comments, which "is particularly evident in poetic language," in that semiotic forces cause "an irruption of the drives in the universal signifying order, that of 'natural' language which binds together the social unit." Indeed, "poetry—more precisely, poetic language—reminds us of its eternal function: to introduce through the symbolic that which works on, moves through, and threatens it"; in its "practices within and against the social order," such language provides "the ultimate means of [the social order's] transformation or subversion, the precondition for its survival and revolution."[7]

A SCIENTIST'S PERCEPTIONS

I begin my examination of Naden's work with "Scientific Wooing," one of four verses contained in the 1887 grouping titled "Evolutional Erotics" in her collected poetry.[8] "Scientific Wooing" is an appropriate starting point for my discussion, since the poem provides an especially striking view of a confident male speaker at ease in the world of science, a confining construction of female subjectivity, the marginalization of women from scientific activity, and a deceptively airy tone. At first glance, "Scientific Wooing" presents an amusing blend of the discourses of science and love in tracing the speaker's early dedication to his absorbing studies, his subsequent attraction to the fair but disconcerting Mary Maud Trevylyan, and a systematic plan to win her affections. Yet, from the opening stanza, the poem subtly signals that troublesome revelations about the masculine perception of women and their separation from the scientific arena will unfold:

> I was a youth of studious mind,
> Fair science was my mistress kind,
>   And held me with attraction chemic;
> No germs of Love attacked my heart,
> Secured as by Pasteurian art
>   Against that fatal epidemic.

7. Julia Kristeva, *Revolution in Poetic Language*, 27, 62, 81.
8. The other poems in this section—"The New Orthodoxy," "Natural Selection," and "Solomon Redivivus"—are also examined in my study. All citations from Naden's poetry come from *The Complete Poetical Works of Constance Naden.*

Drawing upon the conventional dichotomy that allies the male with the mind and the female with the body, the stanza stresses, through its choice of topic for the opening line, the male speaker's acceptance of this cultural truism. Rationality is unambiguously privileged over the emotionality traditionally associated with the body. The speaker invokes the tropes of disease to describe the effects of affection: he refers to the "germs of Love" that attack the heart, the "fatal epidemic" that love precipitates, and his belief that "Pasteurian art" has rendered him immune. Through these tropes, the speaker follows the unpleasant tradition of portraying women as vitiating influences who besmirch, bewilder, and bedevil those men unlucky enough to fall prey to their wiles. Since the speaker, at this point in the poem, has not experienced the distractions of corporeal love, the series of powerful caesuras unleashed in the stanza underscores his resoluteness in pursuing his cognitive interests. The language of desire is wielded only within an intellectual register in these lines, as it is in the following two stanzas; the dream states that traditionally envelop a lover are characterized not by visions of the beloved's face but by a parade of personified chemicals, and the conventional equation of passion with fire is employed only in reference to the speaker's scientific ambitions. Indeed, in choosing emphatic /d/, /t/, and /p/ sounds as he describes "[t]he daring dreams of trustful twenty" that would enable him to "set the river Thames on fire / If but Potassium were in plenty," the speaker displays a surety in achieving his goal that distinguishes him from the humility, wistfulness, and self-abnegation of a typical suitor. That assurance is further conveyed through the speaker's tendency, in this stanza and others in which he is asserting a gritty determination, to adopt predominantly one- and two-syllable words that require particularly forceful pronunciation and protract the reading process, leading us to absorb slowly and in measured tones each insistent word.

The unwelcome emergence of desire for Mary is depicted in especially harsh terms, as the speaker's scientific "yearnings so sublime," with their harmonious sibilance, are violently disrupted by an acoustically powerful predicate; they are "blasted" by the "hazel eyes and lips vermilion" that serve as the poem's first reference to Mary, a disturbing choice of phrasing that firmly connects her to the negative image of the body introduced in the first stanza. Again the alliterative quality of the verse contrasts the dichotomous states of rationality and emotionality:

> Ye gods! restore the halcyon days
> While yet I walked in Wisdom's ways
> And knew not Mary Maud Trevylyan!

The gentle sibilance of the first line of the tercet and the silky /w/ vo-calizations of the next simulate the peace that the speaker derives from immersion in his work, which is aurally convulsed by the final line's se-quence of sharp nasals and aspirates, associated with Mary, that require distinct, discrete, and fierce pronunciation for each syllable. Indeed, the tone becomes vituperative in a subsequent stanza, as the speaker resent-fully exclaims with definitive punctuation, "Away with books; away with cram / For Intermediate Exam! / Away with every college duty!"

The speaker's tone abruptly shifts, however, as he imitates a Petrar-chan lover lamenting his bashfulness, Mary's aloof response to his pres-ence, and his despair that he can "ever dare / To cross the gulf, and gain my Mary."[9] As he describes his beloved, he converts her into the idealized figure of the Victorian woman that the Marian resonances of her name carry: this "fairest fair" is a "worshipped image" that he will "cherish," a "virgin Saint" he now idolizes, and a modest maiden who is "never coy." Through these attributes, the speaker converts the individual Mary into an exemplar of woman, an entity who can be defined and thus presum-ably controlled and contained.

The speaker's uncharacteristic self-abasement is short-lived, though, for he transforms himself from passive admirer into active pursuer once he realizes that Mary's dispassionate response can be supplanted by in-tense affection if he plans his courtship carefully. The apparent irrec-oncilability of rationality and emotionality that surfaced in earlier stan-zas begins to collapse as Mary becomes not simply the object of desire but the object of scientific experimentation. As the poem progresses, the multisyllabic jargon of science is gradually blended with the mellifluous language of love, which the somewhat oxymoronic title, "Scientific Woo-ing," presaged; the speaker compares Mary to a "solar sphere," regrets the lack of a spectroscope to gauge her affection for him, initiates his

9. Albert D. Pionke also makes a Petrarchan connection in noting the speaker's "nod to early masters of the sonnet sequence such as Petrarch, Sidney, and Shakespeare" (" 'A Sweet "*Quod Erat Demonstrandum!*" ': The Poetics of Parody in Constance Naden's 'Sci-entific Wooing,' " 4). Pionke's reading of the poem points to its parodic elements, objec-tification of women, and display of Naden's scientific acumen.

suit "with Optics," intends to win it "by Magnetism," and foresees an ultimate "Chemic union." Mary simply becomes another intellectual puz-
zle, linked to the world of science not as a participant in its language and
rituals but solely as a commodity that is examined, quantified, and regulated. The speaker will manipulate the discourse of science to deceive and
control, as he muses that he cannot "fail to please / If with similitudes
like these / I lure the maid to sweet communion." The vigorous caesuras
that characterized the opening stanza reappear as the speaker stridently
announces his determination to triumph:

> At this I'll aim, for this I'll toil,
> And this I'll reach—I will, by Boyle,
>   By Avogadro, and by Davy!
> When every science lends a trope
> To feed my love, to fire my hope,
>   Her maiden pride must cry *"Peccavi!"*

We have traveled a substantial distance from the vulnerable Petrarchan
lover who had appeared briefly a few stanzas earlier. By invoking the
secular gods of science in the above passage, the speaker not only undermines the quasi-religious hold that the beloved exercised in his previous
idolatry, but he reshapes her from a stainless Marian figure into a re-
pentant Eve whose use of the Latin language of science is limited to a
recognition of her own unworthiness and guilt.

The impassive tone of the detached scientist that the speaker has displayed becomes increasingly disturbing as the poem moves toward its
final stanzas. He will imitate the successful strategies that lower organisms have adopted in the process of sexual selection, craft a "Darwinian
lay" that will point to the naturalness and desirability of his suit, apply
"rigorous Logic" with a calculated mathematical precision to make his
case, and script his words so coldly and designedly that "not a word I'll
say at random." Indeed, this segment hints at an unnerving deviousness
that exists covertly on a narrative as well as sonic level; from the opening
line, the final stanzas are marked by an abundance of smooth /l/ sounds
that seem not only alluringly liquid but distressingly oily. Through his
cunning and "[s]yllogistic stress," Mary will be conquered, signaling her
defeat by the "tearful 'Yes' " and the "sweet" utterance of submission that

would be expected of the paradigmatic Victorian woman who rightly bows to male authority. As in her plaintive *"Peccavi,"* Mary's final words in the poem are limited to her recognition of the male's superior knowledge and position.

As my reading has suggested, the sense of control that Mary exercised over the speaker's emotions in the early stanzas is undermined in significant ways that respond to the Victorian diptych of woman as virgin or whore. First, as we have seen, Mary's awe-inspiring effect on the speaker as an apparent model of ideal womanhood—saintly, unattainable, and chaste—is countered by his reconfiguration of her as an errant and conquerable Eve. Second, the eroticized Mary is reduced to a manageable collection of body parts that are drained of their dangerous and sexual components. The eyes that could suggest an assertive and troubling female gaze in initially "blast[ing]" the speaker's concentration on his studies instead become in his musings the "gentle eyes" that assume a "tranquil gaze" and unmenacingly reveal "[l]ove's vapour, pure and incandescent." The suggestive mouth that could portend an all-consuming and disastrous immersion in desire is neutralized through her faltering and docile responses to the speaker's initiatives.

That Naden is urging us to view the poem not unproblematically as a clever and amusing exercise in melding the discourses of science and love but as a sardonic and angry portrait of masculine conceptions of women is accentuated by a variety of formal qualities. Naden plays with the convention of the romance stanza, dutifully following the six-line framework and standard rhyme scheme of *aabccb,* but departs from the usual tercet sequence of a pair of iambic tetrameters and a line of iambic trimeter. The latter is instead replaced with an unexpected nine-foot line of four iambs and a truncated final iamb consisting of a feminine ending. Moreover, an iambic tetrameter line, in some cases, can be scanned as a nine-syllable line, depending on whether or not one decides to read an occasionally ambiguous word as a synaeresis. As an additional complication of the romance stanza, the first foot in each presumably iambic opening line of a stanza can be scanned instead as a spondee. All of these deviations from the romance form undermine the overall sense of containment and invincibility that the words' denotative and connotative valences seek to assert. With the questionable opening iambs, unstable synaeresis, and insistent feminine endings that transgress beyond the expected endpoint of the meter, the poem conveys not only a sense of protest against its stifling narrative but of subterfuge, defiance, and revolt.

Other formal aspects similarly counter the overall sense of control that the speaker's narrative aims to establish. Though the poem has no extended stanzas, suggesting by their omission that every stanza of the speaker's words is to be viewed as a tightly managed unit dominated by an appropriately masculine rhyme, the tail rhyme of each tercet depends upon a feminine ending. Those tail rhymes seem to defy the abrupt and definitive masculine endings, as if asserting a right to be heard and heeded. In addition, the pairing of the feminine rhymes is inconsistent through a blending of syllabic possibilities, fluctuating among two double-syllable words ("cherish," "perish"), di- and tri-syllabic words ("Davy," "Peccavi") and other unequal syllabic couplings ("crescent," "incandescent"), and even two words and a single word ("began it," "planet"). Such randomness of pattern is seen not only with rhyme but with caesuras, which vary in their intensity and placement throughout the poem, and with enjambment, which periodically evokes erratic and unplanned movement. All of these anomalies war against the speaker's efforts to assert control and resolutely marginalize women through the systematic language of science.

FLAWED FEMALE

Several of the thematic, linguistic, and formal elements that mold "Scientific Wooing" are manipulated in similar ways in "Natural Selection," another offering in "Evolutional Erotics." Again the male speaker exudes remarkable self-confidence, adopts the language of science to describe his courtship, and offers a problematic perspective on women. The unsuccessful suitor of "Natural Selection" defuses the power the inconstant Chloe has exercised through her eventual rejection of his affections by conferring upon her an ethical and physiological inferiority that establishes him as her irrefutable superior. Chloe is recast from desired object into a piece of scientific proof attesting to Darwinian verities. Early in the poem, however, Chloe is crafted as a worthy object of affection who, like the proper Victorian woman, functions as the moral compass in the pair's relationship. Evidencing a "filial regard," of which the speaker approves, for the graves that he ransacks in his scientific pursuits, Chloe displays a principled concern that her lover "ne'er could be true" if he did not respect these ancestral burial places. Yet that supposedly moral stance is immediately dissolved by her paradoxical fascination with such fossils and the unsavory influence she exerts on the speaker, for "Not a fossil I heard her admire, / But I begged it, or borrowed, or stole." Her interest in the fossils is made to appear unwomanly and inappropriate, for it negates the positive moral influence she should wield. Moreover, Chloe is quietly indicted for unwomanliness on another count through the speaker's suspicion that she does not adequately respect his work; she blithely dismisses the repository of his "splendid collection" and temple of science, his study, by disparagingly terming it "a hole."

Through these unseemly allusions, the speaker prepares his readers for Chloe's poor choice in a Darwinian sexual selection, described in the final two stanzas:

> And we know the more dandified males
>   By dance and by song win their wives—
> 'Tis a law that with *Aves* prevails,
>   And even in *Homo* survives.
>
> Shall I rage as they whirl in the valse?
>   Shall I sneer as they carol and coo?
> Ah no! for since Chloe is false,
>   I'm certain that Darwin is true!

In effect, the speaker situates Chloe in an unenviable double bind. On the one hand, a reader can assume that Chloe has followed an unpromising and rarely trodden evolutionary path that allies her more tightly with lower species than with humanity and preordains her line's eventual doom; her interest in the "idealess lad," who is demeaned through his strutting, staring, and smirking, implies that Chloe is no more advanced on the evolutionary ladder than the animal species that likewise choose "dandified males." In arguing that the law governing selection among nonhuman species on the basis of surface qualities "even in *Homo* survives," the speaker intimates with this verb that Chloe's application of the law on such antiprogressive grounds represents a vestigial anomaly rather than a universal pattern. On the other hand, a reader can assume that Chloe has followed the practice of sexual selection but has failed to recognize the speaker as a more desirable specimen who will help lead humanity to the next stage of evolutionary development. The successful suitor lacks the speaker's scientific acumen and intellectual curiosity— "Of Science he hasn't a trace, / He seeks not the How and the Why"—but simply displays evolutionarily unproductive attractions. Chloe's preference is thereby tainted because her criteria for sexual selection are based not on superiority but inferiority. She is unfavorably linked to the body rather than the mind, for the other suitor triumphs solely through his corporeal appeal—the singing and dancing abilities that Chloe values. Whichever of the two scenarios we choose, the effect is the same. In the final stanza, we are left to infer from the Darwinian reference that sexual selection on Chloe's terms is destined for failure, since the process of natural selection is predicated on a species' apt choices in the struggle to survive.

As in "Scientific Wooing," women are marginalized through their depiction as objects of scientific discourse rather than participants in it and as curiosities to be detachedly examined. The sense of power associated with a male speaker is even more apparent in "Natural Selection," however, as a prosodic examination reveals. The eight quatrains, with their pounding *abab* rhyme scheme, exclusively feature masculine endings that suggest through their muscular enunciation that a feminine influence has been successfully excluded, as in the opening stanza:

> I had found out a gift for my fair,
>   I had found where the cave-men were laid;
> Skull, femur, and pelvis were there,
>   And spears, that of silex they made.

Although the lines in each stanza in the poem inconsistently shift between anapestic trimeters and an iamb followed by two anapests, which could seem to signal a disruptive presence that undermines the poem's overall impression of mastery, the curious format instead mimics the randomness of natural selection itself and testifies to the speaker's proficiency and comfort within the scientific realm. Indeed, the fact that the first and final stanzas both feature a pair of anapestic trimeters, followed by an iamb and an anapest coupling, counteracts any supposition that the speaker lacks authority, for the two stanzas serve as inviolable boundaries between which the play of verse is allowed. Like "Scientific Wooing," the poem is dominated by one- and two-syllable words, primarily the former, which lend themselves to the same type of measured and decisive reading of each line, as do the abundance of rugged consonant sounds and the frequent caesuras. On both formal and narrative levels, then, "Natural Selection" decisively establishes science as a masculine purview that provides virtually no opening for a woman.

PRESUMED INFERIORITY

A similarly problematic view of women comes in "Solomon Redivivus, 1886," a third poem in "Evolutional Erotics" with a male speaker. The poem builds upon biblical allusions in that its narrator, King Solomon, was sought out by its silent listener, the queen of Sheba, who wished to question the famed wise man.[10] The speaker adopts a commanding and condescending attitude toward Sheba, a querulously childish figure whose interrogatories precede the poem's opening and initiate the speaker's monologue. He immediately assumes the role of confident superior in identifying himself with the fruits of civilization: aside from his self-perception as a "modern Sage," he is "Seer, savant, merchant, poet"—"in brief," he smugly summarizes, "the Age." He excludes his listener from participation in the accomplishments of the period by firmly situating himself in the subject position, boldly proclaiming, "I am," in the forceful declarative phrases delineating his multiple roles. Sheba serves as a kind of specular entity that the poem establishes through a dichotomy between a privileged "I" and inferior "you," a relationship crafted in part through Sheba's obtuse requests for information with which she is already cognizant, in this reminder of Victorian science's estimation of women as childlike in their mental processes, as well as her Sphinx-like proclivity for posing riddles that the speaker patiently and adeptly answers. Imperious commands further place Sheba in a subordinate position as the speaker physically assumes dominance

10. See 1 Kings 10:1–13.

in demanding that she "sit," metaphorically directs her gaze in warning her to "[l]ook not" upon his glory, guides her behavior in telling her to "[c]ount not" his treasures, and advises her to accept his imperatives to "hear our wondrous tale." As the latter reference indicates, it is the speaker who controls their narrative, while Sheba is relegated to the role of passive listener; even the question that led to the speaker's recitation of their story is presented in his voice rather than hers in the poem's opening lines:

> What am I? Ah, you know it,
> I am the modern Sage,
> Seer, savant, merchant, poet—
> I am, in brief, the Age.

In crediting himself for humanity's progression, the speaker relies upon the Victorian presumption noted in my introduction that evolution favored the male and that the female represented a lesser stage of development. Men, the argument went, were responsible for evolutionary advances on a physiological as well as intellectual level. It is surprising, then, that the speaker identifies Sheba as the one who initiates their metamorphosis from the "soft Amoeba" that was "[u]norganed, undivided" and existing "in happy sloth" to the next evolutionary stage, even though he casts her development in decidedly unflattering terms: she "incurred the odium / Of fission and divorce" and "strayed" her "lonely course." Despite the disparaging characterization, the speaker identifies the female as the one who initiated the series of changes that would transform the pair from one-celled organisms to complex humans. That admission leads us to a parodic reading of the speaker, transforming him from the assured and masterful superior of his female listener that he has crafted in his self-presentation into a ridiculously pompous and ignorant inferior to her. In effect, the poem challenges the masculine scientific view of women as a secondary entity and implies that a reinterpretation of presumably objective precepts is necessary. By so doing, the poem anticipates the prose writings of such iconoclastic evolutionists as Eliza Burt Gamble and David Ritchie, who would argue a few years after Naden's poetry appeared that scientists' conclusions about female inferiority were based on self-serving predispositions rather than careful analyses. We are tempted, then, to interpret the second word of "Solomon Redivivus" in mocking fashion to infer very different connotations for the word's seemingly solemn denotations of rebirth and uncovering.

The poem's form, too, can be productively assessed in this sardonic register. With its *abab* quatrains featuring alternating seven- and six-syllable lines, as in the following example, the poem approximates the scheme of common meter, which in turn conveys the commonality of the speaker's perspective on women.

> Look not upon my glory
>> Of gold and sandal-wood
> But sit and hear a story
>> From Darwin and from Buddh.

Yet in failing to include the final stressed syllable of common meter's paradigmatic *a*-lines of iambic tetrameter, the poem covertly points to the deficiencies in such a view. Indeed, the feminine rhymes of the *a*-lines offer a relentless challenge to the masculine rhymes of the *b*-lines, mirroring the assertion of female importance and vitality that appeared on the thematic plane. In these ways, a female presence is made as significant to the poem as a male one and wars against the speaker's strategy of marginalization.

FEMALE ESSENCE

Despite the quietly empowering message that we may read in "Solomon Redivivus," the sole poem in "Evolutional Erotics" with a female speaker distances her profoundly from the scientific world to provide an inescapably despairing commentary on the relationship of women to that public realm. "The New Orthodoxy" follows a somewhat different trajectory in detailing the relationship of a woman to science in that the speaker chastises her lover for his rumored loss of faith in Darwin, Spencer, and other noteworthy evolutionists. At first glance, we might view Amy, the speaker, as an erudite and independent woman who adeptly demonstrates an understanding of the latest scientific advancements and theories. A Girton graduate, she evidences a comfort with and confidence in such matters:

> Things with fin, and claw, and hoof
> Join to give us perfect proof
> That our being's warp and woof
>   We from near and far win;
> . . . .
> Then you jest, because Laplace
> Said this Earth was nought but gas
> Till the vast rotating mass
>   Denser grew and denser:

Yet that nominally assured self-presentation becomes problematic in light of the speaker's revelatory assumption elsewhere that she is infused with the female essence that Victorians generally considered the defining quality of all women. In the opening stanza, the speaker obliquely aligns herself with traditionally feminine Nature, as did her suitor, in remarking that "I've kept that spray you sent / Of the milk-white heather." Addressing his concern that she has become "too 'advanced,'" Amy seeks to correct the misapprehension:

> Trust me, Fred, beneath the curls
> Of the most "advanced" of girls,
> Many a foolish fancy whirls,
>   Bidding Fact defiance,
> And the simplest village maid
> Needs not to be much afraid
> Of her sister, sage, and staid,
>   Bachelor of Science.

The passage is disconcerting not only because of its subtle link between women and the body in its seemingly offhand reference to "curls," but also because it tends to nullify Amy's intellectual achievements. The qualities of sagacity and steadiness that Amy identifies in the bachelor of science lose much of their impact and import in being presented within an essentialist context that equates women with folly, capriciousness, and illogicality. In characterizing herself as a "sister" to an unlearned rustic, which seems the unlikeliest choice of commonality imaginable for an urbane college graduate, Amy positions herself as simply an exemplar of woman among women.

The ostensible independence that Amy displays in disputing Fred's blithe assumption that the pair will be immediately married, now that he has come of age, also carries disturbing implications. Amy first counters his brusque imperatives that "[w]e will, we must / Now, at once, be married!" with an assurance that appears, through her initial adverbial choice, to be an attempt to silence him: "Softly, sir! there's many a slip / Ere the goblet to the lip / Finally is carried." Yet we can read her response as merely one among several similar pieces of evidence in the poem that Amy is exhibiting not a defiance of the stereotypical role of the Victorian wife but an acceptance of the cultural belief that women serve as the moral authorities within the culture. Although Amy's championship of Darwinism may seem a bizarre manifestation of this gendered function of ethical stewardship, the poem's title leads us to this reading. In labeling Darwinian thought as "The New Orthodoxy," Naden implies that this form of belief has assumed the status of a religion, albeit a secular one. Abundant references in the poem reinforce the connection between Darwinism and religion that the title suggests. Amy refers to Fred, for example, as "a hardened skeptic" in his dismissal of the wisdom of evolutionist T. H. Huxley and his counterparts, chides Fred for his "flippant doubts" as any heretic would be admonished, exhorts him to "pin your faith to Darwin," and reprises that common noun and invokes other devotional terminology in her parting words:

> Yet—until the worst is said,
> Till I know your faith is dead,
> I remain, dear doubting Fred,
> Your believing
>
> AMY.

Amy's ardent advocacy of Darwinism itself serves to situate her within the traditional framework of female moral purity, in that she unswervingly adheres to the doctrines in which she has been taught to believe. No skeptical undertones mar her own presentation of her faith, but instead she emerges as a dedicated apostle and proselytizer of the creed.

The inference that Amy simply performs a traditional role rather than charts new paths for a female subjectivity based on intellectual accomplishment and assertion gains additional credence through the relatively passive and specular role she tends to assume. In the first stanza, for instance, Amy positions herself as reacting to Fred's initiatives instead of asserting her own agency. Thus, she keeps the flowers Fred sent, responds to his concerns that she is "advanced," and "quote[s] the books you lent." This latter reference is particularly important, for it suggests that Amy is less an independent thinker than a mimic who merely repeats the words deemed suitable for her perusal. Fred, in effect, is crafting her views, following the customary male role as the arbiter of the knowledge that a woman can appropriately learn. As a result, Amy's pretensions to intellectuality are drained substantially of their significance, for she can be perceived more as a vessel unquestioningly absorbing male directives than as an independent analyst of ideas.

Elsewhere in the poem, Amy similarly positions herself as a responder to Fred's initiatives and interests. Although Fred never speaks directly, his voice nevertheless dominates Amy's narrative, as he writes, plans, speaks, jests, scoffs, and woos. In each case, Amy is merely the recorder of his directives or opinions, serving as a loyal listener who asserts her own voice only in conforming to his lead. In the final stanza she surrenders any pretense of agency in portraying herself as one ready for his commands and his words: "Write—or telegraph—or call! / Come yourself and tell me all." In her closing comment that "I remain, dear doubting Fred, / Your believing Amy," she reiterates her submission to him; as one who "remains," she occupies a state of passivity, and as "your" Amy, she concedes possession of herself to him.

The poem's prosody reinforces that Amy is a mimic of masculine language and interests who reaches for but cannot attain the knowledge and skill of a male. It is important to assess the poem's formal qualities within the context of the other three works in "Evolutionary Erotics" to gauge appropriately the similarities and dissimilarities between the female and male speakers; if not viewed as part of a whole, the piece would lend itself to a vastly different and, I suggest, misleading reading. In light of the other poems, the prosodic techniques in "The New Orthodoxy" present Amy as a pale imitator of the male speakers with her timid voice and unsure poetic hand. The first clue comes in the overall form of eight-line stanzas rhyming *aaabcccb*. Rather than adopting the vigorous quatrains or ironic romance format found in the other "Evolutional Erotics" works, "The New Orthodoxy" instead employs an anomalous verse form that imitates the eight-line structure of an ottava rima or a triolet but does not conform to the rhyme scheme of either, as if the speaker had only a vague understanding of poetic conventions.

A helpful gloss on this point comes in considering Naden's devotion to form, which is evident in her belief, as R. W. Dale observed in 1891, "that sins against form are unpardonable in a poet."[11] A brief intertextual foray into Naden's "Poet and Botanist" is also instructive in this regard. Like the naturalist, the poet can be a "ruthless" practitioner who metaphorically employs a "cruel knife and microscope" to "work a spell / Of love or fame" and tear apart a bud's "tender leaves" to tell "*His* thoughts, and render up its deepest hue / To tinge his verse." The poet is gendered male in this verse, underscored by Naden's emphatic italics, which suggest a woman's displacement not only from the Victorian world of science but also from the similarly masculinized sphere of literary endeavor into which the intellectually rigorous work of poetic accomplishment, as opposed to the "light" literary efforts conventionally associated with women writers, would presumably fall.

In a related vein, "The New Orthodoxy" is given a decidedly feminized character, for the final line, "Your believing AMY," follows the spacing of a letter in dropping her name to a visual tenth line; to a Victorian mind, of course, private letters—not the weighty tomes of science or elaborately crafted verse—represented one of the few acceptable forms for women's writing. More significant than the epistolary element, though, are the predominance of masculine rhyme in the poem, which appears in all but the *b*-lines, and the presence of an extra syllable in the masculine lines. Feminine rhyme, like the female speaker herself, is made peripheral in the poem, implying only a limited opportunity for a woman to participate in the discourse of science, as well as poetry. The extra beat in the masculine lines, resulting from a clipped initial iamb, further insinuates that the feminine voice is a feeble version of its male counterpart. The aggressive tone of the poems that featured a male speaker, with their determined consonants and bold caesuras, is

11. Dale, "Constance Naden," 518.

not apparent here. Instead, the language seems tentative with its pre-dominance of short rhyming vowels that impart a sense of weakness rather than strength; in the only stanza in which long rhyming vowels prevail, they serve to accentuate a catalog of exclusively male thinkers. A multitude of enjambments, appearing inconsistently and lacking defini-tiveness, also contributes to the uncertain quality of Amy's language. All of these formal moves mirror the equally subtle ways in which Victorian ideology viewed a woman as a tangential rather than central figure who could never gain intellectual parity with the men who would always be evolving beyond her.

A BINARY DISTINCTION

It is appropriate here to turn to the earlier "Love *versus* Learning" be-cause it offers a helpful clarifying perspective on the poems constituting "Evolutional Erotics" through its complementary thematic strains. As the title hints, the poem establishes an unbridgeable distance between the spheres of emotionality and intellectuality for a woman. The 1881 piece relates the musings of a female speaker who recalls her idealized conception of a lover and the subsequent dissolution of her dream as she enters into an actual relationship. In her depiction of the imagined inamorato, the speaker envisions that he would value her intellectual as well as physical gifts. Once the speaker encounters her real suitor, how-ever, that expectation proves chimeric:

> My logic he sets at defiance,
>   Declares that my Latin's no use,
> And when I begin to talk Science
>   He calls me a dear little goose.
>
> He says that my lips are too rosy
>   To speak in a language that's dead,
> And all that is dismal and prosy
>   Should fly from so sunny a head.

Love and learning are mutually exclusive in women, according to the lover's estimation, through the mind/body dichotomy he unquestionably accepts. Under such logic, the "rosy lips" are therefore incapable of uttering learned phrases, and the female brain represents an inappropriate repository of serious thought. The suitor's designation of the speaker as "a dear little goose" diminishes her on multiple levels in its condescending affectional tone, dismissive adjectives, and appalling comparison.

Further distancing the speaker from learned endeavors are her dictional choices in relating her experience, for, as in "Scientific Wooing," the language of science is spoken by the male. She becomes, in effect, merely a conduit for her suitor's words as she indirectly transfers the narrative voice to him:

> He scoffs at each grave occupation,
> Turns everything off with a pun;
> And says that his sole calculation
> Is how to make two into one.
> . . . .
> He says that the sun may stop action,
> But he will not swerve from his course;
> For love is his law of attraction,
> A smile his centripetal force.

The surrender of her voice seems a logical progression when assessed in relation to her similar capitulation to male agency in the poem's early stanzas. An initial assertion of subjectivity and autonomy emerges through a series of statements that begin with a puissant "I" charting the direction of her narrative and guiding our interpretation of events. Yet she proceeds from her strong "I" to one who merely responds to the suitor's actions in her dismal realization that "I saw, and I heard, and I wavered, / I smiled, and my freedom was past." Agency subsequently shifts almost entirely to the male, as signaled by the next lines, in which the speaker laments, "He promised to love me for ever, / He pleaded, and what could I say?" Her loss of agency becomes particularly acute in the penultimate stanza, as her provisional comment that "often I think we must part" is overridden by her capitulation to his "compliments so scientific" that "[r]ecapture my fluttering heart." The phrasing is vexing not only because the image of emotionality implies that the speaker, like the suitor, views herself in terms of the body, but also because the references represent, as in "Scientific Wooing," a masculine manipulation of the language of science to conquer a desired object.

Equally disquieting is the speaker's recognition that the suitor is unworthy of her virtual self-sacrifice through his marked intellectual disparity with her ideal, as well as a suspicion that he is mentally inferior to herself. We can, perhaps, better understand the speaker's acceptance of her flawed suitor in exploring the expectations she held in the poem's opening stanza, for she advises that "I planned, in my girlish romances, / To be a philosopher's bride." Of interest in this revelation is her untroubled acceptance of the Victorian presumption of a woman's proper ambition—the acquisition of a husband. Not until the poem has progressed more than halfway through its narrative does the speaker refer in any detail to her own cognitive abilities, signaling through the delayed placement the secondary importance she accords them, as well as her absorption in and acquiescence to cultural dictates. We are prepared, then, for her unhappy choice of the unsuitable suitor over rigorous intellectual endeavors as the poem draws to its close:

> Yet sometimes 'tis very confusing,
>> This conflict of love and of lore—
> But hark! I must cease from my musing,
>> For that is his knock at the door!

Coupled with the negative implications of her selection on a personal level is the underlying danger that the speaker's choice presents for the evolutionary development of the human species. In general, Victorian culture compels a woman to stifle her own intellectual gifts and assume her destined role within the domestic sphere, even if she is intellectually superior to her mate, as is the speaker in this poem. Such ideology works against the acquisition of adaptive improvements by not encouraging women to choose the most desirable and advanced suitors; moreover, the ideology discourages women from honing their own cognitive abilities.

The culturally crafted opposition between love and learning for a female subject that the poem has drawn thematically is reflected on the formal level, as is the distancing of women from the masculine sphere of the mind. In the first regard, the poem is set in *abab* quatrains with alternating masculine and feminine rhymes to suggest the conflict between the gendered arenas of rationality and emotionality. Yet the masculine *a*-lines carry nine syllables, rather than the eight syllables of the feminine *b*-lines, to intimate that the masculine view of the proper sphere for a woman will prevail, as do the virile end-stops that characterize nearly all of the poem's lines. Like "The New Orthodoxy," the poem hints through its structure that a woman is simply viewed by her culture as a faint mimic of an authoritative patriarchal voice. Though the speaker adopts the quatrain form employed by her male counterparts in "Natural Selection" and "Solomon Redivivus" and gestures toward their stylistic approaches, her version lacks the vigor of the other two poems. Despite the fact that "Natural Selection" has a heavy concentration of anapestic feet and shifts between eight- and nine-syllable lines, as "Love *versus* Learning" does, each of the lines ends with a stress and a masculine rhyme; in "Love *versus* Learning," only the *a*-rhymes conclude with those markers of authority. Similarly, though "Solomon Redivivus" features alternating feminine and masculine rhymes, as does "Love *versus* Learning," the male voice's iambs call more attention to the stressed syllable of each foot than can the female voice's anapests with their two unaccented syllables.

The stanzas quoted above from "Love *versus* Learning" also offer important interpretive clues through their acoustic pattern. Each of the four stanzas in which the speaker merely transmits her suitor's words is dominated by sibilants rather than potent consonants to underscore again that she is an attenuated mimic of a male voice. Only in the final stanza is there an abundance of hard consonants, but they are intermixed with sibilants to convey on an aural level the titular conflict that the speaker undergoes, rather than a powerful female voice:

> Yet sometimes 'tis very confusing,
>   This conflict of love and of lore—
> But hark! I must cease from my musing,
>   For that is his knock at the door!

Ultimately, the vying of those implacable sounds with the softer ones causes the poem to end on a dissonant and unpleasant note that reverberates with the speaker's thematically unsatisfying decision to accept her suitor.

A SCIENTIFIC WOMAN

The portrait of female subjectivity that we have seen thus far in Naden's oeuvre has both drawn from and interrogated Victorian conceptions of womanhood in foregrounding the parameters of proper behavior and interests. In each case, women have been distanced from the world of science in significant ways and prevented from fully participating in its discourses and practices. Yet what are we to make of the unusual woman who defies cultural constraints and plunges into this masculine sphere by adopting science as a profession? In an 1881 poem titled "The Lady Doctor," Naden warns of the exorbitant price that she suggests must be paid. A woman could be perceived as a kind of transvestite, both intellectually and somatically, if she seeks to ally herself with the rationality and logicality conventionally attributed to the male. She cannot comfortably inhabit both the masculine realm of intellectuality and the feminine realm of emotionality; if she chooses the former, the poem cautions, she virtually unsexes herself in the eyes of her myopic culture.

Despite the fact that in the late nineteenth century women did presume to become physicians—medical schools had reluctantly begun allowing women to pursue the vocation at the time Naden was writing, and doctors like Elizabeth Garrett Anderson were making their marks—they often met with disapproval and disdain. To many male physicians and other scientific observers, women who chose to engage in intense intellectual work jeopardized their reproductive capacities because they were unnaturally channeling the body's finite energy and resources into their studies. In so doing, these observers believed, women imperiled future generations of humanity. Even Naden herself was considered to be a female aberration by none other than Herbert Spencer. After her death he opined "that in her case, as in other cases, the mental powers so highly developed in a woman are in some measure abnormal, and involve a physiological cost which the feminine organization will not bear without injury more or less profound."[12]

Told in the third person by an ungendered speaker, "The Lady Doctor" relates the history of the title character as a youthful beauty who rejects her lover, pursues her vocation, disdains marital satisfaction, and gradually changes from beautiful maiden into repellent hag:

12. Quoted in Tilden, "Part III," 89–90.

> Saw ye that spinster gaunt and gray,
> Whose aspect stern might well dismay
>   A bombardier stout-hearted?
> The golden hair, the blooming face,
> And all a maiden's tender grace
>   Long, long from her have parted.

In her youth, before she had decided to pursue a vocation, she is un-problematically associated with the feminine markers of the body and nature: she displayed "[t]he golden hair, the blooming face, / And all a maiden's tender grace"; she conferred "blushing looks, and many a smile, / And kisses sweet as manna"; and "[s]he wandered through the mead-ows green / To meet a boyish lover." Once she has decided to leave her lover, the dissolution of her bond with nature, and inferentially, her link to femininity, is presaged: "She threw away the faded flowers, / Gathered amid the woodland bowers."

Surprisingly, for a brief interlude, the character can combine intellec-tual work with traditional feminine traits and corporeal attractions, as she, "young and fair, / With rosy cheeks and golden hair, / Learning with beauty blended." Yet that unexpectedly harmonious conjunction occurs because, despite her learning, she evinces conventional womanly qual-ities and charms. Again the body becomes a significant trope. She can cure disease through "[a] lady's glance," her eyes prove more effective than quinine, and her smile acts as a tonic. In rejecting love in favor of a profession, however, the character initiates a physical and emotional deterioration, which is couched as a violation of female nature through a muted reference to the natural world:

> But soon, too soon, the hand of care
> Sprinkled with snow her golden hair,
>   Her face grew worn and jaded;
> Forgotten was each maiden wile,
> She scarce remembered how to smile,
>   Her roses all were faded.

Indeed, in the next couplet, the "Doctor she" becomes a witch whose "sole delight" is "[t]o order draughts as black as night"—an unnatural act, as the clangorous iteration of the dental /d/ sounds hints, through which the Medusan physician's "very glance might cast a spell" as she produces her "chill and acrid potions." In violating the conception of female nature she has become unsexed: her appearance is "so grim and stern" that no "heart could burn / For one so uninviting"; she no longer displays a normative woman's "gentle sympathy" but eschews "[a]ll female graces"; and, most ominously, "[s]he seems a man in woman's clothes."

If the reader harbors any doubts that the doctor's unenviable metamorphosis proceeds from her rejection of love in favor of learning, the narrator quickly corrects the misapprehension. We are advised that the character's sad state results from "[t]he woe of living alone, / In friendless, dreary sadness." Particularly troubling, however, is the message that the character regrets her choice:

> She longs for what she once disdained,
> And sighs to think she might have gained
> A home of love and gladness.

The poem thus serves as a warning to other females who might be tempted to follow the doctor's lead in emphasizing that love and learning cannot exist together. In its final stanza, disturbingly titled "Moral," the poem reiterates its distressing message:

> Fair maid, if thine unfettered heart
> Yearn for some busy, toilsome part,
> Let that engross thee only;
> But oh! if bound by love's light chain,
> Leave not thy fond and faithful swain
> Disconsolate and lonely.

As in "Scientific Wooing," the poem adopts the basic structure of the romance form with its six-line *aabccb* stanzas but again plays with the meter, in this case conveying an ironic tone. Though "The Lady Doctor" follows the usual romance pattern in its *a*- and *c*-lines with their iambic tetrameters, the *b*-lines add an extra syllable to the iambic trimeters to conclude with a feminine ending. The stanza's pair of feminine rhymes is overshadowed by the masculine rhymes of the other four lines, however, to accentuate the doctor's more pronounced association with masculinity. Though the *b*-rhymes depend on short vowels, intimating a feminine fragility and softness, long vowels dominate the overall rhyming scheme to impart instead a sense of masculine strength, especially in the stanzas that concentrate on the woman's scientific work.

I wish to return to the first stanza, for it sets the poem's unsettling tone through alliterative and caesural maneuvers. In the first tercet, "Saw ye that spinster gaunt and grey, / Whose aspect stern might well dismay / A bombardier stout-hearted?" the sibilants that generally evoke fluidity and smoothness instead call attention to the character's unseemly attributes—spinsterhood and a dismayingly stern aspect—and resonate with the masculine stouteartedness of the third line. The guttural contrast of the velars in "gaunt and grey" adds a harsh tone to the opening line, as do the interruptions from the light caesura that precedes this phrase and the similarly weak caesuras in the second and third lines. The tercet's enjambed line provides a concussive element with its shift to the onomatopoeic staccato sound of "bombardier," an interesting word choice in view of its inescapable link to the manly arena of war and its insinuation that even this most masculine of men would find the doctor unnerving. The stanza's final tercet continues to jolt the reader through an abrupt tonal change, for the fourth line accentuates the womanly qualities associated with the body—"[t]he golden hair, the blooming face"—that the doctor lacks, in that the line features more euphonious sounds and a caesura that vies with its counterparts in the first tercet to stress femininity. The enjambment of the final line pair—"And all a maiden's tender grace / Long, long from her have parted"—initiates another discomfiting shift that underscores the character's unnatural transformation from womanly model to manly aberration.

A Naden character who adheres to the advice of the final stanza of "The Lady Doctor" and chooses love over learning is the eponymous woman in "The Story of Clarice," a lengthy narrative in which she, in her formative years, lives in isolation with her father "with books for comrades." In the opening stanzas, Clarice is presented as intellectually gifted, yet that precocity apparently precludes the possibility of romantic involvement in distancing her from potential suitors:

> But she, in virgin majesty serene,
>> Whom few had dared to love, and none to woo,
> Wore learning as a long-descended queen
>> Her robes and crown doth royally endue;
> As though what others con with aching head
> This maiden knew by right inherited.

More disconcerting, though, is the negative effect her learning has upon the blossoming of her womanhood, lying latent but thwarted in development:

> Grave was her mouth, and yet was formed for smiles;
>> Pale were her cheeks—how lovely, had they blushed!
> No sweet gay looks were hers, no girlish wiles;
>> Not that her woman's instincts had been crushed;
> But, like azaleas in a darkened room,
> They had not air and light enough to bloom.

Intellectuality is curiously viewed as stunting her maturation; despite her learning, the narrator remarks, Clarice is "so child-like," a conclusion reiterated through a reference to her childish eyes.

Although a suitor subsequently appears, Clarice's preoccupation with learning prevents her from responding appropriately to his romantic initiatives. When he departs after she rejects his advances, Clarice strives to understand the feeling "[t]hat something she had found, and something lost" by immersing herself in the books that "were all her friends" and poring through Virgil, Spenser, and Shakespeare for assistance. Only when the dismissed suitor himself writes a book, which traces his unsuccessful courtship of Clarice, and sends it to her does she begin the process of maturation. The book serves as an intermediary tool for her development in enabling a gradual transition from the lofty realm of the abstract love she had previously known and relied upon to the actual workings of desire that the thinly disguised autobiographical novel represents. Books are subsequently expelled from the narrative altogether, as the expected realization of wedded bliss dominates the final stanzas—a prospect that was presaged when Clarice first visited the ailing suitor: "Then all the wifehood and the motherhood / That in her virgin heart close-hidden lay / Sprang forth."

"The Story of Clarice, like all of the scientifically grounded poems I have explored, conveys a disquieting and binaristic message: a Victorian woman can find little space in which she can challenge and broaden traditional perceptions of female subjectivity. According to the poems, she repeatedly encounters ideological preconceptions that associate a woman with the body instead of the intellect, reinforce her role as moral authority, view her as a specular counterpart to the Victorian male, depend upon an essentialist view that accepts the notion of an enduring female nature, and value her subservience and rectitude. No wonder, therefore, that the intellectually inquisitive woman of Naden's poetry can assert a voice within the realm of science and learning only in unsatisfying ways as an attenuated mimic of patriarchal authority or a virtual transvestite who has surrendered any valid claims to womanhood in the paradigmatic view of her culture. Constance Naden's poetry unmasks the discourse of science as a complicit and duplicitous participant in a Victorian ideology that validates and reconfirms the gendered power relationship through which women are disturbingly marginalized.

3

A Problematic Boundary

Masculinizing Science in Thomas Hardy's *Two on a Tower*

The vivid recognition of science as a male realm that I traced in Constance Naden's poetry becomes not only a heightened but also an obsessive concern with Thomas Hardy's 1882 *Two on a Tower*. In compelling fashion, the novel labors to stake out science as masculine territory and frantically strives to police the boundary, yet feminine intrusion persistently occurs, often even as the novel is in the process of constructing or reinforcing the boundary. Such textual moments reveal a pronounced anxiety over female encroachment, which incessantly threatens to contaminate, undermine, or annihilate masculine scientific endeavors. Despite compulsive efforts, however, *Two on a Tower* reveals that its array of exclusionary practices is destined to fail, for feminine presence is never wholly excised.

This doomed project suggests a variation on the process of abjection theorized by Julia Kristeva, in that a feminine presence is perceived to unsettle "identity, system, order" and refuses to "respect borders, positions, rules." Both attractive and repulsive, the Kristevan abject blurs the distinction between self and other in its menacing play with identity. Though the process of abjection aims to cast out and ward off the feminine peril, the disturbing influence remains, hovering on the border or insinuating its way beyond it. The abject poses "a kind of *narcissistic crisis*," Kristeva says, in that a complete separation from it cannot be sustained. In Lacanian terms, the abject complicates one's passage from maternal connection into the symbolic order, simultaneously demonstrating "the frailty of the symbolic order itself," Kristeva suggests. As Luce Irigaray has observed, the mother is linked to "contagion, contamination, engulfment in illness, madness, and death," and her influence looms as a constant source of danger. In *Two on a Tower*, both individual identity in particular and masculine identity in general are continually threatened by the unruly feminine presence that figuratively invokes the mother. "That other sex, the feminine," Kristeva notes, "becomes synonymous with a radical evil that is to be suppressed."[1]

Despite the novel's intriguing complexities in probing gender and science, *Two on a Tower* failed to garner enthusiastic responses from contemporary reviewers, and its intricacies remained unappreciated. The *Saturday Review*, for example, found the novel "extremely disappointing," though the periodical admired the "striking and imaginative" discussions of astronomy, the particular scientific focus of the narrative. To the *Spectator*, "this is a story as unpleasant as it is practically impossible," lacking "a single gleam of probability." *Two on a Tower*, the reviewer concluded, "as a whole is bad—the worst the author has written." Havelock Ellis thought that the novel "lack[ed] inspiration" and commented that "[t]he astronomical enthusiasm is wanting in spontaneity." More positively, the *Athenaeum* said that "we do not believe that star-gazing has been employed with half the ingenuity shown by Mr. Hardy's lovers." Regardless of such faint or nonexistent praise, *Two on a Tower* devises sophisticated strategies to pursue its ideological agenda.[2]

Two on a Tower explores the complex relationship between Viviette Constantine, wife and ultimately widow of Sir Blount Constantine, and Swithin St. Cleve, an ambitious young astronomer. As the novel opens, Viviette is riding through her husband's property and becomes curious

---

1. Julia Kristeva, *Powers of Horror*, 4, 14, 69, 70; Luce Irigaray, *The Irigaray Reader*, 40.
2. Review of *Two on a Tower* (*Saturday Review*, November 18, 1882), 675; Harry Quilter, review of *Two on a Tower*, 101, 102; Havelock Ellis, "Thomas Hardy's Novels," 125; "Novels of the Week: *Two on a Tower*."

about an ancient tower that she had previously observed but never entered. Though muddy conditions prevent her entry at this point, she eventually returns to the site and encounters Swithin, who has appropriated the tower for astronomical study. Struck by his handsome appearance, Viviette begins a passionate regard for the astronomer, who is considerably younger than she. Viviette makes frequent visits to the tower under an ostensible desire to pursue astronomy as a hobby and serve as a patroness to the impoverished scientist.

The fate of her husband, who had journeyed to Africa for adventure and glory, is uncertain, leaving Viviette as "neither maid, wife, nor widow" (20).[3] Upon hearing a rumor that Sir Blount is residing in London, Viviette convinces Swithin to interrupt his studies and ascertain the truth, but the supposed Sir Blount is not her husband. When Swithin later falls dangerously ill, the smitten Viviette travels to his home and bestows a kiss on the unconscious youth, who eventually recovers and returns to his studies. Viviette subsequently receives word that her husband had died in Africa eighteen months previously, leaving her nearly destitute through his poor management of their financial affairs. Nevertheless, Viviette continues to pursue her supposed interest in astronomy, and her passion for Swithin intensifies. Swithin, however, is oblivious of her feelings and considers Viviette a serious and companionable hobbyist.

Overhearing gossip about himself and Viviette one day, Swithin suddenly realizes that he is passionately attached to her. As he becomes increasingly devoted to Viviette, his dedication to work suffers. Eventually, Swithin believes that marriage would allow him to return to his studies without distraction, and the pair decide to marry in secret. They continue to conceal their marriage, especially from Viviette's brother, who inopportunely arrives for a lengthy visit. Assuming that Viviette is a widow, her brother schemes to marry her to a prominent bishop, whose proposal Viviette subsequently declines. Soon thereafter, a newspaper report announces that Sir Blount had died much later than thought, and Viviette realizes she had still been his wife when she married Swithin. The pair intend to marry again, despite her qualms that Swithin's work is suffering because of her. Before they can remarry, however, Viviette

3. All parenthetical citations come from the 1993 Oxford University Press edition of Thomas Hardy, *Two on a Tower.*

happens upon a letter Swithin had received, advising him that he would be eligible for a sizable bequest from a great-uncle if Swithin refrained from marriage until age twenty-five. The bequest warns Swithin of the harm a woman poses to professional pursuits and blames Viviette specifically, who has become the subject of rumors that have come to the great-uncle's attention.

Though Swithin nonetheless wishes to marry, Viviette continues to fear that she will harm his work and comes to the determination that she will set him free. Despite his disappointment and concern, Swithin decides to travel to the Cape in Africa and explore the southern sky. After his departure, Viviette learns of her pregnancy, which had resulted during the time she thought herself and Swithin married. Viviette frantically attempts to contact Swithin with the news, but his exact whereabouts are unknown. She believes that her only recourse is to marry the bishop, who has renewed his offer, and she accepts him. Three years pass, during which Swithin works assiduously in Africa with much success. While there, he learns from a newspaper report that Viviette has given birth to their son, and he discovers later that the bishop has died. Finished with his African observations, Swithin decides to return to England. Once there he sees Viviette, who has aged considerably, and he realizes he no longer loves her. Nevertheless, he feels obligated to offer marriage because of their history together. Ecstatic at the offer, Viviette swoons and dies. In the novel's final scenes, Swithin encounters an old acquaintance, Tabitha Lark, and the reader is left with the impression that the two will marry.

DRAWING THE BOUNDARIES

Let me turn, then, to the text's assessment of gender and science. Recent critical commentary, especially by Jim Barloon, has pointed intriguingly to the novel's construction of science as a masculine realm. Barloon observes, for instance, that "women are portrayed not only as 'detours' in the advance of science, but as dead-ends"; the novel "affirms the necessity of a realm of 'men without women.' "[4] I suggest that the narra-

4. Jim Barloon, "Star-Crossed Love: The Gravity of Science in Hardy's *Two on a Tower*," 28.

tive's overwhelming concern and feverish attempts to do so deserve additional scrutiny, particularly through an extensive examination of telling passages.

Two on a Tower begins to display its compulsion for establishing science as a masculinist enterprise in the opening chapter by stressing Viviette's separation from the discipline, situating the relationship within a physical register:

> The central feature of the middle distance as [Viviette and her servant] beheld it was a circular isolated hill of no great elevation, which placed itself in strong chromatic contrast with a wide acreage of surrounding arable by being covered with fir trees. . . . This pine-clad protuberance was yet further marked out from the general landscape by having on its summit a tower in the form of a classical column, which, though partly immersed in the plantation, rose above the tree tops to a considerable height. Upon this object, the eyes of the lady and servant were bent.
>
> "Then there is no road leading near it?" she asked.
>
> "Nothing nearer than where we are now, my lady."
>
> "Then drive home," she said after a moment. (5)

As the "central feature" of the landscape, the hill and its looming structure dominate the scene, drawing the eye irresistibly to its contours. The phallic imagery is extensive and insistent, accreting as the description proceeds. Though initially an acclivity of modest height, the landscape takes on multiple phallic permutations as the eye travels beyond a mere "protuberance" to a "summit" and ultimately becomes fixed on a "tower," with its phallic connotations emphasized through repetition of its status as a "column" that extends "a considerable height." In addition, the position of the tower mimics an incomplete stage of masculine sexual penetration in being "partly immersed" in the terrain. The column exerts a power that compels the eye completely, as the predicate "bent" implies through its denotation of forceful or decisive inclination. Moreover, as the "central feature" of a specifically delineated "middle distance," the "isolated hill" suggests both separation from and authority over an observer. Underscoring Viviette's feminine separation from the phallic intimations of the tower is the lack of access to the structure, which she cannot reach from any road. Upon learning this fact, Viviette returns to the domestic realm to which she will be metonymically associated later in the narrative. Upon revisiting the site a short time thereafter, Viviette is prevented from reaching even the margins of the hill because of the sodden earth that impedes passage across the surrounding field. Nevertheless, her eye is again drawn to and arrested by the tower, which compels ocular attention until the site is no longer visible from her moving carriage.

The tower's masculinist connotations become even more pronounced through the patrilineal associations that the narrative immediately proffers to fuse the phallic connection begun by physical description. Not only does the tower stand on "the hereditary estate of her husband," revealing its status as both a current and ancestral marker of male authority, it "showed itself as a much more important erection" than it had initially appeared (6). The phallic overtones of the noun are certainly evident, but more subtle is the column's innate power as intimated by the agency inhering in the phrase "showed itself." Agency is further suggested through the transformation of the noun "erection" to the predicate form of "erected" soon after in adumbrating the tower's origin as not merely a reminder but "a substantial memorial" of an eighteenth-century ancestor, whose masculinity is evidenced by a military career. The early history of the hill itself emphasizes its patriarchal connections through political and additional militaristic links, for it is variously identified by antiquaries—themselves bound to patrilineal heritage by virtue of their occupation—as the locale of an ancient Roman camp, British castle, or Saxon council. A Tuscan example of "classic architecture" (7), the tower is aligned with centuries of patriarchal civilization since the style represents one "of the five classical orders of architecture" (293), all of which would have been crafted by men, and carries implicit connections to the male-dominated culture of early Rome and Greece through evocations of the term "classical." Indeed, "this aspiring piece of masonry," with the adjective conveying both substantial height and lofty ambition, has been "erected as the most conspicuous and ineffaceable reminder of a man that could be thought of" (8), a phrase that again incorporates the erection imagery while conveying both dominance and permanence. The structure is additionally associated with the ultimate

patriarchal figure, as Peter Fjagesund observes in a discussion of the
novel's phallic images, for a cited psalm, uttered by a parson, notes that
"[t]he Lord look'd down from Heavn's high tower."[5]

Furthermore, the masculinist qualities of the tower are foregrounded
by its separation from the surrounding terrain. Though situated within
dense and "pine-clad" vegetation (5), the tower extends above it, "a
bright and cheerful thing" that stretches "unimpeded, clean, and flushed
with sunlight" (7). The liberatory sunlight—a traditionally masculinist image that is specifically gendered elsewhere in the text—appears in
sharp contrast to the overdetermined feminine "*paysage moralisé*" en-
circling the tower's base.[6] Like other *fin de siècle* narratives examined
in critical commentary, *Two on a Tower* imports sexualized imagery
into landscape descriptions to express anxiety over menacingly powerful
women, as if an ominous *vagina dentata* presence lurked within the oc-
cluded space. "[S]pikelets from the trees," though creating a deceptively
"soft carpet" around the tower, conceal a periodic "brake of brambles
barr[ing] the interspaces of the trunks" (7), with the aggressive alliteration of the labial consonants evoking carnivorous flora flexing their
mandibles as they guard against trespassers.

The vegetation serves as a signifier of femininity in part through its
associations to emotionality, even as the flora challenges the masculinized pillar through *dentata* qualities:

> The sob of the environing trees was here expressively manifest,
> and, moved by the light breeze, their thin straight stems rocked
> in seconds, like inverted pendulums; while some boughs and twigs
> rubbed the pillar's sides, or occasionally clicked in catching each
> other. Below the level of their summits the masonry was lichen-
> stained and mildewed, for the sun never pierced that moaning
> cloud of blue-black vegetation: pads of moss grew in the joints of
> the stonework, and here and there shade-loving insects had en-

5. Peter Fjagesund, "Thomas Hardy's *Two on a Tower*: The Failure of a Symbol," 86–
88.
6. The term is used by Sandra Gilbert and Susan Gubar to make a similar point about
the landscape in H. Rider Haggard's *She* (*No Man's Land: The Place of the Woman Writer
in the Twentieth Century*, 2:13). Specifically in relation to *Two on a Tower*, Fjagesund remarks briefly on "the contrast between the tower and the surrounding landscape, which
is typically female" ("Failure of a Symbol," 86). He adds that the tower comes to represent "an erotic awakening" for Viviette.

graved on the mortar patterns of no human style or meaning, but curious and suggestive. (7)

The weeping and moaning of the trees intimate both feminine emotionality and chora-like utterances attesting to a linguistic inability distancing the female voice from the symbolic order. The phallic "thin straight stems" forming "inverted pendulums" convey a feminized mimesis, while the clicking and catching of the branches evoke a conspiratory sororal interaction and communication as the vegetation prevents the sun from a phallic piercing of the moaning nebular mass. Inferences of decay abound as the boughs that erode the tower foster the fecund mosses below, which incessantly invade the manmade structure and shelter insects that continue the devastation. The result is a feminized trace upon the tower "of no human style or meaning," with its "curious and suggestive" appearance (7) seemingly escaping logic and language. So relentless is the process of decay that the stone tablet over the tower door only appears to have once been inscribed, for "whatever it was, had been smoothed over with a plaster of lichen" (8).

The breastlike "rotund hill of trees and brambles" upon which the tower sits is additionally feminized through its contrast to the terrain on which it is situated (7). As an "island" located "in the centre of a ploughed field" that extends many acres, the hill stands in a virtually inaccessible section of cultivated land. The fact that the ground is cultivated carries a masculine valence through the traditionally male ownership of property, yet the tangled section where the tower rests appears to defy attempts at husbandry and order. So difficult to penetrate, the vegetative mass is "probably visited less frequently than a rock would have been visited in a lake of equal extent" (7–8). The markers of feminized nature extend within the tower as well; Swithin had found it necessary to remove "nests and feathers" that had "choked" the column's staircase when he first occupied the structure (11). It is as if the feminine intrudes persistently into the masculine, exerting a continual pressure that threatens male activity; indeed, Viviette's sense of "herself [as] the proprietor of the column and of all around it" (8) underscores that obtrusion, as do the multiple references to the determined gaze that she fixes upon the tower. In a sense, the feminized vegetation imitates the authority and dominance inhering in the phallic tower it surrounds. Not only is the landscape ominously predacious, but it contaminates anything it encircles or touches—in vivid contrast to the tower's "clean" appearance as it is "flushed with the sunlight" in emerging from the ambient landscape (7)—to suggest the contagion typically linked to female presence in *fin de siècle* quest romances.

The gendered oppositions established in the opening passages not only thread through the subsequent narrative but also extend into other areas, persistently seeking to situate science within a masculine realm and position women as a threat to the discipline. Yet, as the essentialized vegetation encroaching on the tower reveals, the boundary between masculine and feminine spaces is neither wholly legible nor inviolable. Nevertheless, the text repeatedly strives to carve out science as a masculine endeavor, even as those attempts reveal the insistent force and destructive intrusions of feminine influence.

PERSONAL VERSUS PUBLIC

As we shall see in the next chapter, which investigates *Heart and Science,* a woman's interest in science is viewed as serendipitous and shallow, stemming not from an admirable dedication to the pursuit of knowledge but narrow selfishness. Viviette's initial foray into the scientific world comes merely by coincidence and a desire to "disperse an almost killing *ennui*" (6), manifested in a "walking weariness" (20) so intense that "[s]he was in the mood to welcome . . . even a misfortune" to alleviate it (6). Viviette had observed the tower from her home "hundreds of times" before the narrative opens, but never had she felt a compulsion to explore scientific possibilities; instead, she is motivated to investigate the structure simply because she anticipated a spectacular view. Although the text seemingly excuses her lack of intellectual curiosity in part because of the problematic relationship with her absent spouse and the tower's links to him, the narrative voice sounds more accusatory than exculpatory.

In contrast, Swithin St. Cleve is drawn to the tower solely for the scientific opportunities it presents. "[R]esolved" to study astronomy and propelled by the desire to attain the title of astronomer-royal, Swithin approaches his sidereal studies consciously and devotedly (12). He envisions himself as "the new Copernicus" (32) and crafts an "air-built image of himself as a worthy astronomer received by all the world" (190). Indeed, the narrator similarly identifies Swithin according to his scientific acumen, for the text is laced with references to "the astronomer."

Although *Two on a Tower* makes references to well-known astronomers, those scientists are exclusively male. The novel ignores contributions by women astronomers, such as Caroline Herschel, sister of famed astronomer William Herschel, and Mary Somerville. Caroline Herschel, however, was not merely the assistant of her brother, and subsequently that of his astronomer-son, but a dedicated astronomer in her own right who identified eight comets, among other accomplishments. Somerville penned books on scientific discoveries for a curious audience. Yet in *Two on a Tower,* a suggestion of female contributions to astronomy would blur the sharp gender delineation the novel strives to enforce.

The initial meeting between Viviette and Swithin underscores their dissimilar interests in the tower through the different objects of their gazes, associating Swithin with the rational world of science—he exudes "scientific earnestness" and a "melancholy mistrust of all things human" (12)—and Viviette within the irrational world of emotion. When Viviette first enters the tower, her gaze is directed to Swithin, who arrests her attention as "an interesting spectacle [that] met her eye" (8); Swithin, placed at the center of the column's summit to accentuate his total immersion within the scientific realm, instead directs his gaze through a telescope.[7] Even though Swithin's unexpected presence causes Viviette to move abruptly and create an audible footfall, Swithin's gaze remains fixed and intense, so much so that his dismissive wave of a hand serves as an interdiction against interruption. As Swithin maintains his gaze on celestial wonders, so undeterred by Viviette's presence that he remains stationary for an "ample time" (9), Viviette's scopic attention remains on him as she examines him minutely and mentally evaluates his physical attributes. Not insignificantly, Viviette's forceful gaze suggests an objectification, feminization, and eroticization of Swithin, a point to which I will return in assessing the deleterious effects of women upon science. At this juncture, however, the vital interpretation rests in Viviette's preoc-

7. For a discussion of the gender associations of rationality and emotionality in the novel, as well as the dearth of female astronomers and a reinforcement of separate spheres, see Malane, *Sex in Mind,* 158–69, 182–89.

cupation not with the attractions of science but of the scientist. Tellingly, her gaze thereafter "never fell upon the Rings-Hill column without a solicitous wonder arising as to what he was doing" (48–49).

The earlier inference that science is a masculine domain becomes more pronounced as the pair enter into conversation. Viviette's ignorance of astronomical fundamentals is manifested in a question she poses, to which Swithin responds "drily" and "not without some contempt for the state of her knowledge" (12). Viviette has "never seen any planet or star through a telescope," and though she professes a fascination with the movements of stars and a desire for enlightenment (12), Swithin remarks upon her "ignorance of the realities of astronomy" being "so satisfactory" that he refuses to correct it without a "serious request" (13). As the exchange between the pair hints, Swithin acts as a kind of gatekeeper to the world of science, controlling access to this rarefied masculine field; only through him can Viviette hope to gain an understanding of astronomical complexities, and Swithin will determine the nature and breadth of the knowledge she can obtain. Thus, Swithin offers to introduce her to the planets and stars she has never viewed telescopically, and in her subsequent travels to the tower her use of the telescope is either attained through or directed by Swithin. In fact, Viviette lacked even a sense of "the grandeur of astronomy until you showed me" its wonders, she informs Swithin (47); she "caught . . . a large spark from his enthusiasm" (51), merely a passive recipient rather than a self-determined agent.

The intimations of emotionality that inform the opening scenes of the novel are manifested more overtly elsewhere in the text to bind Viviette firmly to this essentialized trait. Viviette is governed by "a warm and affectionate—perhaps slightly voluptuous—temperament" (25–26) through which she "dwell[s] . . . on her passing emotions as a woman" (35). Observing Swithin intently and romantically on one occasion as he waxes in eloquent fashion about his work, Viviette "meditatively regard[s] him," evincing "a luxurious contemplative interest" while "in pursuance of ideas not exactly based on his words" (55). "[I]mpressionable as a turtledove" (77), Viviette is marked by an "emotional and yearning countenance" (65). With her "mastering emotions" (141), Viviette is, "by nature, impulsive to indiscretion" (161), for her characteristic tendency is to "counsel her activities . . . by emotions" (231).

Underscoring the essentialist identification of Viviette are occasional reminders that she is a "true woman" (49); she would deem the "remotest
possibility to be the most likely contingency" (49), for example, and as a
"perfervid" woman she displays the "courage of . . . emotions, in which
young men are often lamentably deficient" (115). Not only does Viviette
live by emotion but she dies by it; her death is precipitated by "[s]udden
joy after despair" (281), causing her to produce "a shriek of amazed joy"
and fall lifeless into Swithin's embrace (280).

Swithin's fundamental unfamiliarity with and underlying distaste for
emotionality is made equally emphatic. "[N]o *amoroso,* no gallant, but
a guileless philosopher," Swithin is rhetorically constructed through a
series of facial and cranial elements that each attest to rationality (44).
His lips "spoke, not of love, but of millions of miles"; his eyes "looked,
not into the depths of other eyes, but into other worlds"; and "[w]ithin
his temples dwelt thoughts, not of woman's looks, but of stellar aspects,
and the configuration of constellations." Moreover, Swithin proclaims he
will "never marry," for "[a] beloved science is enough wife for me" (62).
He had "reared himself, in the scientific school of thought" (146), manifested in comparison with Viviette in "his more logical mind" (152). As a
scientific man, Swithin "took words literally," displaying an "inexorably
simple logic" reflective of "natural laws" (279).

The gendered opposition between emotionality and rationality reveals itself, too, in disparate preoccupations with the personal and the
cosmic. These bifurcated interests are particularly evidenced in an early
vignette as the pair converse, when Viviette has visited Swithin at the
tower one evening to ask his aid in ascertaining if her husband is unexpectedly alive and living secretively in London. As Swithin is immersed
in his astronomical observations and attempts to draw Viviette into their
mysteries also, she replies, "It was not really this subject that I came to
see you upon," but "a personal matter" (33). Though Viviette seemingly
recognizes the relative importance of their varied interests in requesting that they "finish this grand subject [of astronomy] first—it dwarfs
mine," the supposition is immediately undercut by the narrator's musings that "[i]t would be difficult to judge from her accents whether she
was afraid to broach her own matter, or really interested in his." Indeed, Swithin's obvious pride in his subject and his assumption that
Viviette shares his engrossment simply "may have inclined her to indulge

him for kindness' sake." For Swithin, characteristically, "the vastness of the field of astronomy reduces every terrestrial thing to atomic dimensions" (221).

The essentialist distinction between the personal and the public realms is drawn not only through such spoken utterances but also through the written word. Viviette's periodic compositions are restricted to feminine manifestations, both in content and form. In every case, Viviette's subject matter devolves around personal issues—avowals of affection, schemes for romantic liaisons, reactions to marital proposals, sacrificial self-denials of connubial bliss, anxiety over an unexpected pregnancy, and the like—and is expressed in an epistolary mode, a traditional feminine vehicle, and usually in casual notes rather than formally crafted letters. Her atypical venturing outside of personal communications comes only through her infrequent role as Swithin's amanuensis, acting merely as a vessel for the transmittal of a male's observations and ideas. Interestingly, the sole reference to Viviette's "writing-room" comes when she receives a parcel meant for Swithin's astronomical work (42).

Conversely, Swithin's writings almost without exception are focused on matters of science, and only rarely do they appear in epistolary form; personal matters are almost wholly ignored, even when a letter is ostensibly written for that purpose. On one such occasion, after Swithin has traveled to London at Viviette's request to search for her husband, he writes only that he has "quite succeeded in my mission" and proceeds to comment about his work; to Viviette's consternation as she pores over his letter, "his mind ran on nothing but this astronomical subject," offering no clues about the results of his journey (39). Unlike Viviette's informal writings, Swithin's notes tend to carry a teleological purpose, in that they represent the basis of further work. Following his sojourn to the Cape, for instance, Swithin amasses for a future treatise "memoranda of observations" so extensive that they "accumulated to a wheelbarrow load" (268). Swithin regularly sends papers to astronomical journals, the Royal Society, or the Greenwich Observatory, and his frequent jottings are invariably devoted to his discipline. With the exception of Viviette's communications, the letters Swithin receives further attest to his immersion in the public realm, for they emanate from scientific or legal sources. Swithin's links to public writing are suggested even by absence; in Viviette's first venture within the tower she finds a blank "scrap of writing-paper" (8), presumably awaiting Swithin's sidereal remarks.

Viviette's connection to reading is even more obscured than to writing. She is so distanced from the former that she relies on a paid companion to read aloud to her, unwilling nevertheless to be even a passive recipient of the written word much less an active creator of meaning. Viviette refuses "to hearken" to her reader, who disgustedly comments that such a feat is "more than a team of six horses could force [Viviette] to do," and after a session is asked "what I've been reading" (19). Books function more as sinister presences than illuminative comforts, for Viviette sprawls in bed surrounded by "immense volumes, that half bury her," as if she were mimicking "the stoning of Stephen" and, in effect, being destroyed by textual antagonists.

On the sole occasion when Viviette actually peers within a text, she does so only through male influence and provision, rifling through the scientific tomes in her husband's library to impress Swithin with her comprehension of his field. Yet the books she avidly peruses in the "awkward dusty" library are hopelessly outdated, serving merely to reveal and accentuate the deficiencies she "learned when . . . a girl" (54), as if a female is irrevocably distanced from the scientific realm. Moreover, though Viviette borrows one of Swithin's books on cometary composition, there is no evidence that she actually reads it before returning it to him. As befitting essentialized woman, however, through the traditional linkage between the female and corporeality, Viviette is adept at reading the body, able to decipher the codes of emotion as expressed on Swithin's face (94). Not surprisingly, Swithin evinces no such feminine acuity, unaccustomed even to "noticing people's features" and rarely so much as "observ[ing] any detail of physiognomy" (158). Instead, he immerses himself in astronomical texts, "seldom read[ing] any other subject" (54).

The gendered distinctions that the text has labored to trace thus far are mirrored as well in the spaces that the characters typically occupy, whereby Viviette is linked to the private world of the home and Swithin to the public world signified by the tower. As Fjagesund also argues, "[t]he two structures are almost personified," with "the column standing for Swithin, and the house for Lady Constantine."[8] Metonymically

8. Fjagesund, "Failure of a Symbol," 88.

associated with the house of her husband, Viviette is comfortable within its confines and rarely leaves its boundaries, venturing beyond its portals or contiguous terrain only to further her connections with Swithin. Generally barred from entering Viviette's home either through his own disinclination or fear of public disapprobation, Swithin finds the house uninviting and suffocating on his rare ventures within. In the feminized world of the home, Swithin strives to distance himself from its female associations.

In one instance, Swithin walks into the home upon Viviette's summons and examines the holdings in her husband's library, a masculine space carved within the feminized structure. Rather than join Viviette for lunch elsewhere in the house, Swithin prefers to dine in the library, an unusual locale for such an activity. His movement beyond the library extends only to an adjacent room, which he enters upon Viviette's urging, as if reluctant to proceed entirely past this physical link to masculine space. Yet, as part of the domestic realm simply by virtue of being contained within it, the masculine space cannot be severed from the feminine; Swithin seemingly attempts to distance himself from domestic connections as he rises "above the embarrassing horizon of Lady Constantine's great house" and rhetorically immerses himself within the world of science, denigrating the obsolete collection of texts he has perused and discoursing on modern scientific theory (54). In a second instance, Swithin accedes to an invitation proffered by Viviette's brother to stay overnight at the home one evening, despite an initial desire to examine certain celestial activities from the tower. Nevertheless, Swithin surreptitiously leaves the home during the night to return briefly to the column and conduct his work within its comforting environs.

As the novel's paradigmatic masculine signifier, the tower is the space that Swithin generally occupies. Indeed, there is "no communication" or path between Viviette's home and the tower (57), as if masculine space must be kept inviolable. Even Swithin's living quarters are extensions of the tower, both literally and figuratively. A cabin constructed next to the tower facilitates Swithin's access to his work, and his chamber within his grandmother's home mirrors the contents of the tower itself. The chamber not only is used as Swithin's study but also is filled with astronomical materials so extensively that the walls are covered by celestial maps and serves as a space "for the manufacture of optical instruments" (70).

FEMALE MENACE

The text's feverish efforts to carve out science as a masculine domain, as the many manifestations of gendered oppositions have illustrated, are undergirded by an obsessive fear that feminine intrusion necessarily brings corruption, contamination, and destruction. Such disastrous effects are demonstrated in part by Viviette's designations as an Eve analogue, a temptress who will cause her Adamic counterpart to stray from righteousness. Before succumbing to Viviette's influence, Swithin's "heaven . . . was truly in the skies," rather than "in the eyes of some daughter of Eve" (44), situating him within a prelapsarian naïveté destined to end. As critical commentary has observed, *Two on a Tower* mimics the crucial Edenic moment when Eve initiates Adam's fall, in this case occurring when Swithin first visits Viviette's home where he corporeally as well as psychologically begins his surrender to feminine defilement. After perusing the texts that Viviette earlier had plucked from "worm-eaten shelves" in the library (51) and agreeing to join her in the adjacent chamber, Swithin "modestly ventured on an apple," an event seemingly preordained when, in childhood, he had frequently pilfered the fruit from the Blount orchards (54). Like the archetypal Eve, Viviette knowingly errs in her temptations of Swithin, self-referentially remarking on one unrelated occasion that "the Eve in us will out sometimes" (97) and presumably "regain[ing] her normal sweet composure about a week after the Fall" (233). Yet all women, not merely the transgressive Viviette, carry an inherent taint, the text insinuates, for the comely presence of Tabitha Lark whom Swithin presumably will marry compels him to join her in a garden where he "strolled out under the apple-trees" (275). Further condemning woman as ensnaring temptress is the narrator's rhetorical musing as to whether "any Circe or Calypso, and if so what one, [would] ever check" Swithin's sidereal pursuits, a prospect the male voice deems a "pity" (44) in creating layers of condemnation through both mythical and biblical figures. As Shanta Dutta observes, Viviette functions as "obviously the eternal 'femme fatale'—of Christian myth and classical legend."[9]

---

9. Shanta Dutta, *Ambivalence in Hardy: A Study of His Attitude to Women*, 59. Scholarship has focused on the astronomer's childlike innocence in prelapsarian terms as

Even before Swithin proceeds from grateful recipient of Viviette's financial largesse to smitten lover, the dangers of female influence in the scientific realm are strikingly apparent. Before agreeing to Viviette's request that he travel to London in search of her husband, for instance, Swithin extracts from her the promise that she will conduct the astronomical observations necessary for his "great theory" on variable stars (37). Without nightly observations, Swithin fears that "the whole of my year's labour" would be wasted, a prospect that Viviette considers merely a sign of masculine selfishness in another manifestation of her distance from the public realm of science. Though eventually agreeing to undertake the observations in Swithin's absence—despite her concern that it would involve "much trouble"—Viviette first asks that Swithin transport the telescope to her home (37). In another reminder of the separate worlds of the home and the tower, Swithin declines to move the apparatus, even though "[i]t *could* be moved" (38). Viviette's promise to make nightly visits to the tower is broken on two occasions, however, seriously jeopardizing Swithin's work. In her blithe response to Swithin's anxious reaction, Viviette displays a feminine lack of interest in and obtuseness to the value of scientific pursuits by commenting that she simply "forgot to go—twice!" (40). Justifying her inaction by saying, "I could not help it," for she "had watched and watched, and nothing happened," Viviette deflects Swithin's disapproval and returns to her customary preoccupation with personal rather than public interests, immediately asking if Swithin has found her husband and causing Swithin to "[lower] his thoughts to sublunary things."

The notion that Viviette's presence will prove destructive to Swithin's work is demonstrated literally as the scene progresses. Like a proud and protective parent, Swithin holds a "carefully cuddled-up" parcel containing a crucial lens for a telescope he hopes to construct, a revolutionary component he deems "a magnificent aid to science."(40). As he accompanies Viviette while she prepares to leave, he places the parcel on a garden wall in a textual gesture toward Viviette's correspondence

well. Barloon, for instance, mentions "Swithin's sexless, prelapsarian innocence" ("Star-Crossed Love," 28), while Dutta comments upon Swithin's "prelapsarian devotion to science" and "the postlapsarian deception of clandestine love affair" (58). For a discussion of the novel's Eve references and Viviette's corruption of Swithin, see Dutta, *Ambivalence*, 58–59.

to archetypal Eve and relaxes his vigilant attention to the packet while making his farewell. When Swithin turns back to the lens for which he had "waited nine months" (41) like an expectant parent, he inadvertently knocks it over the wall and agitatedly watches the precious component shatter on the pavement far below. Viviette's immediate response to his anguish is to make the dismissive comment, "Don't mind it—pray don't!" (42), which underscores Swithin's just-uttered observation attesting to her ignorance of the scientific world as he moaned, "[I]f you only knew what it is to a person engaged in science to have the means of clinching a theory snatched from you at the last moment!" (41). Subsequently, he admonishes Viviette that "you will never realize that an incident which filled but a degree in the circle of your thoughts covered the whole circumference of mine," an assumption that she confirms in writing to him that "I think you were too sensitive to my remark" and attributing his dismay to being "agitated with the labours of the day" coupled with weariness from his nocturnal studies (47).

The episode serves as a prescient glimpse at the ruinous effects of women on scientific endeavor that the text abundantly and obsessively presents throughout the narrative. Once Swithin has become emotionally ensnared by Viviette, his work increasingly suffers as he succumbs to her distracting presence more and more. Rather than immersing himself in his studies, he allows his attention to be focused on Viviette's attractions as his eagerness to establish himself within his profession becomes dismayingly attenuated. Within moments upon realizing his ardor for Viviette, Swithin ignores the prospect of his work being disrupted and damaged, a possibility that even Viviette finds alarming. Fearing that a servant she has sent to the tower will toy with Swithin's materials, Viviette encourages Swithin to return there rapidly to avoid such a disaster; Swithin, however, responds that the servant "may do what he likes—tinker and spoil the instrument—destroy my papers—anything—so that he will stay there and leave us alone" (95). Though Viviette remarks that Swithin was "once so devoted to your science that the thought of an intruder into your temple would have driven you wild," she recognizes that "[n]ow you don't care." Swithin confirms the validity of her comment in answering, "I offer myself, and all my energies, frankly and entirely to you." More ominously in terms of his professional goals, he adds, "Your eyes are to be my stars for the future."

As this incident suggests, the text labors to convey that interests in women and in science are entirely incompatible. Indeed, as Barloon maintains, "scientific pursuit and sexual love are constructed as irreconcilable, even antithetical domains."[10] For the misogynist narrator, the transformation of "an abstracted astronomer into an eager lover" brings the lament, "[A]nd, must it be said? [Viviette] spoilt a promising young physicist to produce a commonplace inamorato" (92). Though Swithin poses the naive query, "[C]an I not study and love both?" Viviette rejoins, "[Y]ou'll be the first if you do."

Despite the fact that a rare comet will soon disappear "for perhaps thousands of years," Swithin finds himself "[s]cientifically . . . but a dim vapour of himself: the lover had come into him like an armed man and cast out the student" (99). The result is that "his intellectual situation was growing a life and death matter," which Swithin himself recognizes in uttering, "I can do nothing! I have ceased to study, ceased to observe." Significantly, Swithin makes the admission in a note to Viviette, adopting her personal and feminized mode of writing, and adds that "[t]his longing I have for you absorbs my life, and outweighs my intentions." Consequently, "[t]he power to labour in the grandest of fields has left me" (99); Viviette, Swithin later comments, has "displaced the work" (100).

The danger of female influence on Swithin's studies is echoed by the narrative's only other scientifically oriented character, Swithin's great-uncle. Unexpectedly offering a bequest to Swithin to conduct his work, the great-uncle, whose association to science has been established by his "long and extensive medical practice" (119) and whose "own scientific proclivities" (120) caused him to become interested in Swithin's career, makes the gift dependent on Swithin's avoiding marriage until the age of twenty-five. Alarmed by the news that Swithin is involved with a woman, the great-uncle warns him that "something in your path worse than narrow means" threatens the young man's work, and "that something was a woman" (121). The great-uncle voices the novel's underlying message

10. Barloon also observes, "If scientific pursuits are 'ennobling,' pursuit of or devotion to a woman is, by implication, the obverse" ("Star-Crossed Love," 28). I agree with Barloon's reading that the novel "subordinates romantic love to the prerogatives of science—or, what is more, that the novel portrays women as impediments to what Freud termed 'the work of civilization'" (31).

in admonishing, "If your studies are to be worth anything, believe me they must be carried on without the help of a woman." He stridently adds, "Avoid her, and every one of the sex, if you mean to achieve any worthy thing." A woman is inherently a threat to scientific endeavor, the great-uncle implies, through an "original disqualification as a companion," which he identifies as "that of sex." Through her presence, Swithin's perspective will be skewed and his work ignored:

> If you attempt to study with a woman you'll be ruled by her to entertain fancies instead of theories, air-castles instead of intentions, qualms instead of opinions, sickly prepossessions instead of reasoned conclusions. Your wide heaven of study, young man, will soon reduce itself to the miserable narrow expanse of her face, and your myriad of stars to her two trumpery eyes. (122)

Though the great-uncle, who pointedly signs his bequest with the identification of "Doctor in Medicine" (123), is characterized in unsavory fashion as "narrow, sarcastic, and shrewd to unseemliness" (119), a "hardened misogynist" whose sentiments thus seem "nothing remarkable" (123), the narrator nevertheless quotes the lengthy document in its entirety; the opinions not only are allowed to stand without rebuttal but are even repeated later. Moreover, the placement of the letter in the narrative flow, inserted shortly after the description of Swithin's actions attesting to the veracity of the great-uncle's predictions, serves to confirm rather than dispute the misogynistic views.[11]

The idea that a woman inherently represents a corrupting influence upon science is underscored with textual evidence that Viviette alters not only Swithin's work habits but Swithin himself. Within moments after realizing he has become enamored with Viviette, Swithin undergoes a decisive change in losing "his natural ingenuousness" (91). Through his "sudden sense of new relations with [Viviette]," Swithin discovers that "[h]enceforth he could act a part." This performative aspect continues,

11. As Barloon comments in discussing the great-uncle's writing, "what is most interesting, perhaps, is not the attitude itself, but how closely it coincides with the narrative point of view" ("Star-Crossed Love," 29). For a discussion of the narrator's comments and misogyny, see Dutta, *Ambivalence,* 59–61. On the female menace to science and the great-uncle's commentary, see also Malane, *Sex in Mind,* 165, 171–74.

for Swithin displays "a disingenuousness now habitual" though nonex-istent before he recognized his affection for Viviette (136). Coupled with the great-uncle's warning that a woman will cause Swithin's scientific ob-jectivity to vanish, the narrative implies that female influence not only impedes scientific progress but also corrodes the scientist himself.

Such an effect is intimated earlier, on a physical plane, before Swithin has realized his ardor for Viviette. Bereft after learning that an important scientific discovery he has made was, in fact, publicized by another as-tronomer six weeks earlier, Swithin flings himself into a clump of heather during a cold March rain and stays in the "humid bed" for a lengthy time (69). The locale is significant because of the strong gender association established earlier between vegetation and femininity, and the reference to the moist bed additionally interjects a sexual note. The erotic connec-tion is reinforced shortly thereafter, when Viviette visits a presumably dying Swithin, "[flings] herself upon the bed," and kisses the barely con-scious man (71). Swithin's eventual recovery proceeds from his interest in a developing comet, which carries masculine connotations that ap-parently counteract the effects of the feminized vegetation that initially felled him. Not only does a comet innately display a phallic shape, the comet that intrigues Swithin reveals an inherent potency and is gendered male. As a servant remarks, "he's getting bigger every night" and is ex-pected to become "the biggest one known for fifty years when he's full growed" (73). The comet instills in Swithin "a new vitality" and "in all probability saved his life" (74), an observation Swithin later confirms in identifying the comet as "[a] reason for living" (82). Not coincidentally, the comet falls "on the wane" after having "waxed to its largest dimen-sions" (99) once Swithin realizes his passion for Viviette.

The text's condemnation of Viviette as representation of woman de-rives not only from her contaminating influence but also from her con-scious recognition of the harm she poses to the young scientist. Like Eve, Viviette allows temptation to prevail. When Swithin ignores the poten-tial destruction that Viviette's servant could wreak by wandering unsu-pervised in the tower, Viviette poses the query, "[W]ho is to blame?" and immediately responds, "Ah—not you, not you!" (95). Though Viviette utters the sentiments with "keen self-reproach in her voice," the nar-rative forecloses a sympathetic reading by stressing Viviette's full com-prehension of her error. Moments later she reacts to Swithin's effusive protestation of affection that "I am injuring you—who knows that I am not ruining your future—I who ought to know better?" (95–96). Viviette functions as the quintessential woman, the bewitching temptress whose allure cannot be resisted, but is demonized even further as one who preys upon an unsuspecting youth. Pleading with Swithin that he promise not to detest her at a later date for having "drawn you off from a grand celestial study to study poor lonely me," Viviette muses, "But you will—I know you will. All men do when they have been attracted in their unsuspecting youth as I have attracted you" (96). The point is restated by Swithin's great-uncle in the bequest, who observes that "[s]he is old enough to know that a *liaison* with her may, and almost certainly would, be your ruin" (122). As an exemplar of womanhood, Viviette is marked by weakness, herself informing Swithin that "I ought to have kept my resolve" and suffered "anything rather than draw you from your high purpose" (96). Periodically through the narrative, Viviette utters similar remarks attesting to a clear recognition of her transgressions, yet she knowingly continues to enact them.[12]

BLURRED BOUNDARIES

Viviette's corruption of Swithin's noble purpose, the novel repeatedly stresses, demonstrates the menace that women pose to the realm of science and the harm that results when feminine influence breaches the boundary of this masculine discipline. Despite the text's insistent efforts to establish and maintain a separation between gendered spheres, the division between them cannot hold, as demonstrated by the landscape both allowing and denying access to the tower. Even the name of the tower, Rings-Hill Speer, suggests the intertwining of masculine and feminine elements, with the hyphenated term evoking with both words the breast-like aspect of the landscape and the following homonym for "spear" hinting at phallic potency and penetration. In effect, the text is

12. Interestingly, several critics view Viviette as being presented sympathetically in the novel. See Richard D. Sylvia, "Hardy's Feminism: Apollonian Myth and *Two on a Tower*," 48; Pamela L. Jekel, *Thomas Hardy's Heroines: A Chorus of Priorities*, 125; Rosemary Sumner, "The Experimental and the Absurd in *Two on a Tower*," 78; and John Bayley, "The Love Story in *Two on a Tower*," 62.

conveying the message that the boundary between masculinity and femininity is inherently unstable; woman, in the person of Viviette, discovers and exploits the fissures between the spheres. In so doing, the female not only jeopardizes masculine endeavors but demonstrates the frailty of masculinity itself, identifying the unsuccessful abjection of the feminine and the ceding of male authority. Let me proceed, then, to representative moments in the text where the distinction between masculinity and femininity is problematized and gender designations confused.

Perhaps the most apparent example comes in the physical description of Swithin in the first chapter, wherein the narrative voice points to the equivocal somatic qualities of the young scientist in detailing both masculine and feminine aspects:[13]

> He was a youth who might properly have been characterized by a word the judicious chronicler would not readily use in such a connection, preferring to reserve it for raising images of the opposite sex. Whether because no deep felicity is likely to arise from the condition, or from any other reason, to say in these days that a youth is beautiful is not to award him that amount of credit which the expression would have carried with it if he had lived in the times of the Classical Dictionary. So much, indeed, is the reverse the case that the assertion creates an awkwardness in saying anything more about him. (9)

Upon initial inspection, Swithin creates a "beholder's first impression that the head was the head of a girl," and he appears a "pretty fellow" (9), so much so that the astronomer's "beauty" leaves an impression "probably richer in [Viviette's] imagination than in the real" (29). In behavior, too, Swithin belies a robust masculinity, as suggested on one occasion by his "wait[ing] as helplessly as a girl" in hopes of glimpsing Viviette as she passes (93).

Rather than display the self-assurance and experience of a mature male, Swithin is marked by an innocence that seems exceptional for a youth on the verge of his majority. The frequent designations of Swithin in terms of his youthfulness serve to situate him as both a boyish adoles-

13. Tess O'Toole sees the early descriptions of Swithin demonstrating his "doubled heritage" in class status as well as his "association with the feminine" (*Genealogy and Fiction in Hardy: Family Lineage and Narrative Lines*, 114).

cent uncertainly poised on the cusp of manhood and an inexperienced Victorian girl kept ignorant of life's realities. Swithin, for example, is termed a "lad" (9) and "laddie" (241), boasts a youthful complexion (9), evidences "childlike faults of manner which arose from his obtuseness to [a] difference of sex" (44), displays a "boyish look" (164), reveals "almost a child's forgetfulness of the past" (192), betrays a "schoolboy temperament" (241), and shows himself "[i]mmature" (234). As Dutta maintains, "Although a youth of 20 is hardly a 'child,' it is surprising to note how often Swithin is conceived of as a 'child.' "[14] In contrast, Viviette is far more experienced, a reflection in part of her greater age but more convincingly her greater awareness of social and sexual mores. There is a curious role reversal here in light of Victorian culture's tendency to shelter the ingenuous female from worldly knowledge and encourage the seasoning of the urbane male. Instead, Viviette not only displays an experiential sophistication that contrasts sharply with Swithin's experiential ignorance, thereby reversing the customary Victorian gender relationship by positioning her as authoritative adult and Swithin as guileless child, but she heightens this psychological division between them by repeatedly infantilizing him. To Viviette, Swithin is her "dear dear boy" (224), who remains "docile as a child in her hands" (151); he becomes her "juvenile husband" (220), as if he were "an innocent youth" whom Viviette "entrapped . . . into marriage for her own gratification" (158) and "led him like a child" (229), for "[s]he in her experience had sought out him in his inexperience" (229). Indeed, a "maternal element" occasionally "evinced itself in her affection for the youth," which "was imparted by her superior ripeness in experience" (231).

Also complicating a reading of Swithin as a robust masculine figure are the linkages established between him and the distant past. In Victorian culture, woman was associated with the ancient, pagan, and mythological world, distinguishing her from the sense of modernity that characterized the civilizing and progressive projects of the male. Yet Swithin periodically is inserted into that antiquated period despite his scientific progressiveness, an interesting textual gesture especially in light of his criticism of Viviette for the obsolete astronomical knowledge she gleaned in her library. He is termed "an Adonis-astronomer" (53) and a

14. Dutta, *Ambivalence*, 63.

"scientific Adonis" (187), an impressionable "youth who looks as if he had come straight from old Greece" (165), and a contemporary version of Eudoxus, a hoary Hellenic astronomer (54).

More telling is Swithin's link to a primitive consciousness, again conventionally associated with the essentialized female. Despite Swithin's comprehension of and comfort with current scientific developments, a primitive superstition of celestial infinitude occasionally emerges. He regrets, for instance, that his former conception of the universe as "grand, simply grand" had been replaced by a sense that "the actual sky is a horror" (33):

> You would hardly think at first that horrid monsters lie up there waiting to be discovered by any moderately penetrating mind—monsters to which those of the oceans bear no sort of comparison.
> . . . Impersonal monsters, namely, Immensities. Until a person has thought out the stars and their interspaces he has hardly learnt that there are things much more terrible than monsters of shape; namely, monsters of magnitude without known shape. Such monsters are the voids and waste places of the sky. (33–34)

Swithin's fear of the universe could, in part, be attributed to the contemporary Victorian theorization of entropy, which would seemingly transmute his apprehensions from the realm of the primitive to the modern, for he cites "the quality of decay" that will eventually cause celestial bodies to "burn out like candles" (34); as Robert Schweik explains, "[i]t is a vision of the ultimate consequence of Kelvin's theory of entropy in the universe that Hardy evoked in the words of his 'votary of science,' Swithin St. Cleve."[15] Yet that modern perspective is far outweighed by Swithin's more antediluvian terror of the unknown, a primordial reaction so intense that it causes him to deem astronomy the sole science "deserv[ing] the character of the terrible" (35). As such, "[i]t is quite impossible to think at all adequately of the sky—of what the sky substantially is—without feeling it as a juxtaposed nightmare," and thus "[i]t is better—far better—for men to forget the universe than

15. Robert Schweik, "The Influence of Religion, Science, and Philosophy on Hardy's Writings," 59. Richard H. Taylor comments on Swithin's "paradoxical mix of scientific rationalism and primitive obsession," which Taylor views as "regressive in personal and social terms" (*The Neglected Hardy: Thomas Hardy's Lesser Novels,* 128).

to bear it clearly in mind!" (35). This "old horror" continues to dominate Swithin's thoughts as his work proceeds and he contemplates "[t]he ghostly finger of limitless vacancy," the "[i]nfinite deeps," and the "unknown tract of the unknown" (268).

Further undermining an assessment of Swithin as an unambiguously masculine figure is the question of entitlement to the tower. As a phallic image, the tower presumably should be unequivocally identified with a male; it was, after all, constructed in memory of a patriarchal representative of the Blount line, and it functions as Swithin's workplace. Yet the title of the novel suggests a joint appropriation of the column in yoking Swithin and Viviette as the "two on a tower," with the preposition implying that both equally dominate the phallic structure. As the pair's opening encounter implies, control of the tower shifts between them, as if possession of this phallic signifier is only provisional and indeterminate. When Viviette first enters the tower, she imagines that she is "the proprietor of the column and of all around it," and a sense of "self-assertiveness" compels her to ascend its height, despite an initial reluctance to do so alone (8). Swithin, she discovers, has "made himself so completely at home on a building which she deemed her unquestioned property" (9). When she queries Swithin as to whether he has "entirely taken possession of this column," he answers "[e]ntirely" with an air of certainty (11). Though Viviette protests, "But it is my column," her response is given "with smiling asperity," a phrase that undercuts her sense of authority even as she is asserting it. Swithin's request that he be allowed to rent the tower continues to complicate the question of control, since Swithin has expropriated the structure, or "entirely taken possession," without actual ownership. Viviette seems to recognize that dominance of the tower is both fluid and uncertain, for she responds, "You have taken it, whether I allow it or not" (11).

Even the astronomical equipment that Swithin values for his work clouds the distinction between masculinity and femininity. With its phallic contours, Swithin's telescope serves as a signifier of male potency, and he is firmly associated with it when Viviette first encounters him staring intently through the instrument, significantly at the masculine image of the sun, and signaling to her not to disrupt his observations. Almost immediately, however, Swithin cedes control of the telescope to Viviette, which in one sense could be considered an indication of his power, since he regulates access to this emblem of male authority; yet the incident more convincingly signals that power over this masculine signifier shifts between them. As Viviette peers through the telescope, the sun "seemed to be laid bare to its core" (11), as if she is probing and exposing the inner recesses of this conventionally masculine image and, by extension, masculinity itself. Indeed, in Viviette's periodic observations through the telescope, whereby "the immensities" that Swithin's "young mind had, as it were, brought down from above to hers," the two individuals "became unconsciously equal" (35).

The fluidity of control over a phallic signifier becomes even more pronounced when Swithin acquires an equatorial, another telescopic mechanism. As a larger and more formidable version of Swithin's telescope, the equatorial seems to serve as an even more impressive representation of masculinity. Viviette attests to that potency in remarking that "[i]ts powers are so enormous . . . that I should have a personal fear in being with it alone," and she expresses "a feeling for this instrument not unlike the awe I should feel in the presence of a great magician" (63). Yet both functionally and nominatively, the device inherently obfuscates the boundary between masculinity and femininity. By definition, an equatorial features two axes of movement, one of which is parallel to the earth's axis and the other perpendicular; through these dual axes, an equatorial suggests an internal opposition, for it shifts between horizontal and vertical planes, mimicking the transfer of control within masculine and feminine domains. With its name a derivative of the word *equator,* the device additionally marks a boundary space between two spheres, literally the northern and southern hemispheres but metaphorically the feminine and masculine. Indeed, Swithin will eventually leave the northern hemisphere, with its multiple associations to Viviette, in favor of the southern hemisphere, where her presence is not somatically in evidence but its traces nevertheless remain. Importantly, he will bring the equatorial with him, where he will install it on another phallic signifier, "a solid pillar," but still gender confusion remains, for the pillar will be located in the traditionally feminine space of a garden (266).

A further occlusion of the equatorial's gender associations emerges through an early question of its ownership, as with the tower itself. Due to Swithin's strained financial circumstances, Viviette offers to fund the purchase of the device, yet she insists that she "vanish entirely from the undertaking" in fear of neighborhood gossip (57). Even as she outlines her plan to Swithin, the ambiguity of ownership is revealed, for she advises him that "[t]he equatorial will arrive addressed to you, and its cost I will pay through you." Once the equatorial arrives, their subsequent exchange, begun by Viviette, continues to cloud the question of ownership:

> "Now are you happy?"
> "But it is all *yours,* Lady Constantine.
> "At this moment. But that's a defect which can soon be remedied. When is your birthday?"
> "Next month—the seventh."
> "Then it shall be all yours—a birthday present." (62)

Though Viviette then assures Swithin that "[t]he possession of these apparatus would only compromise me," and since "[a]lready they are reputed to be yours" so that "they must be made yours," she adds the equivocal comment that "[t]here is no help for it" (62). Despite her offer to transfer ownership to Swithin, the text is silent on whether she acts on the intention.

Another gender confusion emerges over possession of the key to the tower. The provenance of the key further obscures the issue of control and thus the tower's status as an unequivocally masculine space. The key had been ceded to Swithin's great-grandfather by Sir Blount's ancestor, thus being transferred from one male hand to another. Following patriarchal lineage, the key was inherited by Swithin's grandfather and eventually by Swithin himself. Yet before Swithin obtained the key, it fell to his mother's possession, which thus interrupted male transmission of and power over the key. Though the key rested "rusty in its niche" for "thirty or forty years" (12), implying that Swithin's mother never even entered the tower, she nonetheless held control over it as the one who indirectly guarded its portal.

With the key now resting in Swithin's possession, he holds the power over admission to or prohibition from the tower, since the structure is "always kept locked" (11). Though Viviette attempts to enter the tower "to observe the comet through the great telescope" (82), an overdetermined phrase with its references to the dual phallic emblems to which

Viviette seeks access, she is barred from them because of the locked door. Forced to travel to Swithin's abode to request entry into the tower, she asks Swithin's grandmother, in his absence, to advise him that she wishes the door unlocked the next evening. Though Swithin sends a servant to Viviette's home with the key, circumventing her direct request that the door be left unlocked even while ceding the masculine signifier to her, he casts doubt on whether she "could handle the telescope alone" and "with any pleasure or profit to herself" (82). As a result, Swithin travels to the tower the next evening, "[u]nable, as a devotee to science, to rest under this misgiving," where he finds Viviette seated on the observation chair (82); yet there is no indication that she has actually touched the equatorial, much less peered through it, and it is Swithin who "set[s] the instrument in order for observation" (85). It is Viviette, however, who then gazes through the telescope at the comet, now at the most potent stage of metamorphosis, "fill[ing] so large a space of the sky as to completely dominate it."

As we have seen, all of these examples of the instability of the boundary separating masculinity and femininity carry with them the transference of authority from a male to a female register, however ephemerally. Even though these exchanges tend primarily to becloud the vexed issue of power rather than resolve it, simply by virtue of their occurrence the text demonstrates the fragility of male authority. Swithin, for example, is deemed "her astronomer" (70), with the possessive pronoun tacitly situating her within the position of authority. She considers astronomy "my hobby" (57), which seemingly transforms Swithin's labors from serious masculine study to frivolous feminine pursuit and undermines his position of superiority in the process. Though adopting the guise of a generous benefactor who indirectly contributes to important work, Viviette more convincingly suggests a determined manipulator whose financial resources enable her to exercise control.

Nowhere is the frangibility of male dominance more apparent than when power relations are examined at their most primal level, within an economy of sexual desire. Though the many instances of Viviette's attempted or actual appropriation of phallic signifiers have been imbued with a sexual content, my exegetical emphasis has been mainly concerned with the illegibility of gender divisions and their periodic erasure. Yet it is important to interrogate the sexual resonances of Viviette's activities more directly, examining in particular her deployment of the gaze and figurative emasculation of Swithin.

As noted previously, Viviette's first encounter with Swithin is marked by her scrutiny of the astronomer as he peers through the telescope, and he functions as a compelling "spectacle [that] met her eyes" (8). The subsequent description of Swithin's physical attributes serves as a catalog of facial parts, in effect, as the countenance is figuratively broken down to assess each component. This form of objectification, of course, typically is exercised upon female characters in Victorian literature. One is reminded, for instance, of Dante Gabriel Rossetti's examination of an artist's model as a series of body parts in "The Portrait," or Hardy's own paradigmatic maneuvers in depicting Tess and other women who populate his novels. In *Two on a Tower,* the effect of this feminizing move is to fetishize Swithin, transforming him from a vibrant subject to a passive object that can be appropriated, diminished, and contained.

This early scene points also to the text's obsessive interest in ocular terms, images, and actions. The narrative is replete with language that calls attention to the process of observation, both in regard to the astronomical equipment and the main characters' scopic tendencies. Yet those references are neither neutral nor casual, for they are imbued with gender significance. In the vast majority of cases, Swithin's visual activities are centered on scientific study; he cleans eyepieces, obtains lenses, takes observations, wears an "observing-jacket" (53), and has an "observing chair" (82), for example. Viviette's ocular attention is almost exclusively directed to examinations of Swithin that serve as expressions of sexual desire and erotic aggression.[16] As the desiring subject focusing upon a desired object, Viviette performs the role of a Victorian male; she becomes the sexual agent rather than the passive form that is dominated and manipulated. As the older and more experienced of the pair, Viviette is figured as both sexual predator and virtual pedophile.

In one of the novel's most overdetermined episodes, Viviette ventures to the tower and finds a sleeping Swithin prostrate on a rug. A series of

16. See also Sylvia for discussion of the sexualized and emasculating gaze that Viviette trains on Swithin. Sylvia notes, for instance, that "Viviette's gaze and thoughts objectify—and sexualise—the innocent Swithin," and the young astronomer "is a passive object of her desire" ("Hardy's Feminism," 51). See also Malane on "gendered gazes" in the novel (*Sex in Mind,* 187).

sibilants describes her movement, mimicking the sound of a serpent in search of its prey as "a soft rustle of silken clothes came up the spiral staircase" (43). Viviette's scopic attention briefly lights on the work papers and instruments surrounding the unconscious Swithin while she scans the room like a hunter assessing the lair of its quarry. Viviette then gazes "for a lengthy time at his sleeping face," accentuating her assumption of the role of agent and Swithin's status as scrutinized object. With "her eyes . . . fixed on his face," Viviette again assesses Swithin in terms of body parts, as a reference to Swithin's "parted lips" subtly suggests (44). Within moments, Viviette grasps a scissors from Swithin's table and snips a lock of his hair. Critical commentary has pointed to the implications of the act as a metaphoric emasculation or a rape of the feminized youth, which the episode certainly suggests. Richard D. Sylvia observes, for example, that the scene offers a "frank expression of female sexual desire." Barloon remarks that "woman . . . does more than merely 'check' Swithin: she emasculates, or threatens to emasculate him" in this "richly allusive scene." Patricia Ingham cites "a narratorial transposition of gender" in the novel; Viviette "takes all the initiatives" and "[i]n most respects she assumes the male role." Dutta argues that "the suggestion is that by this rape of his lock, Swithin has somehow been betrayed, emasculated, castrated, and that it is Viviette who (in a reversal of gender roles) has taken unfair advantage of him."[17] Adding to the disturbing quality of the scissors scene is the fact that Viviette commandeers Swithin's own implement to perform the act; in effect, she is appropriating the tool of a male to turn it against him, exploiting a moment of vulnerability to assume a relative position of power.

Yet, as the text insists, power flows between the pair in a Foucauldian interchange. Neither female nor male can maintain superiority indefinitely, as another overdetermined episode in the novel stresses. During a rare furtive visit to Viviette's home, Swithin dons her missing husband's clothes for protection against harsh weather as he prepares to make an unobserved departure after Viviette's brother unexpectedly arrives for a visit. Unaware that Swithin has borrowed the clothes, Viviette happens to glimpse him as he quietly attempts to effect his escape. Her response is extreme, for "she raised her hands in horror as if to protect herself from

17. Sylvia, "Hardy's Feminism," 51; Barloon, "Star-Crossed Love," 28; Patricia Ingham, *Thomas Hardy*, 44; Dutta, *Ambivalence*, 59.

him" before "she uttered a shriek and turned shudderingly to the wall, covering her face," as she imagines she is seeing her husband (145). The terrified reaction and defensive posture carry intriguing implications for her relationship with Swithin, who seemingly is transformed into the reviled Sir Blount at this moment. It is as if Swithin becomes a representation of Sir Blount's harsh and unwelcome authority over Viviette as a potent male.[18] An adventurer in Africa, a determined hunter, and a demanding husband, Sir Blount embodies the qualities of the domineering Victorian male exercising control over a powerless wife. In adopting Sir Blount's clothing, Swithin becomes the husband's image, which the newly married Viviette deems "ominous," "ghastly," and "uncanny" (151). Her horror of the apparition could be read as a fear that Swithin will be another version of her first husband who will undermine and negate her own moments of control. Indeed, upon first meeting Viviette, Swithin identified her as the "wife of the absent Sir Blount Constantine" (11), a definition that implies a subordination and possession so pronounced that these effects exist even without the husband's physical presence.

Nevertheless, Swithin is himself defined in the text as Viviette's "juvenile husband" (220), with all of the accompanying associations the phrase evokes as to the complicated nature of the power relations between them. More significant for my purposes are the implications their relationship holds for the world of science. If, as the novel has insinuated, women bring contamination and corruption to the "pure" realm of scientific endeavor, the logical conclusion to draw is that the man of science must escape female influence. In *Two on a Tower*, this assumption is realized in Swithin's eventual decision to leave England and renew his studies in Africa. Within the geographic economy of the novel, Africa represents the site of male endeavor, as scholarship has observed in commenting upon *fin de siècle* quest romances located on the continent. Africa, too, was the destination that the authoritative male figure Sir Blount chose for the typically masculine objectives of discovery, adventure, and self-glorification that critics have associated with expeditions to the continent, and Swithin's goals conform to the pattern.

18. Sylvia argues that the similarity between Swithin and Sir Blount "foreshadow[s] the inevitable destruction of Viviette by way of paternal right" ("Hardy's Feminism," 55). Moreover, "Viviette must be destroyed completely by the male order."

Though to a Victorian mind Africa could represent a remote masculine space, one in which the fantasy of a womanless world could presumably be enacted, as scholarship has asserted, the text conveys the underlying warning that no space is safe from female intervention. For Sir Blount, that lesson comes indirectly after deserting his English wife, in that his subsequent "marriage" to an African woman suggests there is no escape from female presence, which is always a source of danger; marriage, for him, ends in death through his own successful suicide attempt.

The geographic separation Swithin attains in moving to Africa initially appears to belie the supposition that female influence is inescapable. Once Swithin has established himself there, his scientific work flourishes. His travels represent "an awakening," which lead to "an absorbed attention" in his studies of the southern sky as well as "a corresponding forgetfulness of what lay to the north" (262). At this juncture, "women were now no more to him than the inhabitants of Jupiter" (270), yet traces of Viviette's presence nevertheless exist, as the phrase itself subtly suggests in connecting rather than separating womanhood from science. When Swithin's equatorial arrives from England, he notes the "brasses on which [Viviette's] hand had often rested, of the eyepiece through which her dark eyes had beamed" (266). Though he resolves to devote himself to the future rather than the past, Viviette's presence continues to assert itself, most tellingly through the newspaper notice that heralds the birth of their son. Despite "three years of continuous labour" (271) and a gradual attenuation of his memories, thoughts of Viviette periodically intrude. During that time, Swithin nonetheless completed his "barrow-load of precious memoranda, and rolls upon rolls of diagrams," but his scientific work is not finished. Compilation of the data into a finished tract remains, and Swithin decides to conduct this next phase of work back in England. The reminders of Viviette that appeared in Africa, coupled with his return home, suggest that a total severance from female influence can never be effected. Though Viviette's opportune death spares him from an unwanted marriage, he escapes simply from one woman, not women. As his encounter with Tabitha Lark in the garden suggests, Swithin will be entrapped again, with even more ominous results; Tabitha has "joined the phalanx of Wonderful Women, who had resolved to eclipse masculine genius altogether, and humiliate the brutal sex to the dust" (274–75). Moments later, the masculine symbol of the sun itself seems to eclipse by disappearing beyond the feminine symbol of a hill (275).

The reader is left with the impression that the pattern Swithin had followed in his experiences with Viviette will be reenacted in his relationship with Tabitha, thereby suggesting that female intrusion into the male realm of scientific endeavor is an ever-present threat. As the novel has nervously demonstrated, even the most concerted efforts to pursue scientific interests are jeopardized by female presence. Rather than carving out a "safe" space for masculine scientific work, then, *Two on a Tower* carries the message that such an objective can never be achieved, and only extraordinary vigilance can prevent scientific efforts from being utterly doomed.

4

Dangerous Behavior

A Woman's Menacing Avocation
in Wilkie Collins's *Heart and Science*

As *Two on a Tower* frenetically labored to make explicit, science represents a masculine purview from which women are excluded. Although Wilkie Collins's 1883 novel *Heart and Science* conveys the same message, the text follows a different trajectory in pointing specifically and alarmingly to the horrific dangers presumably posed by a woman's actual involvement in science. In this lesser-known but intriguing Collins novel, a woman who becomes an active agent in scientific study is portrayed as a villainous schemer straying far from the ideal of Victorian femininity; indeed, her deviation from idyllic womanhood is attributed directly to her interest in science. A figure of both vilification and ridicule, she demonstrates unwomanly behavior in numerous and varied instances while she pursues her scientific obsession. As the novelistic treatment of an antithetical character reveals, a woman's appropriate relationship to science is to function simply as a passive object to be scrutinized and probed. Thus, the novel validates an essential womanhood and carves no space in which a woman can follow scientific interests.

Heart and Science focuses on the machinations and foibles

of Maria Gallilee, a scientifically inclined and "unwomanly" character whose varied plots demonstrate her cold-heartedness, avarice, and self-ishness. After she is widowed with a son, Ovid Vere, Maria subsequently marries Mr. Gallilee, an ineffectual but kindly gentleman, with whom she has two daughters. Residing in a fashionable London neighborhood, Mrs. Gallilee, under normal circumstances, would have a sufficient income to lead a comfortable life were she not a profligate spender seeking to maintain the appearance of wealth. Science is her passion, and she devotes much of her energy to her studies and interactions with the scientific community, including the unsavory physician Benjulia.

Contemporary reviewers varied in their judgments on whether Mrs. Gallilee had been effectively portrayed. The *Pall Mall Budget* described her as "a badhearted, extravagant, and vain woman," adding that she was a caricature of a Thackeray character. The *Academy* asserted that Mrs. Gallilee is a "less successful" character than Benjulia but noted that neither could "be accepted as a type" and thus offered "no polemical value." In contrast, the *British Quarterly Review* described her portrayal more positively; Mrs. Gallilee displays "the gradual ossification of the heart and healthy sympathies through excessive demand for knowledge and the power it is supposed to bring with it." Her characterization, the reviewer added, provides "a most original study."[1]

The novel concentrates on a relatively brief period in Mrs. Gallilee's unenviable life, following the death of her brother, who had lived in Italy and left an orphaned daughter, Carmina. Under the terms of her brother's will, Mrs. Gallilee is named guardian of the seventeen-year-old Carmina, a gentle and kindly individual whose father has handsomely provided for. Yet under the terms of the will, Carmina's fortune will revert to her aunt should the younger woman fail to marry and have children. As the novel opens, Carmina's arrival in London along with her devoted nurse, Teresa, is imminent. At the same time, Ovid Vere, a promising young physician, is planning a convalescent journey to quell his uneasy nerves and restore himself to sound health. Upon meeting Carmina shortly after she arrives in London, however, he instantly falls in love. Though he does eventually travel to Canada to regain his health,

---

1. "Mr. Wilkie Collins's New Novel," 332, 333; "New Novels: *Heart and Science*," 290; "Novels of the Quarter: *Heart and Science*," 232.

he first becomes engaged to his innocent cousin, who is left in Mrs. Gallilee's care.

Ovid's departure opens the way for Mrs. Gallilee to unravel schemes for undermining his engagement with Carmina and inheriting her fortune. Unsympathetic and cruel, Mrs. Gallilee treats her niece so poorly that Carmina's health suffers, and the young woman attempts to escape. Hearing a rumor that Carmina's father was not Mrs. Gallilee's brother but an attractive medical student, Mrs. Gallilee venomously defames Carmina, which melodramatically causes the niece to fall into a life-threatening illness and severe memory loss. Viciously attacked by Teresa upon hearing the slur, Mrs. Gallilee herself falls ill and her mental health is compromised. Her husband, incensed at his wife's behavior and fearing for his daughters' well-being, whisks them away to a caring aunt and eventually sends Mrs. Gallilee to a private asylum, where she stays for a few months. As Carmina lies dangerously ill, treated by the ineffectual physician Mr. Null and the sinister Benjulia, Ovid learns of her condition and returns home, bringing with him a manuscript from a Canadian doctor who had successfully treated an illness resembling Carmina's. Though Carmina's health deteriorates to such an extent that she believes herself dying, Ovid's loving care returns her to a reasonable level of health, ultimately allowing the pair to marry and have a child. Mrs. Gallilee, meanwhile, is released from the asylum, shunned by her family, and left to pursue her scientific interests.

Luce Irigaray's theorization of women's relationship to language is instructive in assessing Mrs. Gallilee's involvement in scientific discourse through the premise that in Western culture a woman's options for participating in the symbolic order are limited to mimicry and hysteria. Both avenues are followed by Mrs. Gallilee, and both serve to undercut her pretensions to scientific study. Like Dickens's Mr. Pickwick, Mrs. Gallilee becomes a figure of ridicule when her scientific interests are conveyed in the narrative, but unlike him, Mrs. Gallilee is mocked merely because she is a woman, as well as stridently condemned for ostensibly unwomanly pursuits. As a mimic, a woman holds a leechlike relationship to language, reduced to imitation because of her lack of linguistic authority in this masculine arena. Yet underlying the imitative process, Irigaray maintains, is a possibility of menacing power, whereby one can "convert a form of subordination into an affirmation, and thus to begin to thwart it."[2] The narrative's mockery of Mrs. Gallilee for her forays into scientific discourse can be viewed as a strategy to negate the threat of female intervention that she poses, and it is a strategy that apparently succeeds.

To further eviscerate any threat, *Heart and Science* deploys the traditionally feminized illness of hysteria, in effect underscoring Mrs. Gallilee's punishment for intruding into the masculine realm by emphasizing her womanliness. The gender-charged associations of hysteria are even foregrounded when Carmina, as an ideal Victorian woman who demonstrates a conviction that science is a masculine field, falls victim to the illness. Despite these narrative interventions, a sense of feminine menace posed by Mrs. Gallilee cannot be wholly excised, for it seemingly remains just below the textual surface. Suggesting "an impossible and also a forbidden speech," in Irigaray's view, hysteria nevertheless "caricatures and deforms [masculine] language" even through its silence and represents "both a reserve power and a paralyzed power."[3] More ominously, by novel's end, Mrs. Gallilee has recovered her forceful voice.

CONDEMNATION AND RIDICULE

Heart and Science initially establishes the linkage between Mrs. Gallilee and science through multiple references to her extensive learning in the field, attained through determined self-instruction, lecture attendance, research efforts, and discussions with noteworthy professors and other experts. Though generally in an ironic voice, Mrs. Gallilee is variously characterized as "[t]he modern Muse of Science" (178) and a "learned lady" absorbed in "her studies" (198).[4] She boasts a "comprehensive mind" (127) and a "protoplastic point of view" (136). As a woman "superior to the influence of girlish curiosity" (129), Mrs. Gallilee, unlike other females, can "always give [her] reason" for a viewpoint (135), the narrator comments. Moreover, Mrs. Gallilee's "one pride and pleasure in life" is "improving [her] mind" (147), and indeed she is at one point

2. Irigaray, *This Sex*, 76.
3. Ibid., 136, 137, 138.
4. Unless otherwise noted, parenthetical page citations refer to the 1996 Broadview edition of Wilkie Collins, *Heart and Science*.

personified as "Science" (200). As Collins painstakingly remarks in the novel's preface, Mrs. Gallilee's scientific statements are based on fact, accumulated through Collins's "promiscuous reading" resulting in "a long list of books consulted, and of newspapers and magazines mutilated for 'cuttings' "; thus, Collins emphasizes, she is not a "gross caricature," for "not a word of my own invention occurs, when Mrs. Gallilee turns the learned side of her character" to the reader (39).[5]

Mrs. Gallilee's scientific bona fides are tainted, however, not least because of her initial motivation for study. The text suggests that her involvement in science was inherently flawed, for it proceeds from the basest self-interest. Rather than a desire to cultivate knowledge for its own sake or for the betterment of others, Mrs. Gallilee's scientific learning stems from envy, self-aggrandizement, and greed. "From the horrid day" that her sister married a wealthy peer, she "became a serious woman" whose "earthly interests" focused exclusively on "the cultivation of her intellect" (71). Mrs. Gallilee is implicitly condemned not only for this specialized learning but for intellectual development in general.[6]

Since both proceed from the unworthy impetus of the sister's attaining "the prize" from "the race for a husband" (71), the novel hints that women overstep their appropriate boundaries by any serious cognitive pursuits. The text seemingly records in nonjudgmental fashion that within a year Mrs. Gallilee familiarized herself "with zoophyte fossils, and had succeeded in dissecting the nervous system of a bee," yet those studies take on a disreputable cast in that they represent the primary concern of a wife and mother who finds virtually "no counter-attraction in her married life" and tellingly garners "no sympathy" from her first husband. Upon his death, Mrs. Gallilee immerses herself in her studies, "seiz[ing] her exquisite instruments, and return[ing] to the nervous system of the bee" (72), as if her husband's loss was a minor inconvenience.

5. To some extent, Mrs. Gallilee fits Kathleen O'Fallon's description of "the most important of Wilkie Collins' heroines," who "are the daughters of Eve, postlapsarian women with minds of their own" ("Breaking the Laws about Ladies: Wilkie Collins' Questioning of Gender Roles," 228). O'Fallon adds that "Collins is both fascinated and repelled by his strong women" (231).

6. Christine Ferguson rightly notes that Mrs. Gallilee views science "purely as a vehicle for a sort of narcissistic gratification" ("Decadence as Scientific Fulfillment," 473). See also Malane on Mrs. Gallilee's motives (*Sex in Mind,* 132).

As suggested earlier, part of the text's strategy for condemning Mrs. Gallilee's scientific interests comes through persistent ridicule. Though her utterances conform to the vocabulary and trajectory of Victorian scientific discourse, as Collins's preface reveals, they occasionally take on an absurd cast through the inappropriate context in which they appear. As such, Mrs. Gallilee's comments sound like foolish imitation at times rather than thoughtful observations, as if she is merely mouthing scientific terminology with little understanding of its correct application. The multiple references to her as a "learned lady," "muse of science," and similar appellations become both ironic and derogatory when considered in this light. One is reminded of the negative judgment conferred on female intellect by a reactionary and obtuse male character in Sarah Grand's 1893 best-selling *The Heavenly Twins,* in which he avers that a woman "resembles a parrot in her mental process."[7]

The reader's first direct encounter with Mrs. Gallilee sets the novel's derisive tone for her intellectual accomplishments. Arriving at a concert where, unbeknownst to Mrs. Gallilee, her son and niece are also in attendance, she makes a sweeping entrance and astounds the usher with "a little lecture on acoustics" (59). Shortly thereafter, Carmina senses the sinister presence of her aunt, which causes the young woman to faint; Mrs. Gallilee detachedly responds to the situation with a smelling-bottle and the "presence of mind which suggested a horizontal position" (62). " 'Help the heart,' she said; 'don't impede it.' The whole theory of fainting fits, in six words!" In a subsequent conversation, Mrs. Gallilee appears ominously unintelligible to her niece—indeed, "Mrs. Gallilee's science seemed to frighten her" (88)—in rapturously describing a lecture to be attended that day. "We are to have the apparatus, which illustrates the conversion of radiant energy into sonorous vibrations," Mrs. Gallilee tells the startled Carmina. "Have you ever heard, my dear, of the Diathermancy of Ebonite?" Mrs. Gallilee's scientific remarks are more explicitly undermined by virtue of their unconventional subject matter as she later lectures Carmina on the fundamentals of coprolites, which the aunt identifies as "the fossilised indigestions of extinct reptiles . . . , the undigested food of those interesting Saurians" (111–12). Similarly, a professor's ultimate agreement with one of her hypotheses, which seemingly validates her scientific acumen, is converted to absurdity through

7. Sarah Grand, *The Heavenly Twins,* 12.

her ecstatic response. "I have always maintained that the albuminoid substance of frog's eggs is insufficient (viewed as nourishment) to transform a tadpole into a frog," she tells Carmina, beseeching the niece's indulgence for being "carried away by a subject that I have been working at in my stolen intervals for weeks past" (113). Later, this "tender nurse of half-developed tadpoles" shares a most unsentimental observation in lamenting the "idle water" that is "wasted every hour by the falls of Niagara" (128).

Though periodically depicted as an object of ridicule, Mrs. Gallilee is enmeshed in a double bind, for she is also presented—sometimes simultaneously, as seen in Carmina's fearful reaction to her aunt's learning— as a menacing and malicious individual who has traveled far from the Victorian womanly ideal. The novel's title is instructive here, for it presents "heart" and "science" as irreconcilable and dichotomous positions for a woman to occupy. In so doing, the text builds upon the conventional gendered opposition between emotionality and rationality. Though Mrs. Gallilee seemingly views "heart" and "science" as complementary, observing that "my mind must be filled, as well as my heart" (72), the text persistently denies the possibility of such a conjunction for her. Emotionality and intellectuality instead become successive stages in her development, a causal relationship devolving from her scientific interests, as the following passage intimates:

> What a fool she had been, at that early period of her life! In those days, . . . she had flown into a passion when a new dress proved to be a misfit, on the evening of a ball; . . . she had fallen in love with a poor young man, and had terrified her weak-minded hysterical mother, by threatening to commit suicide when the beloved object was forbidden the house. Comparing the girl of seventeen with the matured and cultivated woman of later years, what a matchless example Mrs. Gallilee presented of *the healthy influence of education, directed to scientific pursuits!* (287, emphasis mine)

Mrs. Gallilee's choice of science over heart is deemed a conscious decision, with disturbing consequences. She had, for instance, "deliberately starved her imagination, and emptied her heart of any tenderness of feeling which it might once have possessed"; as a result, "her scientific education left her as completely in the dark, where questions of sentiment were concerned, as if her experience of humanity, in its relation to love, had been experience in the cannibal islands" (67).[8]

"UNWOMANLY" TRAITS

Numerous references to Mrs. Gallilee's lack of feminine emotion and her "hardened nature" (199), implicitly attributable to her immersion in science, punctuate the novel. Upon seeing her niece fainting at their first meeting, for instance, the aunt's "strength of mind" prevented her from likewise fainting (62). Though on one occasion "[s]omething seemed to move feebly under her powder and paint"—a description in itself derogatory—the narrator immediately dismisses the speculation that the "something" could be "[s]oft emotion trying to find its way to the surface" as "[i]mpossible!" (69). When Carmina expounds on the beauty of flowers in the Gallilee household, her aunt coldly responds that "they are part of the furniture" (112). She adds, "I sometimes dissect flowers, but I never trouble myself to arrange them." When her son is planning a convalescent journey, Mrs. Gallilee's initial solution to the caring of his cat is to poison it; she rejects the idea only because her son "was so eccentric in some things, that practical suggestions were thrown away on him" (127). To the sweet and gentle Carmina, Mrs. Gallilee is "a hard, hard woman" (154) and "[c]ruel, cruel creature" (166) who exudes an "icy civility" that Carmina finds "unendurable" (155). To the stern governess, Miss Minerva, Mrs. Gallilee appears "intensely cold and selfish" (170). To her beleaguered second husband, Mrs. Gallilee is "always hard and headstrong" (253). The rare flashes of emotion Mrs. Gallilee displays are mainly associated with a masculine interest in scientific discovery, as seen in her "vivid interest" in reading the professorial missive about

8. Malane also addresses the relationship between emotionality and rationality in the novel, as well as the effects of Mrs. Gallilee's scientific interests and dearth of material inclinations (*Sex in Mind,* 119, 132–35). Tabitha Sparks considers the novel's governess as well as Mrs. Gallilee "examples of the polluting influence of scientific culture upon the construct of Victorian womanhood" and Carmina as "a type of ahistorical femininity" ("Surgical Injury and Narrative Cure in Wilkie Collins's *Poor Miss Finch* and *Heart and Science,*" 25).

the frogs' eggs (111) and in her frequent unsavory plots to advance her objectives at another's expense.

Mrs. Gallilee's "unwomanly" lack of emotion and sympathetic understanding also affects her behavior as a mother, the ultimate role of the Victorian female, of course. Her relationship to Carmina is most instructive in this regard, since it is the primary one studied in the novel. In effect, Mrs. Gallilee merely performs motherhood as she assumes her new role as "a second mother" wherein she "played the part to perfection" (66), albeit briefly. When she is formally given guardianship over Carmina during the reading of her brother's will, Mrs. Gallilee utters the proper sentiments, yet rapacious greed underlies her responses. To each bequest on Carmina's behalf, Mrs. Gallilee seemingly acknowledges her brother's generosity and appears overcome by its breadth, but those reactions are tainted through the narrative context from which they proceed. Shortly before she learns of Carmina's vast annuities for board, education, clothing, and "pocket-money" (80), Mrs. Gallilee belies her words through the language of the body, whereby "the incarnate Devil [was] self-revealed in a human face" (76). "[H]er inbred capacity for deceit was ready for action," the narrator reports, and her "terrible eyes" fix upon the lawyer, who indirectly acknowledges her power. "Even when she hasn't spoken a word," he says, "I have felt her eyes go through me like a knife" (75).

As references cited above have suggested, Mrs. Gallilee's posture of surrogate mother generates anxiety, fear, contempt, and distrust on Carmina's part. In letters to her beloved nurse, Teresa, Carmina records repeated instances of her aunt's malicious behavior, assessing Mrs. Gallilee as a "horrible" individual (167). Indeed, when Mrs. Gallilee self-referentially remarks on her "duty and . . . pleasure to be a second mother," Carmina experiences not only astonishment but a visceral reaction so pronounced that she began to feel an "oppression in [her] breathing" (171). Carmina finds Mrs. Gallilee's "cruelty . . . too much even for my endurance," so much so that the niece is reduced to planning her escape from the household on two separate occasions.

The extent of Mrs. Gallilee's departure from the Victorian maternal ideal is accentuated by comparison to another mother figure, the devoted Teresa. Though marked by a volatile temper and passionate displays of fury, Teresa functions as the paradigmatic mother in exercising those qualities solely as protective measures for Carmina. As the young woman's companion since childhood, Teresa has shepherded her through the trauma of parental death and eased her passage into adolescence. Only Teresa's responsibilities as a wife, facing the imminent death of her sickly husband, can wrest her from Carmina's side once the pair have arrived in England. Teresa acts as confidante, caregiver, and comforter throughout the novel, never swerving from her perceived duties to her charge.

It is fitting, then, that this "true" mother becomes the instrument initiating the downfall of her "false" counterpart. In a seminal scene, Mrs. Gallilee defiles her maternal role on two levels; she defames the reputation of Carmina's biological mother, and she jeopardizes both the physical and mental health of her surrogate daughter. Thus Mrs. Gallilee represents an embodiment not of nurture but of danger. Seizing upon the unsubstantiated rumor that Carmina's mother had had an extramarital affair that resulted in Carmina's conception, Mrs. Gallilee furiously calls her niece an "impudent bastard" (249). Despite Benjulia's attempted intercession with the warning that Carmina is indeed Mrs. Gallilee's blood relative, the enraged aunt continues her verbal assault in hopes of severing the engagement between her son and Carmina. Mrs. Gallilee's frenzied exclamations inveigh against both the natural mother and the daughter to underscore her dual transgressions as maternal substitute. "She's the child of an adulteress!" Mrs. Gallilee screams. "She's the child of her mother's lover!" That the equally cold-hearted Benjulia serves as the agent urging Mrs. Gallilee to "[h]old your damned tongue" is itself significant, for it signals the shift in the designation of the novel's ultimate villain from detestable vivisectionist to destructive mother, as "[t]he demon in her urged her on" and inflamed her desire "to reiterate the detestable falsehood." Yet she is unable to do so, for Teresa grabs her by the throat in a grip like "the claws of a tigress." As Mrs. Gallilee falls senseless, Teresa invokes the ultimate maternal figure, the "blessed Virgin, mother of Christ," to "spare my child, my sweet child!" and confers the heinous appellation of "She-Devil" upon her rival (250). The text leaves no ambiguity as to the seriousness of Mrs. Gallilee's unmotherly behavior; it is so devastating that it initiates Carmina's life-threatening illness and an alarming loss of memory.

Mrs. Gallilee's unsuitability as a mother is evidenced as well through her behavior toward her own children. Her maneuverings to prevent Ovid's marriage to Carmina stem from avaricious self-promotion rather than maternal concern, as Mrs. Gallilee's schemes to usurp Carmina's inheritance demonstrate. Equally telling is her daughters' response when the governess's flight from the household leaves a void in their education that Mrs. Gallilee herself seems certain to fill, a prospect they greet with "terror" (236). So menacing a mother is Mrs. Gallilee that her meek husband is compelled to respond in a dramatic departure from character to assume a protective role over his daughters. Though Mr. Gallilee was "[a]ccustomed through long years of conjugal association to look up to his wife as a superior creature," he finds after her infamous slander "that her place in his estimation had been lost, beyond recovery" (261).

The gravity of this intervention is additionally suggested by Mr. Gallilee's need to move outside the private realm of the household and consult a representative of the legal system. In effect, Mrs. Gallilee's unmotherly transgression is so severe that it cannot be resolved simply through internal domestic measures but must be managed by an outside authority. In fact, Mr. Gallilee and his lawyer, Mr. Mool, share a "common horror" of her behavior (262). So unseemly is her conduct that it carries repercussions for society as a whole, since the Victorian social order is built upon the stability of the family. Even though Mr. Gallilee has been consistently portrayed as so unassertive and ineffectual, and his lawyer so shy and unassuming, that between them they comprised one individual of staunch determination (262), the fact that the two are galvanized into action through Mrs. Gallilee's behavior is itself telling. So, too, is the extent to which the two men feel compelled to intercede. Mrs. Gallilee is not merely rebuked or admonished, but her children are wrested from her influence and spirited away.

Mr. Gallilee's customary tractability, at least until this point, is also to some degree due to the failings of Mrs. Gallilee as a dutiful and submissive wife, certainly as vital a role for the Victorian woman as motherhood in the prevailing ideology. The text implies that she became interested in Mr. Gallilee as a potential husband only because he "drifted across the path of science" (72) and incidentally had fifty thousand pounds that could help her maintain a suitable place in the society she desired. Mrs. Gallilee dominates her husband to an extraordinary degree, cowing him into an emasculating obsequiousness and ineffectuality; her deficiencies

as a wife are periodically displayed through curt dismissals of her husband, decisive orders to him, an apparent reluctance to fulfill her expected conjugal duties, and a host of other infractions equally condemnatory to a Victorian mind. Her scathing tone, dismissive treatment, and
general indifference to her husband all underscore her failure to confer
the respect and exhibit the rectitude expected of a Victorian wife.

More broadly, the Gallilee household takes on elements of the Bakh-
tinian carnivalesque in that it represents a violation of sorts of the Victorian natural order, emanating from Mrs. Gallilee's wholesale assumption of authority and utter lack of interest in maintaining her rightful
place as a constant guiding presence within the home. Mrs. Gallilee's
control over important matters is exercised to such an extreme that it
appears "as if Mr. Gallilee had been dead" (143), and a passing reference
to him as the "master of the house" is followed by a parenthetical exclamation point (181). Yet her power is wielded inappropriately to serve
her own interests. Though Mrs. Gallilee is "as complete a mistress of
the practice of domestic virtue as the theory of acoustics and fainting
fits," her skill in domestic matters is attributable primarily to establishing herself as an admirable figure worthy of entertaining the scientific
community, the only dinner guests specifically cited as enjoying her hos-
pitality (66). Thus, the text enumerates her domestic virtues as dressing
tastefully, supervising creative dinners, heading the table with dignity,
and ensuring the comfort of visitors. Her other domestic strengths—
overseeing recalcitrant servants and uncovering deceitful practices of her
creditors—seem more reflective of Mrs. Gallilee's need to dominate and
discipline than the mere aspiration of managing a well-regulated household. Rather than serve as guardian within the home, she deserts her
family to attend to her scientific interests and inappropriately allows her
servants to fill the void she has left. Her interactions with her daughters
are rare and brusque, leaving them to the guidance and influence of their
governess, a figure whom Mrs. Gallilee distrusts and dislikes.

Not only does Mrs. Gallilee fail to act in her family's interests, she
works directly against them. Her excessive spending augurs a bank-
ruptcy, barely avoided, which would be disastrous for her husband and
children. She actively strives to thwart the path her son has chosen for
his happiness through marriage to Carmina. Mrs. Gallilee's immediate family is not alone subject to her breach of trust, but so, too, is the

brother who depended upon her to safeguard his orphaned child. Rather than bolster the security and stability of the Victorian family, then, Mrs. Gallilee acts to unsettle and undermine it.

Also contributing to Mrs. Gallilee's flaws as a Victorian wife and mother is her lack of religious conviction, which prevents her from occupying her proper role as the moral authority within the household. In line with contemporary reactionary thought, the text suggests that Mrs. Gallilee's atheism stems from her scientific beliefs, for she "knew, on the best scientific authority, that the world had created itself" (288). Only in a momentary lapse when she "completely lost her head" does she utter "Thank God!" (288). So distanced is she from religious ideals that she has an "enemy in the priest" from whom Carmina and Teresa seek spiritual advice; though Victorian England's anti-Catholicism was well entrenched, in this novel Catholicism is viewed instead in a positive light in that it is the religion practiced by the heroine Carmina and her trusted companion, Teresa.

An element of sensation fiction enters into the text's depiction of Mrs. Gallilee as a deviation from the Victorian womanly ideal, for like the notorious Lady Audley, she presents an attractive exterior that obscures an innate evil. Similarly, too, Mrs. Gallilee's nefarious plottings belie the comfortable Victorian presumption that the middle- or upper-class household represents a safe haven, shielded from the hazards and ills of the society at large. Through the schemes of both fictional women, the presumed harmonious and orderly appearance that the home presents to an outside observer is simply a sham, masking the disruption and menace within its confines. As Jenny Bourne Taylor comments in a general discussion of his writing, Collins "transpose[s] the disruptive and disturbing elements of Gothic fiction into the homely setting of the family and the everyday, recognizable world, thus . . . exploiting undercurrents of anxiety that lie behind the doors of the solid, recognizable, middle-class home" and thereby "undercut[ting] the familiarity and stability of that world."[9] The pleasing facade of Mrs. Gallilee, like that of Lady Audley, serves as a kind of synecdoche for the home, through which the seeming stability of the family—and by extension, social stability—is neither inviolable nor intact.

9. Jenny Bourne Taylor, *In the Secret Theatre of Home: Wilkie Collins, Sensation Narrative, and Nineteenth-Century Psychology*, 1.

In effect, Mrs. Gallilee makes herself into a spectacle to be "exhibited in public" (72). Outwardly "still a fine woman" even after being widowed (72), Mrs. Gallilee "dresse[s] to perfection" (59) and boasts stylish hair, a fine complexion, and a blooming countenance (74). Yet these attributes are merely the result of artifice. Her pleasing hair is apparently dyed, and her facial attractions, like her gowns, are achieved through beauty treatments of "Parisian origin." That she resembles "a portrait of the period of Charles the Second, endowed with life" suggests that Mrs. Gallilee is quite literally a product of art. Employing her appearance as a weapon of sorts through which she can "fascinate," Mrs. Gallilee acquires, when necessary, "a flush of health (from Paris), modified by a sprinkling of pallor (from London)" (182). Yet when the facial "paint and powder" begin to disintegrate, "furrows and wrinkles [remain] beneath" (248). She is a Lamia figure whose "awful eyebrows" hold "the sinister fascination of the serpent" (180), and her "glitter[ing]" eyes (193) expose her avaricious desires, which provide the inner stimulus for her to appear "remarkably well" (74).

Underlying all of Mrs. Gallilee's failings as a Victorian female ideal—her lack of emotion and sympathy, her self-interest and greed, and her failings as wife and mother—is her devotion to science. In Victorian terms, she has been "unsexed," for she has stripped herself of the vital attributes that constitute the essential female in embracing the masculinist pursuit of science. Mrs. Gallilee thus anticipates the figure of the "unsexed" woman who would be the subject of extensive nonfiction writings by biologists, psychologists, and physicians especially within the decade following publication of *Heart and Science*.

GUILT BY ASSOCIATION

Part of the way the novel vilifies Mrs. Gallilee comes from her association with and admiration for the distasteful Benjulia, a medical doctor specializing in disorders of the brain and nerves who has turned to unsavory experimentation as his life's work.[10] "[O]ne of Mrs. Gallilee's old

10. Christopher Kent reads Benjulia as the personification of "a hostile attitude towards science in its strongly materialist form" ("Probability, Reality, and Sensation in the Novels of Wilkie Collins," 63). For a discussion of Benjulia and other "decadent" scientists, see Ferguson, "Decadence."

friends," Benjulia is a shadowy individual about whom "[n]obody seems to know much" (97). Isolated in a desolate area that "nobody can discover," Benjulia exhibits a "mania" for mysterious chemical experiments about which he refuses to speak. A gigantic six feet, six inches, Benjulia is a towering and frightening presence, so "hideously" emaciated that he is called "the living skeleton" by his many enemies (95). With "great gloomy gray eyes," "protuberant cheek-bones," and a sinister complexion suggestive of gypsy origin, Benjulia creates a "startling effect" and presents a "weird look" (95). Benjulia seems Gothic in appearance, "the sort of man whom no stranger is careless enough to pass without turning round for a second look" (95).

Benjulia's unsettling demeanor serves as a somatic marker of his intrinsic evil, for he is an avid vivisectionist. Yet the parallels to Mrs. Gallilee are clear. Her "inestimable friend" (127), equally "hard-hearted" (158), practices his shameful art solely for self-aggrandizement—Mrs. Gallilee's own underlying motive for scientific study—rather than any altruistic concerns. Seeking the "grandest medical discovery of this century" (190), this "scientific savage" (214) is wholly obsessed by vainglorious ambition:

> Am I working myself into my grave, in the medical interests of humanity? *That* for humanity! I am working for my own satisfaction—for my own pride—for my own unutterable pleasure in beating other men—for the fame that will keep my name living hundreds of years hence. . . . Knowledge for its own sake, is the one god I worship. Knowledge is its own justification and its own reward. . . . Knowledge sanctifies cruelty. (190)

Indeed, Benjulia's cold-heartedness extends beyond animals. He blithely informs his brother, "[I]f I could steal a living man without being found out, I would tie him on my table, and grasp my grand discovery in days" (190). His encounters with acquaintances are startling in their remoteness; on one occasion, for instance, Benjulia's disturbing eyes observe Teresa as they would "any inanimate object near him" (96). When he tickles Zo, the Gallilees' younger daughter, with whom he has a bizarre quasi-friendship, he monitors her reactions "with as serious an interest as if he had been conducting a medical experiment" (96).

Similarly, his rare patients, chosen only for their interest as unusual specimens, are examined with a detached scrutiny lacking any element of humanity. When called in for consultation after Carmina falls dangerously ill, for example, Benjulia allows her condition to worsen simply because she presents a challenging case, justifying his neglect of his patient in the name of medical progress. His rationale "not only excused, but even ennobled" his behavior, he believes, through its "scientific connection with the interests of Medical Research," an endeavor so revered that it requires capitalization as would a deity (255). In the economy of the text, characterizing Benjulia as a vivisectionist carries the strongest possible indictment.[11] An antivivisectionist physician, for example, remarks upon "the false pretences, under which English physiologists practice their cruelties" and "propose[s] to drag the scientific English Savage from his shelter behind the medical interests of humanity, and to show him in his true character" (189). Not insignificantly, the seriousness of Benjulia's transgressions as a vivisectionist is foregrounded in having his closest relative, his older brother Lemuel, serve as the instrument seeking the physician's exposure.

As cultural scholarship has shown, the Victorian debate over vivisection was particularly heated in the latter half of the nineteenth century. Antivivisectionists, with Frances Power Cobbe as their prominent spokesperson, urged the total prohibition of such animal experimentation. Though the 1876 Cruelty to Animals Act put into place various regulations on animal research, vivisection was not banned. Collins, an ardent antivivisectionist, continued to oppose it. Collins's stance did not escape Victorian commentators on his novel. The *Fortnightly Review* asserted that "Mr. Wilkie Collins has been upon the war-path. It is as clear as possible that he said to himself, Vivisection is a horror and an abomination, and I will smite it hip and thigh." However, the reviewer was not impressed by Collins's treatment of the subject, noting that "the serious novel of vivisection, fair-minded and properly informed, based upon large opportunities for study of the theory and for observation of the practice of it, founded faithfully upon life, instead of extracted from the depths of the author's moral consciousness, still remains to be written."

11. As Steve Farmer observes, the novel is an antivivisectionist tract, replete with the most compelling arguments of the day in condemnation of the practice (*Heart and Science,* 187).

The *Athenaeum* commented that Collins "has hampered himself with trying to write with a purpose."[12]

Like Collins, many nineteenth-century observers vigorously assailed vivisection. Vernon Lee, for example, found vivisection morally reprehensible, arguing in 1882 that "honour rejects vivisection as an unjust and cheating practice," which "is contrary to the nature of the highest result of our gradual evolution." Lee assailed the "wholesale and profitless agony" that vivisection involved, arguing that "we are laying obliterating fingers upon those delicate moral features which have thus slowly and arduously been moulded into shape." Physician Elizabeth Blackwell termed "this method of investigation" as "a grave error" and pointed to "the intellectual fallacy which underlies this method of research." Blackwell added that vivisection involved "a twofold fallacy, resulting from the differences of organization in different classes of living creatures" as well as "the fact that when any organ is injured, it is a process of destruction or death—not life—that is exhibited." As late as 1895, Cobbe would point to "the frightful callousness wherewith . . . agonies have been multiplied and prolonged by vivisectors." Cobbe reminded the Victorian public in emphatic italics that "[o]ne thing only I have directly insisted on": animals have the "right to be exempted from the *very worst evil which can be inflicted upon them,*—namely, Torture," which Cobbe argued was "assuredly the minimum of all rights."[13]

The fact that ardent vivisectionist Benjulia is one of Mrs. Gallilee's most cherished friends serves as a kind of metonymic indictment of this female scientific advocate. Unlike her husband, who instinctively distrusts Benjulia, or her son, who finds Benjulia so disturbing that he begs his mother to prevent the scientist from associating with Carmina, Mrs. Gallilee welcomes the vile practitioner into her home. A frequent visitor, Benjulia on occasion wanders through the household unsupervised, free to interact with Carmina as well as Mrs. Gallilee's impressionable daughter Zo. Allowing Benjulia open access to the home serves as more damn-

12. "Theories and Practice of Modern Fiction," 880; review of *Heart and Science* (*Athenaeum*, April 28, 1883), 214. For background on Collins and his views on vivisection, see Farmer, introduction to *Heart and Science*, 17–19.

13. Vernon Lee, "Vivisection: An Evolutionist to Evolutionists," 804; Elizabeth Blackwell, *Essays in Medical Sociology*, 2:36; Frances Power Cobbe, "The Ethics of Zoophily: A Reply," 499, 502.

ing evidence pointing to Mrs. Gallilee's shortcomings as the guardian and moral authority of the household.

Moreover, Mrs. Gallilee's unwomanly character is displayed as well through her mere association with a vivisectionist. As critics have noted, the Victorian antivivisectionist cause attracted many women, in part because they recognized unsettling parallels between the exploitation of animals and of women. Coral Lansbury argues that Victorian women viewed themselves in an analogous position as mistreated animals, with many female antivivisectionists perceiving "their own condition hideously and accurately embodied in the figure of an animal bound to a table by straps with the vivisector's knife at work on its flesh." Concern for animals seemed to the Victorian public a feminine quality that tapped into the wider vein of sympathetic feelings in women. Cobbe would assert that "I do not in the smallest degree object to finding my appeals on behalf of animals treated as womanly"; instead, she said, "I claim, as a woman . . . to have the better right to be heard in such a cause than a man." Cobbe added, "If my sex has a 'mission' of any kind, it is surely to soften this hard old world, such as men . . . have left it."[14]

In freely associating with the vivisectionist Benjulia, Mrs. Gallilee is implicitly acting against the interest of her more enlightened sisters. That Benjulia has not been openly exposed as a vivisectionist seems almost incidental, since other characters are instinctively repulsed by him and sense his intrinsic evil; furthermore, based on her unwavering coldness, one assumes that Mrs. Gallilee would approve of Benjulia's work in the name of science. As her son Ovid muses, if the widespread suspicion that Benjulia's "chemical experiments" were merely "a cloak to cover the atrocities of the Savage Science" was in fact true, the information "would only raise the doctor in his mother's estimation" (136).

Despite Benjulia's despicable activities, the novel suggests that Mrs. Gallilee is even more blameworthy. Though he literally has blood on his hands (185), Benjulia does, at moments, reveal glimpses of humanity.[15]

14. Coral Lansbury, *The Old Brown Dog: Women, Workers, and Vivisection in Edwardian England,* 84; Cobbe, "Ethics," 497. The stance of many fervent antivivisectionists, Lansbury adds, was "a direct consequence of what they had seen done to poor women in the charity wards of public hospitals" (84).

15. In a letter to Frances Power Cobbe, Collins described his characterization of Benjulia: "I shall be careful to present him to the reader as a man not infinitely wicked and

He remarks, for instance, that his latest experiments "horrified" him, as he witnessed a monkey's "cries of suffering" and "gestures of entreaty" (191). "I would have given the world to put him out of his misery," Benjulia recalls, though he resisted the impulse in service to "the glorious cause." On another occasion, Benjulia mulls the concept of love and wonders, "Might he have looked higher than his torture-table and his knife? Had he gained from his life all that his life might have given to him?" (247). Additionally, in his final moments before committing suicide in his laboratory, Benjulia mercifully destroys several experimental subjects and frees the rest. Each of these acts carries a vestige of self-reflection and a fleeting possibility for redemption through recognition of transgressions. Yet no such epiphanic moments arise for the immutably cold Mrs. Gallilee. In fact, Benjulia himself eventually deems her an unwanted companion whom he adamantly endeavors to avoid. He considers her "a scandal-mongering woman" to whose level he prefers not "to lower himself" (195), and he comments after Carmina is defamed that he "desire[s] to hold no more communication with [Mrs. Gallilee]" (254).

FEMININE IDEAL

As crucial as Mrs. Gallilee's linkage to Benjulia is the absence of a similar connection to Carmina, since the niece serves as the exemplar of womanhood in the text and a forceful contrast to the unfeminine Mrs. Gallilee. To the *British Quarterly Review,* "Carmina is an admirable creation— sweet, tender, and true, whose touch converts nearly everything and everybody to show their best sides."[16] Befitting a Victorian heroine, judged in part by a desirable appearance, the first extensive description of Carmina concentrates on her physical charms. Though merely "a slip of a girl—and not even a tall slip," and "too thin," Carmina nevertheless boasts "attractions [that] were sufficiently remarkable to excite general

---

cruel" but "in some degree, an object of compassion as well as of horror" (quoted in Farmer, *Heart and Science,* 370).

16. "Novels of the Quarter, *Heart and Science,*" 232. Less effusively, the *Pall Mall Budget* opined that Carmina was "an amiable and attractive heroine enough," though she was "given to fainting and brain fever to a more than eighteenth-century extent" ("Mr. Wilkie Collins's New Novel," 332–33).

admiration" (52–53). Before enumerating those attractions and noting their deficiencies, however, the narrator judges Carmina's appearance according to a standard of female beauty, detailed as a series of body parts presented to a male gaze:

> The fine colour and the plump healthy cheeks, the broad smile, and the regular teeth, the well-developed mouth, and the promising bosom which form altogether the average type of beauty found in the purely bred English maiden, were not among the noticeable charms of the small creature. . . . She had very little colour of any sort to boast of. [Her] hair was of so light a brown that it just escaped being flaxen; but it had the negative merit of not being forced down to her eyebrows. . . . There was a delicacy of finish in her features—in the nose and the lips especially—a sensitive changefulness in the expression of her eyes (too dark in themselves to be quite in harmony with her light hair), and a subtle yet simple witchery in her rare smile, which atoned, in some degree at least, for want of complexion in the face and of flesh in the figure. Men might dispute her claims to beauty—but no one could deny that she was, in the common phrase, an interesting person. Grace and refinement; a quickness of apprehension and a vivacity of movement, suggestive of some foreign origin; a childish readiness of wonder, in the presence of new objects—and perhaps, under happier circumstances, a childish playfulness with persons whom she loved—were all characteristic attractions of the modest stranger. (53)

Though deviating from a specific standard of beauty, Carmina does display qualities associated with the quintessential Victorian woman—a feminine frailty, a refined demeanor, the light hair typical of the stereotypical "good" woman of fiction, the quick perception viewed by contemporary science as a quality of the female in contrast to the deeper judgment of the male, and an innate capacity for bewitchery, among others.[17] Moreover, she demonstrates a childishness, remarked upon

17. Philip O'Neill observes that Collins's nonfiction writing about women demonstrates "a call for the defence of an essential femininity" and that Collins "is not a feminist by any means" (*Wilkie Collins: Women, Property, and Propriety,* 183, 187). As Sue Lonoff notes, "dozens of casual comments throughout the novels reinforce traditional views of woman's weakness, her foibles, her inferior status" (*Wilkie Collins and His Victorian Readers: A Study in the Rhetoric of Authorship,* 139).

twice in one sentence, that conforms to both traditional and scientific conceptions of womanhood while offering an implicit contrast to the very unchildlike Mrs. Gallilee. Indeed, references to Carmina's childishness permeate the narrative to emphasize the point firmly. As we have seen, scientific discourse noted strong similarities between women and children, while men were distanced from both groups in terms of intellectual development. With Mrs. Gallilee's decided intellectual abilities, she would appear to the Victorian mind as a masculine anomaly, further distancing her from ideal femininity.

The opening pages of the novel establish as well other behavioral dissimilarities between Mrs. Gallilee and Carmina, foregrounding the latter's emotional, sympathetic, and compassionate nature to position her as an emblem of woman. Shortly after arriving in London, Carmina encounters a starving dog, and her "gentle heart gave its pity to this lost and hungry fellow-creature" (57). Almost immediately the dog is killed by a passing cab, which "struck the girl's sensitive nature with horror," so much so that she became "[h]elpless and speechless," "trembled piteously," and required the restorative effect of a glass of water. Carmina is so affected by the incident that she refuses soon after to enter a cab, fearing that "[w]e may run over some other poor creature" (58).

Carmina's innate qualities, her presumed "essence," all reflect positive female values to a Victorian reader. Her "sweet young face" (80) serves as a somatic marker of her intrinsic goodness and a signifier of her "gentle, just, and generous nature" (235). Her youth, remarked upon as frequently in the novel as her childishness, attests to an unbesmirched purity, revealed physically through her "innocent eyes" (118). Despite these qualities demonstrating her meekness and unworldliness, Carmina's "fine spirit that was in her fired . . . eyes" (115) suggests a righteous determination, a staunch and unwavering sense of propriety that is displayed in her dealings with her aunt. Carmina's salutary traits bring forth the highest qualities in others, as her interactions with the stern and self-acknowledged wicked governess reveal; Carmina's "higher and better nature," Miss Minerva comments, "has opened my heart to tenderness and penitence of which I never believed myself capable" (173).

Carmina also exhibits essentialized womanliness in recognizing and admitting to the kind of intellectual deficiency approvingly attributed to the Victorian female. Unlike the erudite and studious Mrs. Gallilee, Carmina is continually characterized as a mediocre intellect who cannot hope to plumb complex subjects. In fact, she appears "as unintelligent as Zo" (88), speaks "as simply as a child" (116), and recognizes Mrs. Gallilee's "superiority" (124). Carmina admits, for instance, that she failed to learn piquet because she is "too stupid" (123), and the infinitely more involved world of science is far beyond her capacities. Informing her aunt that "I am so ignorant," Carmina is led to examine a scientific tome solely because of its pleasing binding and can understand its subject matter only when Mrs. Gallilee explains it, "lower[ing] herself to the level of her niece" (111). Carmina's beloved Ovid similarly "lowered himself to the level of a girl's intelligence" to communicate with her, choosing the undemanding and feminine "language of romance" as his vehicle (108). The governess views Carmina as "simple" and wonders if she can "ever see below the surface," a speculation that Carmina is not capable of comprehending (118). Carmina even admits that she is "not clever enough" to match her father's "eye for character" (156). As baffling to Carmina as the language of science is the language of law, so unintelligible that it is "an unknown tongue" (170). She tells her nurse that she found even a letter from a lawyer inaccessible, for "[t]he strange words, the perpetual repetitions, the absence of stops, utterly bewildered me." Since both scientific and legal language belong to the male-dominated public sphere, Carmina's inability to access the mysteries of these languages serves as approbation rather than condemnation in the novel; her inaptitude firmly places Carmina in a tightly defined domestic sphere.

Because Carmina is depicted as a paragon of feminine virtues, her fearful reactions to and obtuse understanding of science suggest that these are the appropriate responses of a woman. Moreover, the valorized position for women, *Heart and Science* cautions, is to serve as the passive object of scientific study rather than as an active agent of scientific endeavor, in a definitive contrast to Mrs. Gallilee, which the lengthy section tracing the onset of Carmina's illness and her eventual recuperation makes clear. Carmina becomes completely and rightly dependent on *men* of science once her illness strikes, as they examine, probe, and treat her virtually inert body. That Mrs. Gallilee is herself the instigator of Carmina's illness seems uncoincidental, as if the aunt's active pursuit of science, on some level, is responsible for the tragedy and thus disaster must ensue from this transgression of gender roles.

Even before Mrs. Gallilee delivers her scandalous speculation on Carmina's parentage, her negative effect on her niece's health is evident, for Mrs. Gallilee's coldness and cruelty initiate the nervous condition that will become so seriously complicated. Earlier, medical assistance was necessary to treat Carmina's "nervous prostration" (243), which indirectly serves as an indictment against the aunt by again demonstrating her deficiencies as a guardian of her family; allowing Benjulia unrestricted access to Carmina in his role of medical consultant causes her condition to worsen. Not only do his "dreadful eyes" heighten her dangerous excitement (245), he refuses to intervene when Mrs. Gallilee's "silent and sinister entrance" into the sickroom unnerves Carmina (248). Instead, Benjulia detachedly "waited, in the interests of physiology, to see how the new nervous excitement would end" (248).

As befitting a woman's passive relationship to science, Carmina represents merely "an object of medical inquiry" to Benjulia (243); also appropriate is the feminine nature of her ailment, which intimates that she is "on the verge of hysterics" (244). Soon thereafter, Mrs. Gallilee's appalling remark on Carmina's illegitimacy creates a "complicated hysterical disturbance" (280). Feminist critical commentary has documented the long-standing gender connections of hysteria, of course, stemming from its ancient origins as a sign of a wandering womb and its more modern associations to a feminized emotionality and cultural anxieties about gender roles. Nineteenth-century scientists certainly weighed in on the issue and pointed to female linkages of the disease. *The Cyclopaedia of Practical Medicine* in the early 1830s observed, for instance, "evident signs of the activity of the uterine system" that were associated with hysteria, which served "to connect the two circumstances together in the firmest manner." The text added that hysteria "exercis[es] its wide influence on the susceptibilities of a nervous system by nature too easily affected by all impressions," a position that coincided smoothly with Victorian beliefs that women possessed more active and unstable nervous systems than men. An 1853 text titled *On the Pathology and Treatment of Hysteria* noted that the "considerably greater" emotionality of a woman compared to a man leads her "to feel, under circumstances where the latter thinks," which also taps into Victorian views of emotionality and rationality. Repression of sexual passion by the "unmarried and chaste" female contributes "immensely to the forces bearing upon" her. As C. S. Wiesenthal comments, "Carmina's dramatic symptoms . . . represent a plausible repertoire of the types of hysterical conversion symptoms being studied at the time by great theorists of the disease."[18]

Carmina's "hysterical disturbance" degenerates into a nearly paralytic state, which also provides a significant commentary on a woman's proper relation to science as passive object rather than active agent. Immediately following Mrs. Gallilee's heinous charge of illegitimacy, Carmina responds with "[a] ghastly stare, through half-closed eyes, [that] showed death in life"; she becomes "[r]igid, immovable, . . . voiceless and tearless" (250). Though later she briefly revives somewhat from her state of "partial catalepsy" (253), Carmina suffers a "melancholy relapse" of "simulated paralysis" in which the young patient "lay still as death" (298). In that state "[h]er eyes never moved," and "her hand showed no consciousness of . . . touch" (298). Through her paralysis, Carmina becomes almost literally an object of science—inert, unresponsive, incapable of acting on her own volition, and utterly reliant on the medical men who treat her. This debilitating paralysis itself carries gender implications, not only because it derives from a hysterical reaction to a severe shock, but also because Carmina's case replicates that of two Canadian women who had themselves been the object of medical scrutiny and, in a sense, became a kind of literal object when transformed into the content of a medical text.[19]

Even though Benjulia strays far past the appropriate boundaries in his management of Carmina's illness, his actions are instructive, for to a lesser extent all medical men in the novel—and, more broadly, in Victorian society as a whole—view a woman patient as a phenomenon to be analyzed and probed. An ethical physician would certainly con-

18. John Conolly, entry in *Cyclopaedia of Practical Medicine*, 185; Robert Brudenell Carter, *On the Pathology and Treatment of Hysteria*, 190–91; C. S. Wiesenthal, "From Charcot to Plato: The History of Hysteria in *Heart and Science*," 259.

19. Wiesenthal points out that *Heart and Science* is "replete with 'excitable' women" and adds, "Clearly portrayed as mad and hysterical victims of their own ungovernable passions, Collins' women reveal themselves as essentially creatures of the 'heart' " ("From Charcot to Plato," 259, 260–61). See Malane on Carmina's intellectual limitations, as well as their relationship to her illness (*Sex in Mind*, 124–27).

demn Benjulia's "dread of a commonplace termination to an excep-
tionally interesting case" (254) and revile Benjulia's expectation that
Carmina would "take her place, along with the other animals, in his
note-book of experiments" (280), but parallels are evident in other respects. Undoubtedly, the intellectual challenge of an unusual illness, on
some level, transforms a patient from a person to a noteworthy case that
suggests stimulating "new ideas" to the physician, as it does for Benjulia (255). Benjulia's seemingly innocuous command to "[d]raw up the
blind" because he "want[s] to have a good look at her" (280) underscores
Carmina's status as an object subjected to an extremely penetrating male
gaze. Observation becomes "investigation" (280), a term that implies an
intense search into the mysteries of the female body. Carmina is acted
upon by not one but three medical men, all of whom seek to probe
somatic secrets.

IDEAL MAN OF SCIENCE

Though Benjulia, like Mrs. Gallilee, exemplifies an irreconcilability between "heart" and "science," the novel does not make the reductive claim
that the two realms are necessarily incompatible. Instead, the characterization of Ovid Vere provides an instructive illustration of their harmonious conjunction. Not coincidentally, of course, is this embodiment of
"heart" and "science" a male; as the text has abundantly warned through
its characterization of Mrs. Gallilee, and the absence of any positive female figures with scientific leanings, such a concordance is impossible
for a woman to achieve. Her role, Victorian culture would expect, would
merely be to channel her scientific capabilities into the education of her
son; in effect, she would function simply as the biological vessel for the
transmission of scientific acumen to Ovid and provide the necessary
nurturance to develop his intellectual potential to the fullest. In demonstrating intellectual capacities of her own, Mrs. Gallilee belies physiological laws and cannot be allowed to thrive within the economy of the
novel. As Francis Galton remarked in 1869, "A mother transmits masculine peculiarities to her male child, which she does not and cannot
possess." He claimed that "there exists no criterion for a just compari-

son of the natural ability of the different sexes," even though his study sample was "too small to warrant any very decided conclusion."[20]

Ovid's successful incorporation of heart and science is established in the novel's early chapters and reiterated periodically to underscore the plausibility and desirability of melding the two. As C. S. Wiesenthal observes, Ovid is the "normative ideal of Heart *in* Science."[21] At age thirty-one, the novel reveals, this member of the Royal College of Surgeons is "devoted heart and soul to his profession" (45), a choice of phrasing that smoothly blends emotionality with the intellectual demands of his career. Even as a relatively young medical man, Ovid demonstrates an impressive expertise, commented upon by a "great physician" who claims that Ovid "is on the way—already far on the way—to be one of the foremost men of his time" with "no common medical career before him" (48). Yet Ovid displays an acute sensibility that distinguishes him from the equally expert Benjulia, positioning Ovid as the embodiment of appropriate emotion and Benjulia as entirely deficient in this human quality. In one telling example in which the pair are in conversation, Ovid unexpectedly grabs Benjulia's arm and, "with a sudden outburst of alarm," warns the older man to "[s]top!" in an unsuccessful effort to prevent him from stepping on a wayward beetle (103). Benjulia's reaction to Ovid's "abortive little act of mercy" is speechless amazement as he muses upon "an adult male human being (not in a lunatic asylum) anxious to spare the life of a beetle," especially one that is not even an unusual specimen.

Though Ovid had displayed a Benjulia-like "abrupt" manner in earlier encounters with patients, he brings warmth and compassion to his work once he encounters Carmina; he demonstrates "a silent gentleness which presented him in a new character" and confers "a patient attention wonderful to see" (67). Ovid's dramatic alteration, the text implies, derives from Carmina's influence as a womanly ideal who performs her proper role in bettering those she encounters, as if unwittingly preparing for her future as a wife and mother. Before Ovid met Carmina, the primary female influence upon him was Mrs. Gallilee, and the shift in his character serves as yet another indictment of her as both woman and

20. Galton, *Hereditary Genius*, 55–56.
21. Wiesenthal, "From Charcot to Plato," 261.

mother. Once distanced from Mrs. Gallilee, Ovid can develop into the model physician, as seen in his later treatment of Carmina, when he brings her from the brink of death to the best state of health possible after the horrible shock she had received. Importantly, Ovid places the blame for Carmina's illness firmly on his mother's behavior.

Also indicative of Ovid's status as an admirable practitioner of science is the contrast between his mode of treatment and that of Benjulia in addressing Carmina's illness. Not only did Benjulia encourage the hapless ministrations of fellow physician Mr. Null, allowing Carmina to deteriorate for a "vile end of [Benjulia's] own" (306), but his underlying rationale in treating her was to further the goals of his vivisection work on brain disorders. Ovid, however, depends upon the findings of the physician who had treated and written about the two Canadian women suffering from hysteria, a physician who was adamantly opposed to "the useless and detestable cruelties which go by the name of Vivisection" (307). Instead, the Canadian physician based his treatment protocol exclusively on "the results of bedside practice." A vivisectionist, this physician avers, is "a man in a state of revolt against God" (308) who cannot "justify deliberate cruelty in the means" to achieve any end, whatever its "asserted usefulness" (307). Significantly, Ovid's publication of the deceased Canadian physician's manuscript becomes the causal agent in Benjulia's suicide, for that text negates the effects of Benjulia's own scientific efforts and precludes the intended publication of his own discoveries.

Ovid's recognition not only of Benjulia's harmful medical treatment of Carmina but also the "ignorant treatment" of the "incompetent" Mr. Null (306) provides further proof of both the young man's scientific acumen and Mrs. Gallilee's perfidy, for Mr. Null's lack of medical effectiveness is made abundantly clear in his approach to Carmina's condition. Null's imprecise diagnosis of her illness as "[s]ome nervous prostration" and his proposed ineffectual cure of "the air of the seaside" cause the astute Benjulia to discern Null's "mental calibre at its exact value, in a moment" (243). So unskilled is Mr. Null that his "course of action could be trusted to let the instructive progress of the malady proceed" for Benjulia's loathsome edification, "without a suspicion of the nervous hysteria which . . . threatened to establish itself, in course of time, as the hidden cause" (255). So obtuse is Mr. Null that he "never had an idea of his own, from the day of his birth, downward" (296), and he is "incapable of stepping beyond his own narrow limits, under any provocation whatever" (297). Yet the astute Mrs. Gallilee allows the self-serving and ineffectual Mr. Null to provide continuing care to Carmina, presumably because his inept treatment could eventually rid Mrs. Gallilee of her niece.

LOSS OF REASON

With her many failings as a woman, wife, and mother—all traceable to her interest in science—Mrs. Gallilee must, in the logic of the text, be punished. Like Carmina's life-threatening illness, Mrs. Gallilee's deterioration stems from the pivotal scene in which she impugns Carmina's parentage. Immediately following the remark, shrieked in "a frenzy of rage," Mrs. Gallilee utters "a screaming laugh" before Teresa attacks her (249). The text's phrasing is important, for it introduces the element of madness.[22] In the context of Victorian responses to female madness, frequently attributed to unruly women who challenge their restrictive role within the domestic sphere, as critical commentary has demonstrated, Mrs. Gallilee would indeed appear mad. Not only does she fail Carmina as a surrogate mother through this incident, but she subsequently fails again as a wife; Mrs. Gallilee's condition worsens to the point that she responds to her husband with a similar "shriek of fury" (301), which serves as the impetus for her temporary removal to an asylum.

Nineteenth-century medical writing on hysteria is again instructive in providing a lens through which to read *Heart and Science,* for Mrs. Gallilee exhibits symptoms that suggest the disease, but the cause of her hysterical behavior is far different from that of her intellectually deficient niece. *The Cyclopaedia of Practical Medicine* noted that "excessive study" could also cause hysteria to develop, as did Thomas Laycock's 1840 *Treatise on the Nervous Diseases of Women,* which cautioned that "[t]he relations of hysteria to the present modes of education are of great

---

22. Wiesenthal also makes this connection, noting that "[e]ven the 'intellectual' Mrs. Galilee succumbs in the end to a temporary but full-blown mania: a 'violent madness' à la Bertha Mason, during which she is also confined in an upstairs room, and flies at her husband with 'a shriek of fury' when he attempts to see her" (ibid., 260). See also Malane on Mrs. Gallilee's madness (*Sex in Mind,* 134–35).

importance" and warned that "forced mental training" led to "irritabil-
ity of the brain." F. C. Skey similarly noted in 1867 that hysteria "often select[s] as its victim a female member of a family exhibiting more
than usual force and decision of character, of strong resolution, fearless
of danger, bold riders, having plenty of what is termed *nerve*."[23] Mrs.
Gallilee's fascination with learning, and the rigorous mental training required for successful scientific study, thus would provide sufficient cause
for developing hysterical symptoms.

The irony of Mrs. Gallilee's deterioration is that the actions of this
woman of reason cause her to lose her reason. After being struck insensi-
ble by Teresa's attack, Mrs. Gallilee gradually revives but "look[s] wildly
round the room" (251) in another reminder of madness. Though apparently recovering her mental faculties—characteristically, "[h]er first
thought was for herself" upon reviving (251)—Mrs. Gallilee has begun
a progressive decline, so much so that she requires her husband's assistance to retreat to her bedroom, where "she lay helpless" with "her
authority set at naught" (257). Physically as well as mentally attenuated,
this formerly "ready and resolute woman" finds that "the mere effort
of decision" is an excessive strain (258). Her enfeebled mind manifests
itself in "the difficulty she found in expressing her thoughts," which is
so uncharacteristic that it "even startled stupid Mr. Null" (292). Her
customary "loud and hard" voice, a marker of her previous authority,
becomes "strangely subdued" (290) and "[e]ven . . . failed her" on one
occasion (258). The woman of reason becomes unreasonable to such an
extent that she falls to her knees, begging her servants for prayers as she
laments, "I don't know how to pray for myself. Where is God?" (295).
Forcibly restrained, Mrs. Gallilee is so unhinged that even the dense Mr.
Null can recognize that "[s]he is out of her mind."

Though "the measures taken to restore Mrs. Gallilee to herself" at the
asylum are surprisingly successful, she rarely speaks; on the few occasions she does, "her mind seemed to be occupied with scientific subjects" (311). No mention of her family is made, a disturbing omission
that is expected to be cured within months and allow her to return to
her home, "as sane a woman as ever." Again suitable in light of Victorian estimations of madness, the fact that Mrs. Gallilee rechannels her
thoughts into scientific matters serves as a marker of continued insan-

23. Conolly, *Cyclopaedia,* 186; Thomas Laycock, "A Treatise on the Nervous Diseases
of Women," 189; F. C. Skey, quoted in Taylor, *In the Secret Theatre,* 69.

ity, whereas concern for her family would signal a restoration to mental health. In a gap of the text, Mrs. Gallilee is allowed to leave the asylum, even though her interest in science remains intact and a devotion to her family unrealized—indeed, once home, "[m]essages from her husband are as completely thrown away on her . . . as if she was still in the asylum" (326). Though presumably cured sufficiently to enable a return to society, Mrs. Gallilee's reasoning continues to appear impaired; as lawyer Mr. Mool, trained in logical thought, assesses the situation, Mrs. Gallilee "declares herself to be an infamously injured woman" and, in fact, "proves it, from her own point of view." To Mrs. Gallilee's twisted reasoning, the events that she had set in motion transform her from victimizer to victim: she was deserted by her husband, her children are removed from her and fail to write, her niece plotted to run away to Ovid after defaming her aunt in a letter, and her son chose the ungrateful Carmina as his wife. Mrs. Gallilee's sole shortcoming, in her skewed judgment, rests in what she dismissively terms a loss of temper in her infamous remark to Carmina. The aunt implies that her action was justified in view of the information she had, still questions the veracity of the evidence proving Carmina's legitimacy, and again shifts the blame to others for her presumably trivial misstep. As Mr. Mool recounts her self-justification to Mr. Gallilee in urging the beleaguered husband to separate legally from his wife, the disgusted lawyer repeats her words:

> "Am I to blame," she said, "for believing that story about my brother's wife? It's acknowledged that she gave the man money—the rest is a matter of opinion. Was I wrong to lose my temper and say what I did say to this so-called niece of mine? Yes, I was wrong, there: it's the only case in which there is a fault to find with me. But had I no provocation? Have I not suffered? . . . I owe a duty to my own self-respect; and that duty compels me to speak plainly. I will have nothing more to do with the members of my heartless family. The rest of my life is devoted to intellectual society, and the ennobling pursuits of science." . . . I declare to you, my flesh creeps when I think of her. (326)

In the final paragraphs of the novel, Mrs. Gallilee is contentedly "At Home to Science," entertaining "[p]rofessors of the civilised universe" with a derogatorily termed "perfect Babel of names" (327). Though ostensibly a solemn gathering of intellectual luminaries, the evening's events are described in terms more parodic than praising; Mrs. Gallilee, for instance, "solved the serious problem of diet" for turning tadpoles into frogs "with such cheering results that these last lively beings joined the guests on the carpet, and gratified intelligent curiosity by explorations on the stairs." Relaxing after the guests have left, bereft of her family, Mrs. Gallilee ironically utters her final words, and those of the novel as well: "At last, I'm a happy woman!"

JEZEBEL AND HER DAUGHTER

The text's unequivocal message that scientific interests are wholly improper for women's indulgence resonates with Collins's 1880 novel, *Jezebel's Daughter,* which offers an instructive gloss on the 1883 *Heart and Science.* The earlier novel similarly features both a menacing woman with links to science and a young paragon of virtue, in this case a daughter. The widow of a chemistry professor and as extravagant as Mrs. Gallilee, Madame Fontaine plots to marry off her daughter Minna to the comfortably situated Fritz Keller, whose father vigorously opposes the marriage because of the mother's reputedly scandalous behavior. Using poisons that her deceased husband had wanted posthumously destroyed, Madame Fontaine attempts first to murder the elder Mr. Keller and then poses as his savior by applying an antidote her husband had also developed, winning Mr. Keller's gratitude and approval of his son's marriage. Subsequently, Madame Fontaine attempts to murder Mr. Keller's business partner, whom she fears will undermine the marriage plans, but accidentally kills herself instead with another of her husband's poisons, for which there is no antidote.

Unlike Mrs. Gallilee, Madame Fontaine does not have an avid interest in science; her relationship to it is more indirect, deriving from her subversion of her scientist husband's wishes about the disposal of his chemicals. He had directed that upon his death, his chemicals should be given to another professor who would destroy the chemicals so no one would be injured, but Madame Fontaine thwarted his wishes by retaining the most dangerous materials. As in *Heart and Science,* we see a gendered contrast between positive and negative relationships to science. Professor Fontaine's motivation for working with the poisons derived from an interest in finding antidotes for "the good of my fellow-creatures" (50); his wife's motivation proceeded from an interest in harming her fellow creatures.[24] He is termed "a wonderful man" by one character, "the greatest man in Germany" (381).

Critical commentary on Collins's oeuvre in general and *Jezebel's Daughter* in particular offers helpful perspectives from which to view the complexities of the novel. As Jenny Bourne Taylor comments in a discussion of Collins's fiction that certainly applies to *Jezebel's Daughter* as well as *Heart and Science,* "[m]any of the later novels seem to be concerned not with creating a range of possible meanings, but with narrowing meanings down." Most pertinently to my analysis, "science itself comes increasingly to be used as a monolithic form of power and manipulation—an externalized source of melodrama and horror," Taylor remarks. The characterization of Madame Fontaine fits with Patricia Frick's notion that "Collins occasionally fell back on two standard conceptions of the magdalen: the man-trapping jezebel and the madonna/whore" in his fiction. Moreover, as Keith Reierstad points out, Madame Fontaine's criminality is related to "a megalomaniacal desire to exercise power over others" and suggests "the ultimate falsification of the maternal role and the domestic ideal." Indeed, the *Spectator* review of the novel, though finding Collins "nearly as entertaining as he ever was," took issue with his characterization of Madame Fontaine, whom the reviewer believed was given too much credit for being a devoted mother. "[W]hy should Mr. Collins try to make us believe that Jezebel, the modern Lucrezia Borgia, who will poison you as soon as look at you, is . . . redeemed . . . by the supremacy of her maternal affection?" The reviewer added that the tendency of fiction to unearth "exquisite traits of generosity, tenderness, and nobility in natures the most lost and degraded" is merely "a cheap and tawdry form of sentimentality."[25]

Like Mrs. Gallilee, an attractive exterior conceals the corrupted nature of Madame Fontaine. Variously termed a "truly grand creature"

24. Parenthetical page citations refer to the Peter Fenelon Collier edition of Wilkie Collins, *Jezebel's Daughter.*

25. Taylor, *In the Secret Theatre,* 211; Patricia Frick, "The Fallen Angels of Wilkie Collins," 345; Keith Reierstad, "Innocent Indecency: The Questionable Heroines of Wilkie Collins' Sensation Novels," 59; review of *Jezebel's Daughter* (*Spectator,* May 15, 1880), 208, 209.

(25), "remarkable" woman (75), and "glorious creature" (86), Madame Fontaine boasts "profuse black hair" (75) and a "well-rounded figure," along with "the supple grace of all her movements" and "the command-ing composure of her expression." In addition, she is "perfectly dressed" (76) and exhibits an "exquisite charm of her voice and manner." As in the 1883 novel, however, a disquieting gaze warns of a demonic personality; her "furtively cruel" eyes (75), the male narrator comments, "seemed to be looking straight into my heart, and surprising all my secrets" (76). Ad-ditionally, Madame Fontaine displays "serpentine graces" (205) that pre-figure Mrs. Gallilee's own Lamian qualities. Madame Fontaine is seem-ingly an embodiment of the sublime; her touch creates "a strange sense of disturbance, half pleasurable, half painful" (80). Moreover, despite her womanly appearance, Madame Fontaine exhibits masculine quali-ties in her "strength of mind" (55), a voice "as firm as the voice of a man" when conveying a resolute determination (107), and a crossed-handed pose like "the great Napoleon" (110).

In contrast, her daughter is a Carmina-like character. Termed "the sweetest girl living" by her future husband, the eighteen-year-old Minna is "gracious, delightful, desirable" (25). Virtuous, "singularly delicate" (67), and "innocently frank" (79), Minna appears "too exquisitely sen-sitive, for the rough world she lives in" (82). Unlike her mother's "in-describable witchery of . . . manner" (75), Minna is distinguished by "modest and ladylike" behavior (64). With "lovely" (68) and "soft sen-sitive eyes" (64), Minna's gaze displays none of the aggressive and trou-bling qualities that typify her mother's unsettling look. The daughter's countenance radiates with the "heavenly light of true and generous feel-ing" (282).

Other parallels to *Heart and Science* also emerge in *Jezebel's Daughter*. Like Mrs. Gallilee, Madame Fontaine is deemed mad, in this case by a male character who himself had been driven mad. "Bedlam is the only place for her!" he exclaims (268). Asserting that there is "no possible mistake" in his assessment of Madame Fontaine's condition, he adds, "If there's a creature living who thoroughly understands madness when he sees it—by Heaven, I'm that man!" (270). Yet madness is feminized in this novel, as in *Heart and Science,* because his condition resulted to some extent through Madame Fontaine's actions. Her madness additionally carries a pronounced gender link to hysteria. She exhibits "hysterical excitement" through a "frantic fit of laughter" (267) and even remarks upon being "a little hysterical" (235) in her behavior with her daughter.

The portrait of Madame Fontaine drawn in *Jezebel's Daughter* provides a kind of prototype for Mrs. Gallilee, but the connection between female involvement in science and unnerving behavior is made far more explicit in *Heart and Science*. The 1883 novel serves, then, as a strident warning to a Victorian society enthralled with the workings of science that it must guard against women entering this masculine domain, even as mere amateurs. In portraying Mrs. Gallilee's unsettling failures as a wife and mother through her avocation, *Heart and Science* implies that disturbances to the basic unit of society, the family, hold ominous repercussions and jeopardize the stability of Victorian culture as a whole.

5

"Escaping" Gender

The Neutral Voice in Marianne North's
Recollections of a Happy Life

For a Victorian woman devoted to science, a clear dilemma existed. How could she resolve the seemingly inherent contradictions that these dual conditions of gender and avocation posed in a culture that denied women an intellectual equality with men on the basis of biological determinism? For the narrative voice of Marianne North's massive travel memoirs, the apparent solution is to enact a psychological denial and virtual erasure of her gender status. This prolific botanical painter attempts to transcend gender in the three-volume *Recollections of a Happy Life*, I suggest, by assuming an ostensibly neutral voice within a theoretically genderless space. In effect, the narrator labors to step outside of gender to become neither a male nor female entity but one that is emptied of its gendered content altogether. The neutralization project is doomed, of course, for a subject can never fully step outside of gender status, despite intensive efforts marshaled in the process. Nevertheless, North's persona pursues a range of stratagems to attain an idealized state of gender indeterminacy, deploying a complex array of techniques to manipulate, reshape, and reject essentialist associations. Yet in attempting to cast off gender, North becomes trapped in rhetorical binds and ideological pitfalls that produce a callous, racist, and misogynist voice.

An unusual figure in Victorian culture, North achieved fame and respect as a worldwide traveler, painter, and naturalist whose posthumously published memoirs trace her experiences spanning almost a quarter of a century.[1] Traveling primarily alone across six continents, North not only painted hundreds of natural scenes and plants, eventually given a permanent home in a gallery at Kew Gardens, but also participated in the collection and identification of specimens—several of which were named for her—as one of Kew's many informal representatives throughout the empire. Born into a privileged household with enviable connections to prominent figures in science, government, and the arts, North developed an early interest in botany through the influence of a father whose own fascination with plant life was evidenced by several greenhouses and enthusiastic amateur study. As the *Journal of the Royal Horticultural Society* remarked, botany "played a large part in the North family life, and plant-collecting expeditions on the mountain slopes of Europe became an annual event." Initially traveling with her father across Europe and beyond, North continued her explorations after his death, undertaking numerous journeys throughout the empire and elsewhere. Though she intended to edit the memoirs herself—thereby wholly controlling the narrative voice—and even tried unsuccessfully to publish a far lengthier version than the finished text, she died before the project could be completed.[2] Her sister Catherine, spouse of John Addington Symonds, assumed the editorial duties and published the first two volumes in 1892, which met effusive public regard, and the similarly well-received third volume a year later.

The *Athenaeum*, for example, appraised the first two volumes as "fascinating" and "in the first rank among the records of travellers' experiences." Noting that the texts contained "not a page which has not some

1. Marianne North's two-volume *Recollections of a Happy Life* chronicles travels in the 1870s and early 1880s; *Some Further Recollections of a Happy Life* traces earlier travels, from 1859 to 1870. All parenthetical citations refer to these texts; volume numbers are included where necessary to differentiate the two texts in *Recollections of a Happy Life*, while parenthetical citations to *Some Further Recollections* are indicated with the abbreviation *FR*.

2. Alvide Lees-Milne, "Marianne North," 232. For a history of the writing, editing, and publishing of the *Recollections*, see Brenda E. Moon, "Marianne North's *Recollections of a Happy Life:* How They Came to Be Written and Published."

special charm," the *Athenaeum* spoke approvingly of the "recollections of a noble and gifted woman" of "genius and enthusiasm," whose career was unlike that of any other woman. The third volume received an even more commendatory review, in which a "great traveller" of "wonderful strength and courage" was applauded for the "wit and liveliness" of a "most delightful and refreshing volume." *Nature* designated North "an accomplished and faithful painter of plant and animal life" in its positive 1892 review and complimented the subsequent volume in 1893 as displaying "[t]he same freedom in style and criticism" as its predecessors.[3]

In an obituary, the *Athenaeum* remarked that "the world is poorer" for North's death and added a series of accolades. North "was a woman of versatile genius" who demonstrated "force and nobleness of . . . character," a "clear incisiveness of . . . intellect," and expressed herself with "power rather than the grace of reticence." The often scathing tone of North's observations was ignored, however, for the *Athenaeum* commented that the "large-hearted tenderness and delicacy of feeling of the woman was always keeping in subordination and restraint the masculine element."[4]

VICTORIAN TRAVEL WRITING

To assess North's narrative voice most productively, it is first necessary to contextualize her memoirs within other contemporary travel accounts. Modern scholars have interestingly commented on the ways in which Victorian travel writers and their precursors constructed themselves autobiographically on the basis of gender and other significant factors such as their representation of the authority of empire. Though critics disagree in important ways on the gendered elements of women's travel writing, two common strains of thought appear. For many women travel writers, the solution to a problematic gender status in a traditionally male endeavor was to adopt the narrative stance of a white male, whereby

3. Review of *Recollections of a Happy Life* (*Athenaeum*, February 27, 1892), 269, 270; review of *Some Further Recollections of a Happy Life* (*Athenaeum*, June 17, 1893), 755; "The Travels of a Painter of Flowers," 602; "Earlier Recollections of Marianne North," 291.

4. "Miss Marianne North," 319.

they could align themselves with the projects of empire, speak author-
itatively of a traditionally male experience, reconfigure themselves intermittently into the opposite sex to establish a distance from unwomanly behavior, or make their primary identification with race rather than
gender.

In her seminal study, Mary Louise Pratt adumbrated an array of characteristics that surfaced in a variety of male explorers' writings, which
were approached from aggressively imperialist perspectives. Pratt notes,
for instance, that male travelers "homogenize[d] the people to be subjected," transmuted them into "a collective *they*" or "iconic *he*," and
accorded them a "pregiven custom or trait." Male writers ignored "domestic settings," so much so that "one is hard pressed indeed to find
even an interior description of a house." Moreover, these travelers "es-
theticized" landscapes, accreted meaning through elaborate infusions of
modifiers, avoided scientific terminology, favored a "monarch-of-all-I-
survey" perspective, displayed a "rhetoric of presence," and positioned
themselves on promontories in one of the many signifiers of dominance
that inform the accounts.[5]

Conversely, Pratt sees a self-identification of the "indoor world" as the
"seat of the self" in women's writings, with interior "refuges" connoting
a "site above all of solitude." Pratt observes, "If the men's job was to collect and possess everything else, these women travelers sought first and
foremost to collect and possess themselves." In fact, "[t]he masculine
heroic discourse of discovery is not readily available to women."[6]

Feminist critics of Victorian women travel writers have offered
variations on Pratt's schematic. Dea Birkett, for instance, argues that
"[w]omen travellers felt they had to act the part of male explorers," a difficult task always complicated by gender status, and evaded criticism of
their unfeminine behavior by assuming "a temporary male status." The
masculine characteristics women travelers displayed could be bracketed
off by "attributing them instead to an amorphous masculine culture."
Catherine Barnes Stevenson also cites the "sexually ambiguous position"
of women travelers who had "the license to behave like men at moments
when 'typically' female conduct would have been not only ludicrous but

5. Mary Louise Pratt, *Imperial Eyes: Travel Writing and Transculturation,* 63–64, 159,
204, 205, 213.
6. Ibid., 159, 160, 213.

dangerous." Skin color was of paramount importance, Birkett explains, for "[t]he community of racial status surpassed all other divisions of gender, class, and nationality."[7]

Birkett contends that female authors "saw the foreign worlds through white masculine eyes" with scarce interest in "female culture and family life," rather than revealing a "'feminine eye' and attention to domestic detail." For other women travel writers, however, the solution to their vexed gender status was to speak from a decidedly female perspective, deflecting criticism by embracing rather than rejecting femininity. Because of the "different discursive frameworks and pressures" of colonial women travelers, Sara Mills observes, their accounts "tended to be more tentative" in proclaiming the "'truths' of British rule" and generally avoided homogeneous racial accounts while identifying Others as individuals. These writers also privileged "personal involvement and relationships with people of the other culture." As Mills maintains, women writers tended to spurn or modify the voice of "the bold adventuring hero of male travel texts" and opted for "other narrative roles"— nurturing maternal figure or philanthropic sympathizer, for example— lacing their memoirs with self-effacing remarks and penning their accounts "very much as 'feminine' women." Moreover, Stevenson points out that women travelers wrote for "a predominantly female audience interested in both the minutiae of everyday domestic life and the writer's psychological reactions to a new environment," while Maria H. Frawley cites the tendency of women travelers to focus on the trauma of "leaving home." Travel writing enabled women "to establish a voice of authority unavailable in any other genre," notes Lila Marz Harper. An alternative narrative position offered by Susan Morgan holds that North's texts "lined up not as masculine or even male-identified discourse but as a version of the new kind of feminine discourse." North's writing, Morgan maintains, evidenced a "'new' kind of female, indifferent to the private sphere, yet contributing her feminine vision to the great work of sustaining and extending British power in the public sphere."[8]

7. Dea Birkett, *Spinsters Abroad: Victorian Lady Travelers*, 136, 137, 192, 115, 123; Catherine Barnes Stevenson, *Victorian Women Travel Writers in Africa*, 4.

8. Birkett, *Spinsters Abroad*, 167, 192; Sara Mills, *Discourses of Difference: An Analysis of Women's Travel Writing and Colonialism*, 3, 21, 22, 44; Stevenson, *Victorian Women*, 9; Maria H. Frawley, *A Wider Range: Travel Writing by Women in Victorian England*, 26; Lila

Though I agree with Morgan that North's writings provide "significant modifications of the rhetoric of nineteenth-century British women's travel discourses," demonstrate a "nonparticipation in the conventions of feminine dependency" whereby "[h]er writing breaks out of . . . familiar gender prescriptions," and complicate "ideological expectations about female self-representation," I am suggesting a different scenario at work in North's *Recollections,* whereby the narrative voice adopts neither a feminine perspectival orientation nor assumes the persona of a white male.[9] Missing from the *Recollections* is a sense that North wishes to enact a kind of transvestitism that would allow her to speak as a man or that she desires to speak as a woman. The narrator thus does not fit the profile of the woman traveler who suspends femininity intermittently to engage in masculine exploits and maneuvers and then returns to a woman's voice, demeanor, and concerns. Instead, the narrator seeks to transpose the voice into a white *gender-neutral* entity who elides definitive categorization. One is reminded of North's early comment that a "poor old parrot took a fancy to me" until "it found out I was only a woman, and liked me no more" (*FR*, 313); the narrative voice seemingly seeks to excise any taint of womanhood that would evoke similar sentiments in her own species. It is as if the narrator participates in a form of "decorporealization" to negate the gendered body and metamorphose into a neuter voice.

At first glance, one might surmise that an "ungendered" voice in Victorian culture is simply a male voice, the presumably normative articulation for universalized human experience. Yet if we examine the traits attributed to masculine travel writing by the above critics and others, we see that most do not apply to North's text. The *Recollections* only occasionally locate the narrator on promontories, convey not a sense of mastery over the landscape but of appreciation, describe panoramas succinctly rather than applying dense layers of modifiers, avoid presenting the landscape as a female body to be penetrated and vanquished, and deploy rather than shy away from scientific language. Though North does adopt the various imperialist tropes that collaborate to confer an

---

Marz Harper, *Solitary Travelers: Nineteenth-Century Women's Travel Narratives and the Scientific Vocation,* 16; Susan Morgan, *Place Matters: Gendered Geography in Victorian Women's Travel Books about Southeast Asia,* 122, 127.

    9. Morgan, *Place Matters,* 118, 119, 130.

impression of homogeneity in the Other's land, this authorial predilection seems more a factor of nationalist egocentrism than of gender, especially since many women's travel writings participate in that project as well.

Perhaps we can attribute North's attempts at gender nullification, at least in part, to experiences in her early years, specifically parental relationships. North reveals a distinct identification with patrilineal heritage, obfuscating and nearly effacing her matrilineal connections. Indeed, the first volume of the memoirs opens with a recapitulation of ancestry, tracing North's lineage from her "progenitors," all of whom derive from the paternal line (1:1). Though North mentions her mother's earlier marriage in passing, the father's influence is so dominant and formative that she observes, "My first recollections relate to my father" (5). Characterized as "from first to last the one idol and friend of my life," without whom North "had little pleasure and no secrets," the paterfamilias became North's traveling companion and confidant until his death as she approached middle age. Indeed, Molly Dickins points out that "[w]hether there was ever any other man in her life except her father Marianne gives no hint; but the probability is that her father's companionship was all she wished for." Though her dying mother insisted that North never abandon her father, the daughter's intense affection intimates not so much a sense of filial duty as unshakable emotional attachment. In a family with no sons, North became, in effect, both a daughter and a surrogate son who invariably sought the father's approbation and affection. Such a role would insert her into a kind of gender indeterminacy, compelling her to act the part of the dutiful daughter while receiving the attention and cultivation reserved for a beloved male heir. North's nickname of "Pop" is particularly significant in this regard, for it conveys a "sexually ambiguous" quality, as Birkett observes, that is shown so strongly in the strategy of gender nullification underlying the memoirs.[10]

The reluctance to assume a female voice can be readily attributed, of

10. Molly Dickins, "Marianne North," 320; Birkett, *Spinsters Abroad,* 27. For a discussion of North's close affiliation with her father's ancestry and lack of interest in her mother's, see Birkett, 4–38. Birkett makes the unnerving observation that father and daughter registered as "Mr." and "Mrs." in their travels (5). North's sorrow about her father's death was "unnatural," Birkett comments, and "not simply explained by the loss of a loved parent" (37, 38).

course, to the delimiting historical and cultural inscriptions traditionally imposed upon the female body, through which a woman is defined, contained, and molded into a social entity. In this regard, Elizabeth Grosz points to "the ways in which the body must be psychically constituted in order for the subject to acquire a sense of its place in the world and in connection with others,"[11] and in Victorian culture a woman's body certainly relegated her to an unenviable positionality. The materiality of the body thus absorbed, shaped, and generated perceptions of subjectivity. As has become a verity in Victorian scholarship, the female body was inextricably linked with weakness, emotion, irrationality, ignorance, reproduction, and a host of other qualities that comprised the cultural estimation of woman.

Perhaps the desire to separate herself from the associations to the female body helps explain North's dismissive attitude about the limits of her own, typically female, education. She speaks condescendingly of both governesses and schools, and she attributes her knowledge to self-education. "Governesses hardly interfered with me," she says, for "Walter Scott or Shakespeare gave me their versions of history, and Robinson Crusoe and some other old books my ideas of geography" (1:8). Recognizing that she "was very uneducated" and was therefore sent to school, North nevertheless recalls that "[t]he teaching was such purely mechanical routine" that "[a]t last the happy time came, and I left school" (13). She compensates for her lack of formal education by claiming that "a really distinguished woman needs no colleges or 'higher education' lectures" (91).

By affecting a gender-neutral voice, the *Recollections* narrator can elide, at least rhetorically, the otherwise inescapable connections that the body would signify. In so doing, the narrative voice seemingly can construct an alternate subjectivity and thus a differing perception of the "reality" into which the subject is inserted. Through this psychic dissociation, the narrator can operate under the illusion that gender can be dismissed, shed like an unwanted skin. The narrator thus becomes not a woman masquerading as a man, a male mimic, or a victim of hysteria, as Luce Irigaray has characterized options available to a female, but an entitled and appropriate participant in the symbolic order. The voice

11. Elizabeth Grosz, *Volatile Bodies: Toward a Corporeal Feminism*, xii.

therefore struggles to evade the essentialist taints that would marginalize, stifle, and disempower, presumably enabling it to enact an abjection from its own material form. We see in *Recollections* an effort to undergo not the kind of gender performance that Judith Butler has identified as a means of conforming to cultural expectations but a gender *nonperformance*, which, of course, is a gender performance in itself. Butler speaks of the body "becom[ing] its gender through a series of acts which are renewed, revised, and consolidated through time," yet North's narrative voice strives for a veritable disavowal of gender by severing customary expectations. As Butler also comments, "[o]ne is not simply a body but in some very key sense, one does one's body," and applied to North's memoirs, the doing of the body translates into a kind of erasure of the body.[12]

Even the overall structure of the narrative contributes to the project of gender neutralization. At first glance, the narrative seems to conform to the practices of other women writers, for North chose the "odyssey" format that Stevenson identifies as the one preferred by women travelers over the quest-romance genre typified by male adventurers. Stevenson further distinguishes the two approaches in summarizing that males "write formal, distilled autobiographies in which the primary concern is an objective evaluation of the significance of the whole life (or journey)," while "[w]omen, in contrast, produce more private, fragmented episodic autobiographies . . . which impose no overarching design on their lives or travels." As Mills similarly notes, "[G]ender shapes the parameters of the possible textual structures within which writers construct their work."[13]

North's memoirs are indeed fragmented, not only when the *Recollections* are assessed collectively but even on a more particularized level. Transitions between paragraphs are an exception rather than a tendency, for instance, and a reader struggles to determine geographical as well as personal context when scenes shift rapidly from one locale and acquaintance to another. The structure of individual paragraphs is often bewildering, for they tend to branch into myriad directions without warning.

12. Judith Butler, "Performative Acts and Gender Constitution: An Essay in Phenomenology and Feminist Theory," 274, 272.

13. Stevenson, *Victorian Women*, 8–9; Sara Mills, "Knowledge, Gender, and Empire," 30.

Though part of the disjunction may be attributed to her sister's editorship, North undoubtedly favors a heterogeneous instead of a formally rigorous structure. As the *Athenaeum* stated in an 1892 review, "a few more months spent in editorial work might have been well spent." Nevertheless, North's narrative departs from Stevenson's paradigm in that an overall purpose does become evident, precisely in the narrative's incessant efforts to construct its voice as gender-neutral.[14]

Though North's memoirs are nonfictional, the narrative configurations of fiction can be usefully mapped onto her work, since in a broad sense she is constructing a story. Modern critics have written convincingly about the gendered elements of narrative forms, identifying a masculinized linear pursuit of desire that ends in a release of textual energy or a feminized open-ended textuality that allows for continuous expulsions of that force. North's *Recollections* cannot be neatly identified in either way, for the three volumes blend elements of masculine and feminine narratology through a diffuse agglomeration of plot trajectories, picaresque episodes, forward movements, and recursive paths. The result is a narrative that, because it displays both masculine and feminine components, can be classified in neither category.

SELF-CONSTRUCTION AS AN ARTIST

Let me turn, then, to North's central strategy of gender neutralization. Linking the disparate elements of the narrative is an incessant attempt to obfuscate, disrupt, and negate the boundaries between masculinity and femininity through a steadfast self-positioning within the context of Work, a concept appraised so highly in Victorian culture that the Carlylean term associated with duty, morality, and religiosity seems to demand capitalization. To construct her identity within the realm of Work, North's narrator follows the intertwined trajectories devolving from the pursuits of painting and of science, both of which offer compelling

14. Review of *Recollections* (*Athenaeum*), 269. Moon points out that the published text was "a very different work from that which Marianne intended" ("Marianne North's *Recollections*," 503). Observing that North "was not an accomplished writer," Moon comments that "[s]he had no idea of punctuation, capital letters, or paragraphs." Moon also remarks on editorial deletions "at times making the text confusing and the chronology perplexing" (504).

ambiguities that foster the project of gender indeterminacy. As critical commentary has shown, a Victorian woman could participate in either activity without affronting cultural expectations; dabbling in natural history was as unthreatening as pursuing the traditional feminine accomplishment of painting, for neither necessitated a departure from a strict definition of a woman's appropriate domestic sphere. Yet the two activities were also pursued by the male professional, which firmly located them in the public realm. North occludes the distinction between an acceptable amateurism and a troubling professionalism in both areas, attempting to negotiate a space separate from the two spheres by draining the activities of their gendered components.

For the economically comfortable Victorian woman, painting could be an occasional pursuit, an enjoyable hobby that helped to occupy the leisure time in a wife and mother's uneventful day. For North, however, painting functions as an all-consuming labor inextricable from the cultural associations of Work and is specifically designated by the term, as when she notes the "abundant work" confronting her in "painting different orchids and other flowers" (1:125) or underscores that she "was soon hard at my usual work again, painting" tropical flowers (90). North's interest in her art serves not simply as an avocation to amuse and distract, but as the driving force of the narrative. The episodic collection of incidents that the memoirs relate is made to cohere through the narrative mechanism of desire that is here manifested through an endless, unquenchable search for subjects to capture aesthetically. North's *Recollections* literally trace the Work of art, not simply the making of works of art, and thereby give form to an otherwise scattered account. Each drawing acts as a kind of signifier in an endless chain, leading to the next sketch, and the next. This *Künstelrroman*-like memoir confounds simplistic and unequivocal conclusions that would define North as strictly a feminized amateur or a masculinized professional. Though she does not sell her paintings, she exhibits them; though she enjoys painting, it is a compulsive interest; though she travels as a private individual, she receives much indirect governmental assistance; and though she draws for self-fulfillment, her paintings carry botanical value.

The *Recollections* invariably construct North as a committed and single-minded worker who moves determinedly from one aesthetic possibility to the next, constantly battling against time in her efforts to capture a scene effectively. In the hills of India, for instance, North "did not let the time be wasted, but worked very hard" (2:28); on another day, North felt she "had no time to rest, though very weary" and "wandered out to work again" (78). Such reminders of the passage of time or schedule-like accounts punctuate the narrative as North attempts to capture diverse arresting scenes. She remarks of her stay in Jamaica, for example, that she "could not waste time, so took my painting things and walked off to finish my sketch" (1:85); that she devoted a month to "incessant painting" (84); and that she "painted all day, going out at daylight" (83). Similarly, in Brazil, North "worked every day and all day," so much so that she was "far too tired to pay evening visits" (118) and interrupted a walk by sketching for a precisely designated two hours (124). In India, she discovers "incessant ready-made pictures, if I had but time to paint them" (2:5). Surprisingly, despite North's repeated references to "work," she gives few details about the actual artistic process. As Dorothy Middleton observes, "Though telling us much of where she went and of how she got there, Miss North says very little about her methods of work."[15]

Nevertheless, North enhances her self-construction as an artist through her frequent designation of herself by that term and by an implicit self-inclusion in ungendered generalizations about these practitioners. A residence provides "a rare home for an artist to settle in," and she "soon fell into a regular and very pleasant routine" (1:143); an intriguing vista provides "a spot for an artist to spend a life in," as does a nearby site (187); and a town offers "a most enjoyable place for an artist" (350). Moreover, locales are presented in regard to their aesthetic value, described as if captured and framed by an artist's eye. North typically saw "endless studies everywhere" (2:16), and a scene "crammed with subjects for painting" (55). Artistic challenges are carefully noted, as in the difficulty of capturing heat and glare (1:188) or in representing a view that "needed the hand of a Rembrandt to paint it properly" (*FR*, 189). Also occasionally evident is North's sense of artistic superiority, as when she sniffs that another artist saw "nothing but the *same* green!" (1:296).

15. Dorothy Middleton, *Victorian Lady Travellers*, 70. As Suzanne Le-May Sheffield also notes in a discussion of the point, "North relished her work for work's sake" (*Revealing New Worlds: Three Victorian Women Naturalists*, 98–99).

Further complicating a precise gender categorization of North's activities is the unusual form her art took, which offers a helpful gloss on the construction of the memoirs' narrative voice. As scholars have noted, the harmless sketching acceptable for a Victorian female tended toward delicate renderings, muted coloring, and sentimental subjects such as winsome children. For a woman intrigued by nature, the common mode of artistic expression was a pleasing landscape or, less often, a study of a detached specimen of a plant against a neutral background—the kind of artwork North's sister made, as Birkett notes. Women favored the dainty medium of watercolor with its gentle shading and tranquil tones, generally leaving the vibrant power of oil and canvas to the professional male artist. North, however, chooses the latter as her aesthetic vehicle to craft a definitive and distinct style. North revealed a "passion" for oils, as Laura Ponsonby comments, and preferred them over the watercolors previously employed. North viewed oils as " 'a vice like dram-drinking, almost impossible to leave off once it gets possession of one.' "[16]

Rather than the subtle shades typically associated with a Victorian woman's artwork, then, North frequently opts for bold, startling colors that seem to issue a visual challenge to an observer. The paintings often evoke power and aggression, blending the concepts of the beautiful and sublime in a way that defies the distinct gender designations Edmund Burke imposed in his definitions of the two states.[17] Though the delicate shapes and textures of plant life are captured in exquisite detail in North's superbly executed and extraordinarily compelling paintings, the pictures also overwhelm a viewer, as if they were attempting to assert dominance. Not only does the vigorous pigmentation generate this effect, but so does the perspectival disorientation the paintings create. The observer is situated too close to the plants for visual comfort; one

16. Birkett, *Spinsters Abroad*, 105; Laura Ponsonby, *Marianne North at Kew Gardens*, 15. See also Sheffield, *Revealing New Worlds*, 107–16.

17. Birkett similarly describes North's paintings, with their "vivid strong oils," as an "unfiltered reaction to the force of colour and vitality in the world about her" (*Spinsters Abroad*, 105); the paintings rendered the "force of colour in tropical vegetation" more effectively than the watercolors of an "amateur, middle-class female dabbler" (107). Barbara T. Gates offers a somewhat different interpretation of the sublime in Victorian women's depictions of nature (*Kindred Nature: Victorian and Edwardian Women Embrace the Living World*, 167–81). Gates defines the sublime as stressing "not power *over* nature but the power *of* nature in a given place, and not a rhetoric of presence so much as a rhetoric based in absence, especially absence of the self" (170).

wishes to step back from the striking scenes and the veiled menace they project. Flowers, for example, fill and extend beyond the frame, as if they are combatants seeking to conquer anything in their path. They exert control over the foreground with their forceful lines, appearing to reach out and intrude ominously into a viewer's personal protective space. The pictures do not passively accept an observer's gaze but instead issue a defiant invitation to it. As a result, painting after painting leaves the viewer feeling vaguely overshadowed, unsettled, and disconcerted as well as overcome by spectacular beauty.[18]

Many of the paintings create their disquieting effects by fixing attention on foreground plants that far exceed the expected scale, dwarfing mountainous terrain or other sizable natural elements. A study of water lilies, for instance, presents them in arbor-like proportions, thrusting forth enormous flowers and buds whose pads each seem the size of an entire pond. A painting of a lotus displays one flower dominating the foreground so extensively that it occupies an enormous area of the picture, compelling an observer to focus solely on its ominously assertive countenance rather than the tiny plants at its base or the minute leaves of a neighboring tree. A rendering of rhododendron features vibrant plants extending downward in forceful fashion to obscure all but a small section of sky, hills, and trees reduced to miniature size in comparison. Often, masses of tendrils or enveloping foliage threaten to absorb and swallow the observer as well the other elements, inanimate or human, depicted in the scene.

Indeed, in the relatively few paintings in which human life appears, the plant life generally assumes a confrontational stance, hanging menacingly or extending voraciously over unsuspecting individuals and groups. A massive ficus, for instance, seems prepared to sweep its branches across the canvas and crush the workers below it, some of whom are huddled beneath its vast, sinewy trunk. In another landscape, a dense grove of palms, breadfruit trees, and other large vegetation seems poised to overrun the dirt paths winding through it as it obscures the many Javanese workers toiling in its reach. A baobab of a third painting dominates a royal garden so completely that a palatial residence in the

18. For an analysis of the paintings, such as the relationship between people and nature, as well as between foreground and background, see Sheffield, *Revealing New Worlds*, especially 122–30.

background seems of no more consequence than a rustic hut, and the dark patches of color on an entranceway only barely resemble human forms. As these depictions suggest, plant life reduces human life to inconsequentiality, so much so that individuals become almost invisible as they blend into vegetation or other components of a scene. In many of the pictures, only vigilant scrutiny allows an observer to detect signs of human presence, for North's coloration not only camouflages but also flattens individuals to make them even less significant against the backdrop of the multidimensional and apparently mobile plant life by which they are seemingly consumed. As *Nature* remarked, "[i]n nearly all the pictures, plants have supplied the motive, the other objects represented being mere accessories."[19] Humanity becomes passive in these works, acted upon by the vegetation that represents the only active agent in a curious reversal of customary expectations. It is as if the botanical subjects of North's work not only overshadow but diminish and nearly obviate the material form of the human body. So obscured are these forms that an observer frequently struggles to determine if a smattering of color is actually representing a human shape.

Even more significant is the virtually genderless quality of the depicted figures. Faces are customarily without features, and a variety of headgear often disguises persons even more fully. Clothing tends to enshroud its wearers so amorphously that sexes become indistinguishable and humanity becomes merely a series of sexless shapes. Occasionally, clothing is made to confuse even more, as in the ficus picture, which features a young rajah whose garb would appear to a Briton as a girl's dress and hat. Through these artistic maneuvers, gender becomes meaningless, bracketed off so frequently and effectively that one focuses only on the deft execution of the Work itself. In a metonymical way, the genderless quality of the aestheticized forms serves to extend to their artistic creator as well. Instead of a feminine artistic eye, the observer senses a detached human presence examining plant as well as human life with the coolness of a sexless scientific practitioner.

In a seemingly contradictory respect, however, the depicted plants themselves carry a marked sexual suggestion. Modern critics have com-

19. W. Botting Hemsley, "The Marianne North Gallery of Paintings of 'Plants and Their Homes,' Royal Gardens, Kew," 155–56.

mented on the sensuality of North's paintings, and the description is by no means inaccurate. Yet, rather than calling attention to distinct sexual identities, the paintings seem to convey an amorphous erotic tone. In an intriguing way, the sensual quality serves to promote instead of undermine North's project of gender indeterminacy, for the reproductive aspects of botany—"the lurid world of plant sexuality," as Londa Schiebinger characterizes the Linnaen approach to botanical study— were ignored by women who thought such matters indelicate and inappropriate to discuss.[20] In heralding rather than hiding the sexual component of plant life, North further distanced herself from the mainstream response of the modest Victorian female.

Many of the paintings North mentions in her memoirs are inspired by scenes in domestic gardens, which presumably would carry a feminine connotation. Gardens, of course, represented a female space through their contiguity to the home and their taming of nature, freed of the dangers associated with the landscapes traversed by male adventurers.[21] Yet North's memoirs effectually situate gardens in a realm of gender indeterminacy. Depictions of gardens that appear at first glance to derive from a feminized effusiveness about the glories of nature instead function as preludes to an analysis of their applicability to her work. "The views from the verandah and lovely gardens, of the broad river, distant isolated mountains, and glorious vegetation, quite dazzled me with their magnificence," North writes on one occasion but immediately adds, "What was I to paint first?" (1:238). Through two prevalent but independent maneuvers, the narrator detaches the garden from domestic connections that would otherwise link North to Victorian femininity.

The first approach involves an emphatic rejection of any interest in the domestic locale itself that does not pertain to the furtherance of her work. One house, for instance, "was most comfortable and unpretentious," with a spectacular view that offered "endless studies everywhere"

20. Londa Schiebinger, *The Mind Has No Sex? Women in the Origins of Modern Science,* 242.

21. For a discussion of the domestic quality of gardens, see Birkett, who argues that colonial versions represented "the final frontier to the surrounding threatening and encroaching foreign beyond." Birkett observes that the "gardens which tempted the women travellers were not the well-tended beds surrounding colonial houses but the great unpruned beyond" and could be considered "the border between European culture and the society past its gates" (*Spinsters Abroad,* 96–97).

(2:16). The memoirs are marked by an utter lack of attention to the details of interior spaces for their own sake; in the few cases where a room is accorded any description unrelated to North's work, the motivation can be traced not to a feminized fascination with the home but an imperialistic condescension, a British egocentrism, a distaste for the accouterments of domesticity, or a validation of her powers of endurance. Domestic spaces carry significance only insofar as they allow access to exterior spaces, often mediated by windows, verandas, and other borderline sites, or as they provide a haven from severe weather to finish work begun outdoors.

In perceiving the home as a vehicle for pursuing her work, North obscures the distinction between feminine and masculine space to create, in effect, a gender-neutral locale that extends to the gardens themselves, which are further voided of their essentialist content through the discerning evaluation of their aesthetic possibilities. One garden, for example, is remarkable for its "foreground studies—ferns, aralias, daturas, and areca-palms growing in a half-wild and most picturesque way" (1:289). Moreover, gardens are defeminized through the many scientific names and particulars of natural history sprinkled in their descriptions. A feminine attention to detail instead becomes in North's memoirs evidence of an acute power of observation associated with both the devoted artist and the probing scientist, as in the following paradigmatic passage:[22]

> One balsam was of a cream-yellow, with a deep claret-coloured throat inside and out, and there were lovely turquoise berries on another plant, shaded from blue to green, as the real turquoise is. I found, higher up, a beautiful blue creeper, like a gentian—*Crawfurdia speciosa,* with its buds set between two leaves. The bells were two inches long, shaded into white at the neck like the common gentians, and of the same waxy material. Another new idea to me was the poppy, *Meconopsis Wallichii,* the flowers as large as our field-poppy, but of the most lovely pale blue with a gold centre, growing on branches from a central stem of brown velvet a yard

22. Morgan makes the point that "North's writings bring together in one constitutive discourse the apparently opposite visions of a feminized appreciation of, and even joyous love for, the multitudinous details of the human as well as the natural world with a masculinized 'objectivity' and indifference" to people (*Place Matters,* 132).

or more high. As they faded, all the leaves and stalks turned from
green to gold and brown, and were covered with hairs. (2:31–32)

The second strategy by which the gendered content of the garden
is nullified comes through North's numerous visits to formal botanical gardens. As with domestic gardens, the botanical collections are notable for their furtherance of North's work, for she sketches repeatedly
in these sites. Yet the value of a garden is heightened by virtue of its status as a public space. These gardens are inextricably connected to the
pursuit of pure knowledge in the field of natural history, the promo-
tion of economic projects through the British trafficking in plants, and
the extension of colonial influence through the empire's network of gardens. In fact, observes Lucile H. Brockway, "[t]here is no way to draw
the line between science, commerce, and imperialism in the work of
the Kew collectors."[23] Adding another dimension to the public quality
of the gardens is their habitual connection to prominent scientists or
government officials in North's memoirs. Her extensive and extended
studies of botanical gardens often take place in the company or under
the auspices of an eminent individual—invariably a male, which further detaches a garden from feminine associations—who sweeps away
obstacles to North's unwavering commitment to painting. She recalls,
for example, that in one Brazilian area she traveled at six each morning
to the botanical gardens, where her all-consuming work was eased by
the director's allowing her to keep her painting materials at his home
(1:118). In Java, North works daily at the "famous" garden nearby, later
dining with the governor-general at his "grand palace in the midst of the
garden" where "great men" were in attendance (256). A "dear old gentleman" in Ceylon, the botanical director, accompanies North for a lengthy
walk around the gardens, displays "his exquisite collection of butterflies,
and promised to give me some of his spare ones" (305), and arranges for
her to work in a nearby garden "in undisturbed quiet" (306). In none
of these encounters does North hint that she is perceived as a woman;
instead, the *Recollections* painstakingly construct her as a gifted artist

23. Lucile H. Brockway, *Science and Colonial Expansion: The Role of the British Royal
Botanic Gardens,* 84. Brockway explores the profound influence Kew exercised in the
colonial enterprise (7). For a discussion of Kew's role in imperialism, see Susan Morgan,
introduction to *Recollections of a Happy Life,* xxviii–xxxiii, xxxv).

seemingly devoid of gender affiliation whose work is assessed solely on its merits.

In calling into question the gender designation of a garden, then, North rhetorically creates a space in which the divisions between masculinity and femininity are indistinguishably overlapped. Yet North also *physically* created such a gender-neutral garden space in which her work could be displayed and admired. As North carefully records in the memoirs, she supervised the design and construction of a gallery for her paintings in Kew Gardens, and the edifice itself additionally obscures the distinction between private and public space. Initiated by North, the gallery could be considered a private space filled with a woman's drawings, which she personally selected and arranged; yet as part of Kew, with its far-reaching influence on British economic and colonial interests, the gallery could be interpreted as a public space, especially since it was created specifically for the purpose of public appreciation and enthusiastically supported by Kew's director as a valuable archive for vanishing plant forms. As Ponsonby remarks, "Sir Joseph Hooker stressed the importance of the paintings as an historical record, particularly as many of the plants 'are already disappearing or are doomed shortly to disappear before the axe and the forest fire, the plough and the flock, of the ever-advancing settler or colonist.' "[24]

Moreover, the gallery disrupts associations between North's work and female accomplishments in her intentions to emphasize the scientific underpinnings of the paintings.[25] She planned, for instance, to affix "an enlarged map of the world on the ceiling, coloured according to the geographical distribution of plants"; "to add an index of fruits painted by myself . . . and twelve typical trees"; to construct a dado of "woods from all parts of the world"; to develop a catalog and provide information on the plants (2:211); and to organize the plants by their geographical locations (330). North followed a similar approach when her paintings were exhibited by the Kensington Museum. She cataloged "the 500 studies" she lent the museum and added "as much general information about the plants" as she "had time to collect," for "people in general [are] wofully ignorant of natural history" (1:321).

24. Ponsonby, *Marianne North at Kew,* 119.
25. Birkett also makes this point in asserting that North was "discreetly presenting herself before the public not merely as a painter, a female dabbler in artistic pursuits, but as a professional in the scientific field of botany" (*Spinsters Abroad,* 207).

Supplementing North's self-construction as a dedicated artist is an almost obsessive effort to record the many instances where her work is accorded effusive regard, in an unspoken contrast to the polite compliments bestowed upon a female dilettante. Periodically, North mentions passersby, casual acquaintances, and interested friends, both male and female, who praise her sketches, as if to establish in a gender-neutral register the widespread recognition that her work achieved. More compellingly, she relates the profound esteem her art garners from recognizably discerning sources—authorities in natural history, reviewers of her exhibitions, and other renowned artists—as if to create a kind of specular image whereby her determined positioning of herself as a serious artist is not merely reflected back to her but amplified in the process. One motive for this defensive posture could stem from North's lack of formal training in art. She alludes only briefly to her limited training in noting she "had some lessons in flower-painting from a Dutch lady, Miss van Fowinkel, from whom I got the few ideas I possess of arrangement of colour and of grouping," and "a few lessons" from another artist "in water-colour flower-painting" (1:26–27). North's sister expressed the belief that North "was intolerant of 'Rules' in all things . . . , exceedingly and scornfully sceptical as to rules in art: for instance, the limitations and laws of composition in painting. She painted as a clever child would, everything she thought beautiful in nature, and had scarcely ever any artistic teaching" (2:336).

In addition, North's defensive maneuver suggests not so much a blatant egotism as a means to deflect or diffuse potential criticism of her paintings as mere "women's work" and instead attest to their aesthetic and scientific validity. North recalls, for instance, that "[a] most enthusiastic botanist came to see me" (2:277), who "watched me at work, much pleased to see his dear aloes at last done justice to" (278); a "great authority on all sorts of natural history" and fellow artist journeys from the countryside solely to visit North (247); and an assortment of botanical directors and other notables enthusiastically collect specimens for North to render.

Similarly, North comments that the *Pall Mall Gazette* urged that her paintings be displayed at Kew, observes that "a very distinguished writer" was "impressed . . . so much" with North's work "that he wrote a long flourish in the newspaper" (2:317), and mentions that a director of an Australian botanical garden "put a paragraph about my paintings in the local paper, which induced a little boy to ask, 'What will they do with you when you return to England, will the Queen knight you?' " (109). At a showing of North's Australian paintings, she remarks that "I was treated like a lion, and interviewed in turn by everybody," after which her work was scrutinized "with real interest" by "the greatest of living landscape-painters" (208). North recounts, too, the Kensington Museum's avid interest in exhibiting her paintings and an overheard conversation in which an official claims, "We must have those things at any price" (1:321). Such self-promotional notations permeate the *Recollections* with a curious blend of humility and braggadocio; though she assumes a somewhat modest tone—opining of the museum officials' interest in her paintings, for instance, that "I was only too happy that they thought them worth the trouble of framing and glazing"—she nevertheless carefully records rather than omits the numerous incidences of lavish praise, as if to deny that her work is simply an inconsequential conglomeration of readily dismissible "female accomplishments."

SELF-CONSTRUCTION AS A SCIENTIST

An analogously paradoxical mixture of modesty and pride characterizes North's self-positioning in the realm of science. Although she designates herself as "an amateur collector of a frivolous nature" (*FR*, 134), this humble estimation is resolutely undercut by her concerted efforts to establish her bona fides as an observer, authority, and innovator. The memoirs, both overtly and subtly, labor to establish North not merely as a skillful painter but as an accomplished *botanical* painter. She presents herself as a devoted student of botany, as well as other branches of natural history, whose lack of formal knowledge in the field is compensated for her zealous absorption of its intricacies. On occasion North mentions, in apparently casual fashion, that she has diligently pored over botanical tomes and hearkened intently to experts eager to share their learning. North recalls, for example, that she "spent a pleasant evening with a heap of valuable botanical books" (1:178), gazed upon a table filled not simply with "valuable botanical books" but also "MSS" (1:327) attesting to serious study, and deemed Alfred Russel Wallace's treatise on natural history "a Bible" (1:282). North prizes her acquaintance with a deputy governor who "knew more about the plants and trees than any one I met in India" (2:7), converses with "another walking botanical dictionary" (2:9), resides with "one of the best naturalists" in Chile (2:327), and also laments the absence of "some intelligent botanical companion to answer my many questions" (1:151). North further cultivates her botanical acumen by sedulous examination and dissection of species she encounters in noteworthy professional collections as well as serendipitous discoveries in the field. Despite her offhand self-designation as an amateur, North obviously prides herself on a knowledge gleaned so assiduously that a particular plant that habitually "deceived botanists" was ultimately identified correctly by herself (2:274). In addition, North carefully mentions the various plant species named after her by Kew director and botanical luminary Joseph Hooker. The self-deprecation that characterizes narratives by other Victorian women travelers such as Mary Kingsley emerges only perfunctorily in North's *Recollections,* as if an attempt at scientific modesty is *de rigueur* but undesired.[26]

North's self-characterization as an amateur naturalist serves another function, for the term confuses gender identity by positioning North's pursuits within a class register. As Morris Berman has argued, "the wealthy amateur" who engaged in scientific study was admired because of a perceived aristocratic link; both men and women could follow that avocation because it simply was considered enjoyable.[27] North's enviable economic situation certainly placed her in the category of a "wealthy amateur," for she apparently is able to travel worldwide at will without financial worry. In designating herself as an "amateur collector," North can tap the cultural approval for this activity of the upper classes and thereby minimize gender identification.

The term *amateur* thus is disingenuous when self-applied by North, for the *Recollections* strive to present her as anything but a scientific trifler. Part of the way North establishes her scientific credentials, albeit indirectly, is by closely allying herself with the scientific community. She repeatedly alludes to conversations and encounters with Victorian men of science and, in effect, "borrows" their ethos by so doing. In none of these encounters with scientific figures is there any reference to North's

26. For a discussion of the "self-effacing pose" adopted by Kingsley and other women travel writers, see Mills, *Discourses,* 83.

27. Berman quoted in Morgan, *Place Matters,* 98; Morgan, 99.

being viewed as a woman in a male field, nor is there a sense that she perceives herself as an exceptional woman treading on forbidden turf. Instead, the narrative voice is again notable for its tone of gender neutrality, as if North viewed herself as an unsexed cipher psychically and physically divorced from sexual classifications. References to notable figures such as Charles Lyell, Asa Gray, and Francis Galton abound, as if by mentioning her association to them she is obliquely signaling their approval of her; lesser figures of whom her audience would be unaware are identified by their accomplishments, as is one host, a "Mr. G," who "was one of the first explorers in Western Australia" and who related "a story of his having to speak at the Geographical Society on his election as a Fellow" (2:120).

North's relationship with Darwin is particularly informative, for she first accords him ebullient praise and later relates his admiration for her work. Darwin "wanted to see me," North writes of "the greatest man living," whose advice that North venture to Australia and paint its plant life is heeded "as a royal command" (2:87). Though North subsequently relates that Darwin displayed "in a few words how much more he knew about the subjects [of her Australian paintings] than any one else, myself included," she implicitly conveys his decisive approval and admiration of her work by including the fact that "he insisted on packing my sketches and putting them even into the carriage with his own hands" (215). Inserted into the memoirs by North's sister is a note from Darwin, in which he stated, "I am so glad that I have seen your Australian pictures" (216). Commenting that he was "often able to call up with considerable vividness scenes in various countries," Darwin wrote to North that "my mind in this respect must be a mere barren waste compared with your mind."

An important consideration in examining North's self-positioning in the scientific arena is the state of Victorian botany itself during this period. As Ann B. Shteir has explained in a book-length study, efforts to professionalize botany, like other scientific disciplines, became a priority as the nineteenth century progressed. Botany had had a particularly curious, and feminized, history in the latter part of the eighteenth century and the first third of the next century. Women occupied leisure time with field study, plant collection, illustration, and other related activities. An interest in botany was especially cultivated in women during this period and "became increasingly a feminized area, . . . part of both education and recreation."[28]

The result of this feminization of botany, Shteir reports, was a concerted effort to move to greater professionalization, whereby "women were pushed to the margins of an increasingly masculinized science culture." As one prominent botanist had argued in 1829, "It has been very much the fashion of late years, in this country, to undervalue the importance of this science, and to consider it an amusement for ladies rather than an occupation for the serious thoughts of man." Women (and other amateurs) became increasingly marginalized from the burgeoning botanical science after 1860, Shteir points out. Nonetheless, botany still carried a feminized taint, as an 1887 essay titled "Is Botany a Suitable Study for Young Men?" suggests. Physician J. F. A. Adams argued that:

> An idea seems to exist in the minds of some young men that botany is not a manly study; that it is merely one of the ornamental branches, suitable enough for young ladies and effeminate youths, but not adapted for able-bodied and vigorous-brained young men who wish to make the best use of their powers. I wish to show that this idea is wholly unfounded, but that, on the contrary, botany ought to be ranked as one of the most useful and most manly of studies, and an important, if not an indispensable, part of a well-rounded education.[29]

In view of the growing professionalism in the discipline, North's avid interest in botanical study presents a curious situation. As a woman and an amateur botanist, North seemingly would be excluded from the realm of "serious" science and instead inserted into the world of "polite" science. Yet North's memoir positions her in the former arena. Again the strategy of gender neutralization is important, for by rhetorically presenting North as an ungendered entity, the narrative voice seeks to complicate, and even erase, the distinction between amateurism and professionalism. As a "neutral" voice, the narrator strives to relocate botanical study from a gender register to an ungendered and thus nonrestrictive space.

28. Ann B. Shteir, *Cultivating Women, Cultivating Science*, 4, 5, 50.
29. Ibid., 103, botanist quoted, 156–57, 168–69; J. F. A. Adams, "Is Botany a Suitable Study for Young Men?" 116.

Assuming an ungendered voice also seems to provide North, on the surface, a mechanism for aligning her with the scientific dictums about "inferior" womanhood that would otherwise exclude her on the basis of sex. In so doing, however, North becomes enmeshed in an extremely troubling rhetorical trap. To distance herself from other women in a Victorian scientific economy, North apparently felt compelled to adopt a racist stance and implicitly identify herself by her presumably superior racial status rather than by gender. As Susan Morgan asserts, "North's rhetoric . . . supports the belief that evolution provided some kind of 'objective' evidence" that the British had evolved to a greater degree in comparison to other groups. North "saw darker foreign peoples not only as subhuman but as even lower evolutionarily than monkeys."[30]

As we have already seen, late-century science, following Darwin, postulated an evolutionary continuum based on sex as well as race, situating the white male as the most advanced member of the human species and relegating women and nonwhite men to a lesser developmental category; these latter groups would never be able to achieve cognitive equivalency with their more evolved counterparts. As women and nonwhite men evolved over generations, white men would invariably be attaining a more sophisticated level of development as they likewise evolved, allowing them to maintain their status at the apex of the human species. Darwin, for instance, noted the distinction between the intellectual traits of the sexes, concluding that certain attributes demonstrated by women were "characteristic of the lower races, and therefore of a past and lower state of civilization."[31] Herbert Spencer and other prominent Victorian scientists proffered similar analogies to identify perceived differences between white males and their supposedly inferior counterparts, deeming such characteristics as acute perception, intuition, and impulsiveness attributed to the latter as indicators of diminished mental capacity.

In view of the scientific discourse, it is perhaps not surprising, though certainly no less reprehensible, that the *Recollections* are infused with an overt, pronounced, and appalling racism. Proceeding from a racist stance ostensibly establishes an unbridgeable gap between the narrator and these disempowered groups, showing not a condemnatory commonality but a distinct dissimilarity. As North travels from one coun-

30. Morgan, introduction to *Recollections,* xxxvi.
31. Darwin, *Descent,* 587.

try to another, then, each Other is harshly diminished in some respect. Part of the ideological power released through this strategy stems from North's adoption of the tropes of travel writing, primarily surfacing in the memoirs of prominent male Victorian explorers, that conform seamlessly to the scientific views of a white European superiority—specifically British, in North's case. As Pratt has demonstrated, Western travel writers employed a range of rhetorical techniques to place themselves in a position of power through both visualizing and obscuring the Other. Most importantly for my analysis, the Others of the *Recollections* gain visual prominence as homogeneous masses, picturesque spectacles, and unseemly primitives loaded with superstitions and barbaric customs, yet they also recede into invisibility when the landscape, presented both as a broad expanse and as myriad differentiated elements, seizes ocular attention.

Throughout the *Recollections,* the Other is identified by consonant somatic markers. In Brazil, for instance, a biweekly "review of the blacks" at one house showed them "all dressed in a kind of uniform": women wore "red petticoats and white dresses, with red stripes for good conduct, bright orange and red turbans and blue striped shawls, which they arranged over their heads in fine folds"; men wore "red caps, blue jackets, and white trousers, with medals pinned on for good conduct, and a general grin passed over the faces" (1:147–48). In India, "500 coolies packed" on a boat like commodities "were graceful figures of a beautiful dark bronze colour, very shiny, and loaded with bangles on arms and legs," who "seemed always to live and to laugh on nothing" (323). In Jamaica, women were "loaded with bangles and nose-rings," making them "picturesque" (106)—a demeaning adjective that appears abundantly in the memoirs.

Especially troubling, however, are descriptions of locales in which people and other sights are blended almost interchangeably—within a paragraph and even within a sentence—so that the Other becomes simply another object to be visually consumed and figuratively appropriated. In one "wonderful little house," for example, a catalog of its furnishings includes "plate, linen, knives, a clock (going), telescope, piano . . . , and a nice tidy woman and family in the yard to get all I wanted" (1:95). Observing workers, North comments that the distinctive grass of the area "had been imported from India with the Coolies and Mongeese" (106). As North assesses the artistic potential of a scenic area, the Other becomes a part of the landscape, indistinguishable from surrounding natural elements:

> There were many curious and grotesque old tree-trunks down there, with snake-like roots stretching over the ground, and arched buttresses, from which the floods had washed away the sand and earth at different times. Graceful little black children were running in and out of the water, bathing and splashing one another. Fish, too, were jumping out of the clear water, which ran rapidly over the golden sand. I went there very often afterwards to sketch. (97–98)

Pronominal references also contribute to the sense of homogeneity and marginality that such depictions evoke. The Other is identified by the ubiquitous *they* that Pratt sees demeaning difference in the genre of travel writing, along with the more unnerving pronouns of *this* and *it*, which may even lack an antecedent to append a further layer of objectification to the term. "There was a small black imp called Ida," North recalls in one description that is so animalistic that a reader must infer from various clues that Ida, repeatedly designated as "it," is indeed a person (1:109). Characterized as "the pet of the house," Ida "ran in and out with as much freedom as the dogs." Moreover, "[i]t liked riding on horseback, and was not averse to strong spirits," which made the "[p]oor solemn little atom . . . more hideous than ever."

The degrading material portrayals of the Other assumedly serve as damning somatic evidence of an intrinsic inferiority that is proclaimed more directly as well. American Indians, for example, are "as near to animals as mortals can be" (1:75); Brazilian blacks were "not capable of ambition or forethought" (1:48); Zulus are "the merriest savages" North ever encountered (2:276); and in Borneo comes the realization that "all semi-civilised races delight in playing with fire, just as children do" (2:93). The *Recollections* are infused with references to the Other's supposedly lesser mental capacities, in many cases invoking comparisons to monkeys, as Morgan has noted, to conform to prevalent evolutionary theories.[32] Demeaning and sweeping characterizations of the Other's traits replicate the impression of homogeneity created in the

---

32. Morgan, *Place Matters*, 129.

physical descriptions of unindividuated masses. In scene after scene, the Other is vilified in horrifying terms.

Even when the descriptions are not caustic, the Other is universalized to occlude differences within a particular group. Thus, "[t]he Malays are a gentle race" (2:93), Chilean Indians are "a noble race" (2:320), and Egyptians "had that calm soft type of countenance that marks the old statuary of their country" (*FR*, 115). Manners and customs descriptions also abound, reminding us of Pratt's observations on the way in which the Other was generalized in travel books. North asserts, for example, that "[t]he Pondo natives are well worth the journey to see," as she proceeds to describe in detail their unusual hair arrangements and her interest in sketching such a curious sight (2:263). Although North occasionally refers to people as individuals, few are presented in a positive light and even in those cases her comments tend to be condescending, as in comparisons of the Other to children reminiscent of Victorian missionary discourses.

North even goes so far as to advocate slavery, a telling indication of a dehumanization process brought to an extreme manifestation. Morgan points to "the rhetorical shock" that North's comments about slavery produce, which "depends in part on its being narrated by a woman's voice, albeit one self-identified as belonging among the scientists. That voice challenges conventional cultural expectations about sympathy being a feminine trait."[33] North describes the situation in Rio, for example, as follows:

> [T]hough laws are passed for the future emancipation of these slaves, it will be a very gradual process, and full twenty years will elapse before it is entirely carried out. It would have been better perhaps if our former law-makers had not been in such a hurry, and so much led away by the absurd idea of "a man and a brother." I should like some of the good housewives at home who believe in this dogma to try the dear creatures as their only servants. . . . It is a mistake to suppose that slaves are not well treated; everywhere I have seen them petted as we pet animals, and they usually went about grinning and singing. (1:120–21)

33. Ibid.

In fact, North suggests that slavery offers a vehicle to save Others from themselves. "In the 'good old days,'" she argues, "when black babies were saleable articles, the masters used to have them properly cared for"; in contrast, contemporary "mothers didn't see why they should be bothered with them now" (148). Observing a slave dealer in charge of a roomful of youths, North opines that "[t]hese boys looked very happy, and as if they enjoyed the process of being fatted up" (156).

SEPARATION FROM "WOMANHOOD"

Although other Victorian travelers expressed a deeply ingrained racism in their memoirs, North's version appears excessive for the period and the genre; as Morgan comments in discussing North's Brazilian travels, the opinions, "even in Victorian England, were conservative and reactionary." Yet that very profusion offers a clue to racism's rhetorical function in furthering North's project of gender neutralization. Not only do the racist observations aim to align North with the scientific conclusions about the evolutionary progression of civilizations to position her as an ungendered "white" voice, they serve also to distance her from the cultural verity that women were the moral authorities of Victorian society—in effect, performing a kind of gender erasure that severs a crucial link to "womanhood." Indeed, a distinctly agnostic tone surfaces in the memoirs. North dismisses her mother's spiritual leanings in insisting that "I could never quite see the benefit" of religious instruction (1:9), avers that a parson "bore me no malice for not going to church" (2:131), imagined while taking a bath that "I soaked off a certain quantity of the puritanical atmosphere which had so oppressed me" (2:190), and "breathed more easily when I escaped" a Calvinistic community (2:228).[34] North's narrative shows no intersections with the projects of the angel of either the house or the empire. The abolitionist fervor of an Elizabeth Barrett Browning, for example, is nowhere visible in North's writings; indeed, in the Rio passage above, North explicitly

34. Ibid., 128. North's antireligious sentiments separated her as well from women botanical enthusiasts whose writings followed the "pious and evangelical tone" that Shteir identifies in the 1830s–1860s (*Cultivating Women*, 197). For a discussion of North's views of religion, see Sheffield, *Revealing New Worlds*, 94–95.

assails women who adhere to antislavery sentiments. Nor is there any hint of the philanthropic zeal that many forthright Victorian women showed in their efforts to improve the plight of such disparate populations as the urban poor, child workers, or "fallen" women. Instead, North exhibits a remarkable coldness to human suffering and death, asserting in one case that "we had more dead Chinamen on board than was altogether agreeable to our noses" (1:212).

This striking lack of a feminized tenderness and nurturance emerges in other respects, too. It is as if North seeks to excise almost any trace of "womanliness" by targeting every essentialist association accepted by Victorian culture and nullifying any suggestion that she embraced or exhibited such traits. In sum, the narrative voice denies that North is a woman speaking from a positionality of womanhood. For example, unlike many female Victorian travel writers, North reveals no feeling of commonality, however tenuous, with women of the colonial world on the basis of shared gender concerns.[35] Absent is even a veiled sympathy for colonial women who are marginalized in either analogous or disparate ways from their female counterparts in England. Rather, some of North's most vitriolic observations of the Other are uttered about women, particularly in the homogeneous descriptions that wind through the narrative.

In another important respect, too, does North separate herself from the compassionate womanhood so revered by Victorian culture. In numerous episodes, North displays not simply a lack of interest in children but a pronounced dislike. Although English children are generally exempt from scathing criticism, the Other's children rarely are, as the description of the ill-fated Ida suggests. Children are frequently presented as encumbrances—noisy, unmannered, and annoying. Yet there is a type of child who escapes North's disapproval, which serves as another revelatory manifestation of the narrator's strategy of gender neutralization. Children are implicitly categorized into two groups: those who disturb and impede North, and those who indirectly assist in the narrator's self-construction as a dedicated naturalist and painter. The "good" child finds North a nest to sketch, speaks knowledgeably of local

35. For a discussion of the attitudes of Englishwomen toward females in colonial culture, see Antoinette Burton, *Burdens of History: British Feminists, Indian Women, and Imperial Culture, 1865–1915.*

plants and birds, or collects unusual specimens. The child's value devolves not from an intrinsic maternal warmth but an ability to contribute to North's work.

North's narrative further reveals her almost wholesale self-severance from the feminized proclivity to emotionality, the essentialist sign that conventionally separated women from the intellectual acuity associated with men. The icy tone that allows the narrator to remark detachedly about such subjects as the advantages of slavery and a trafficking in wives is broken only to assert authority or to herald an important discovery integral to her work. North periodically becomes enraged to compel "idle natives" (1:305) or recalcitrant innkeepers to follow her dictates in a most unfeminine show of assertiveness, and her sole displays of unrestrained pleasure or longing, indicated by a propensity for "screaming," derive from the sighting of an aesthetic or scientific rarity. North recalls, for instance, the discovery of "real pitcher plants (*Nepenthes*)" that caused her to scream "with delight" (233), a reaction that greets glimpses of a chameleon, a tortoise crab, and various other species of plant and animal life, which are all identified either by scientific name or precise description of distinguishing features. Emotion thus enters the plane of intellectuality, attesting not to a manifestation of feminine unrestraint but an ungendered response to an object of appropriate wonder.

Only rarely does North allude to the fact that she is indeed a woman, and even in these instances she usually conveys the impression that she is markedly different from and superior to her biological kind and thus, inferentially, cannot be categorized among them. She represents the sole woman on a train, avoids fainting (unlike the other females present), wins over a Russian misogynist, and in repeated ways sets herself apart from womanhood. On the few occasions where her self-referential comments about womanhood do not aim to separate North from her sex, she generally either highlights a positive attribute, as in the phrase "sketching woman" (2:69), or alludes to the demeaning perceptions that motivate her more typical desire of gender abjection, such as an acerbic comment about Turks having no "horror of a woman drawing them" because women have "no soul" (*FR*, 186–87). Rather than view herself as a woman, exceptional or otherwise, North more compellingly labors to deny she is a woman. Her overwhelmingly pervasive strategy is the rhetorical construction of herself as an ungendered body—in a sense, disembodied. The narrative voice either distances North entirely from essentialized traits, both somatic and behavioral, or recasts them to create a gender-neutral persona. Sexuality is excised; she proclaims herself too old for marriage (2:72), for example, and disdains any trappings designed to attract or allure.

Additional attempts to enact a virtual disembodiment, in a gender economy, proliferate. Perhaps most intriguing are North's continual references to the physical hardships suffered while unearthing and depicting interesting species and landscapes. The emphasis here is not on the body as a female site but as a *human* form whose endless trials and mishaps transcend the realm of gender. The corporeal tribulations that beset North seemingly occur in an ungendered space wherein biological sex carries no meaning. Instead, physical hardships serve as rites of passage that establish North as a worthy practitioner of art and science, one who has faced and overcome each challenge that confronted her. It is not as if North enacts a form of transvestitism in which she temporarily becomes a male body that confronts obstacles in the manner of a quest romance hero like an Allan Quatermain, who psychically transforms a landscape into a female terrain that can be entered and conquered.[36] Nor is there a sense, conversely, of a female acting against a masculinized panorama of control and command. Rather, the tone of gender neutrality seen elsewhere in *Recollections* obtains here as well, for the landscape and the hazards that inhabit it are accorded no sexualized qualities, nor is the body itself conceptualized as anything other than a desexualized entity that rarely displays fear or anxiety.

A certain breeziness attends North's often casual recitations of danger. One night in Jamaica, for instance, "the rats came and ate holes in my boots, which were very precious and not easily replaced"; the incident gives rise not to a feminized horror of wandering vermin but to a pragmatic resolution to place the boots "on the top of the water-jug during the rest of my stay on the island" (1:103). A treacherous traverse over "crazy wooden planks" in Brazil, which North found "startling enough,

---

36. Women travelers tended not to adopt the sexual topography, as Mills remarks (*Discourses*, 82). Morgan also notes that North's "narrative does not use the language of sexual desire to represent North's experiences in the contact zone" (*Place Matters*, 119). In a related vein, Margaret Strobel points out that "women's travel narratives incline less toward domination and more toward discovery" (*European Women and the Second British Empire*, 36).

at first," becomes merely an inconvenience that "one soon learned to think nothing of," as does the host of venomous snakes that North "soon forgot . . . existed," even though she "heard occasionally the rattle near me" (146). "[E]ndless" spiders crafted webs "so thick and strong," North relates, "that they gave my face quite a cutting sensation as I rode through them" (150–51). Mounting an unruly horse, North "felt sure death was coming, and felt quite comfortable, but thought he was a long while about it" (283). On many occasions North dismisses warnings of peril and repeated admonitions not to venture into hazardous areas, recounting either that no such difficulties presented themselves or that she persevered where others refused to tread. In scene after scene, North records the discomforts and risks she experienced as an artist and collector, not as a *female* practitioner of those activities.

Not unexpectedly, a feminine preoccupation with dress is reshaped in the memoirs into a practical concern that stresses initiative and cleverness. Following a mishap in which her suitcase dropped into a harbor, North comments:

> Everything was thoroughly soaked, and had to be spread out separately to dry, all my paints, paper and dress (only one), for we took the least possible luggage, and yet had everything we really needed, even luxuries (?), including a bonnet, whose crown I used to stuff with a compact roll of stockings and cram into a hole left for it amongst my underclothing, just big enough to contain it: when taken out it would be damped and set in the sun, with the stockings still in its crown, and it stretched itself into proper shape again, and was the admiration of all beholders. (*FR*, 1)

Other rare references to clothing foreground a motive of necessity or scientific curiosity rather than a desire for self-aggrandizement. She explains that she is compelled to hire a tailor because her "dresses were becoming very ragged" (1:240), and she justifies a needlework project that involves affixing the unfeminine ornamentation of "2000 beetles' wings on some silk to trim some future dress with," by the fact of "the colours being even more marvellous than the sea at Aden" (2:82). Similarly, a feminized pleasure in the frivolous pursuit of shopping is transformed in the memoirs into an opportunity to augment knowledge of natural history. North's purchases are limited to an array of birds, shells, and other artifacts for study by herself or others.

North's compulsive efforts to disassociate herself from "womanly" traits and interests lead her into another dismaying and extreme rhetorical maneuver, however. A distinct strain of misogyny runs through the *Recollections,* as North dismisses and disdains the women she meets. More often than not, North marginalizes other women by almost erasing their presence in the various scenes in which they briefly appear. Emphasis is placed on the husbands or fathers of the numerous families with whom she visits or stays, as if the wives or daughters were merely peripheral entities to be itemized as would be a plant or animal species that blends into the background of a scene. The women typically represent encumbrances who delay or interrupt North's efforts to collect and paint, and a note of pride enters the memoirs when North successfully eludes them. The few women who escape such disparaging treatment, like the rare children who gain North's approval, tend to contribute in some way to North's artistic and scientific pursuits.

The narrative voice thus stands outside of its own gender in an oddly disjunctive way, creating the illusion of an objective observer casting a harsh judgment on a foreign species. Diminutives are copiously sprinkled into the narrative, as women are characterized as "little," commonly in a suggestive phrase that identifies them inconsequentially as a "pretty little wife," which resonates disturbingly with the periodic references to the "wives" of various birds North glimpses. Scathing criticism is accorded through dismissive predicates, modifiers, and clauses to women who "cackled" (2:2), to "unthinking, croqueting-badminton young ladies" who so "aggravated" North that she "could hardly be civil to them" (2:31), to gossiping females such as one acquaintance who was "delighted to get a new talking-post" (2:154), to a group of women "all serene and happy, but not entertaining" (2:226), to an Englishwoman who "had to sit at home half the day because her hair was not done" (*FR,* 119–20), and to the vast majority of other women she meets. The cumulative thrust of such remarks is that of a narrator who doggedly locates each example of stereotypical female behavior and then ridicules it relentlessly, divorcing herself from any empathy with or connection to it.

Moreover, an unmistakable note of condescension frequently threads through portrayals of women who seemingly escape harsh judgment. Recalling the "magnificent" gowns of an aristocratic group residing in India, for example, North comments that one peer's wife was "herself so hung with artificial flowers that she made quite a crushing noise whenever she sat down" (2:8); a "poor secluded woman" for whom North felt "real pity" delivered the narrator from "the trouble of amusing her" as the woman, "loaded with ornaments," listened attentively to her husband (1:328). Even on the uncommon occasions when North avows admiration, conventional descriptions of women as self-effacing, nurturing, and objects to be gazed upon proliferate, as in a vignette of one Englishwoman, who "had the good art of making others shine" and was noteworthy for "that wondrous smile and look of sympathy on her beautiful face" (2:215).

Also suggesting a gender disassociation are North's frequent attempts to separate herself from any hint of commonality even with other women noted for their scientific acumen, artistic ability, or travel accounts.[37] The rare exceptions to this approach tend to involve famous women who praise North, such as photographer Julia Margaret Cameron, described as "full of clever talk," whose characterization of North in a letter "might serve as an elegy" (1:314–15). The prominent female traveler and watercolor painter Constance Gordon Cumming, however, is dismissed with the nonchalant comment that "I got quite tired of her name" (1:303). Although North writes of her initial meeting with this woman "who had so long haunted me (by name) in various corners of the world, and for whom I had often been taken" (2:212) that "I felt when I saw her that it was no small compliment to have been taken for her," North immediately relates an anecdote that casts Gordon Cumming in a ludicrous light. Similarly, when asked in India by an interpreter if she were a disciple of one prominent woman, North conveys her distaste for the affiliation by relating the interpreter's unambiguously negative reaction to the same query (2:70).

These varied interactions with other women, both ordinary and extraordinary, thus constitute another mechanism for distancing the *Recollections'* narrative voice from essentialist associations. In all of the nar-

37. Birkett explains North's reaction as "continually having to fight off other women travellers' intrusion into her own sphere" and cites the examples of both Constance Gordon Cumming and Isabella Bird (*Spinsters Abroad,* 139).

rative strategies I have explored, North carefully negotiates a rhetorical space through which she attempts to blur gender boundaries or obliterate them altogether. Immersed within a culture that limits women's opportunities and possibilities so drastically, it is not surprising that North would psychologically endeavor to step outside of gender and inhabit a free space devoid of the essentialist traits and determinism that would otherwise constrain her. North's sparse references to her mother's life reveal a marked distaste for the "dreary" existence that awaited a conventional Victorian woman, and North apparently perceived the maternal experience as an admonition. As her memoirs reveal, North responded to that prospect not by surrendering to but by attempting to nullify gender, allowing her to become, at least in her own mind, a member of neither sex.

6

Evolutionary Mediation

The Female Physician in Charles Reade's
A Woman-Hater

With popular novelist Charles Reade's compelling 1877 novel, *A Woman-Hater,* I shift attention to the challenges facing a Victorian woman seeking to be recognized and accepted as a professional scientific practitioner, in this case as a physician. Though the narrative is sympathetic to the young woman's plight, the text nevertheless follows a pronounced—and troubling—essentialist vein in arguing that women are innately qualified for medical practice due to their widely recognized proclivities for acute observation, domestic talent, and other distinctly feminine traits. *A Woman-Hater,* I suggest, hints at a curious progression in presenting a "manly" female physician as an intermediate evolutionary form that augurs promisingly for the eventual development of a "womanly" physician who will combine the impressive intellectual talents attributed to men with the ostensibly natural female proclivities deemed valuable for the medical profession.

Julia Kristeva's theorization about women's relationship to the symbolic order offers a useful overall gloss for the novel, in speculating that "a woman cannot be part of the temporal symbolic order except by identifying with the father." If a woman "shows any sign of that which, in herself, escapes such identification and acts differently," Kristeva comments, she reveals a connection to the unconscious, to that which the symbolic order aims to suppress.[1] *A Woman-Hater*'s unfeminine physician, Rhoda Gale, can be viewed as striving to identify fully with the father as a means of entering and remaining within the symbolic order; signs of womanliness would attenuate that linkage and reinforce associations to the repressed and gendered unconscious. In a sense, Rhoda is presenting a performance, mimicking a man, to gain the acceptance she desires. Interestingly, she speaks more than any other character in the novel, given a lengthy first-person commentary, as she demonstrates a masculine facility within the symbolic realm. Yet, as I mentioned, the novel paradoxically considers feminine traits as positive characteristics for medical study. *A Woman-Hater* resolves the inconsistency with the message that an eventual evolutionary combination of masculine and feminine qualities will produce the perfect physician.

Hélène Cixous's assessment of the "other bisexuality" also provides a helpful hermeneutic lens in her postulation that each individual carries "the presence of both sexes, evident and insistent in different ways." As a survival strategy, Rhoda must bury the feminine aspects and foreground the masculine, since the male has "been trained to aim for glorious phallic monosexuality" rather than evince any feminine qualities. If we view Rhoda as a kind of evolutionary bridge, then the more developed form will evidence "the nonexclusion of difference or of a sex" in a bisexuality that "does not annihilate differences but cheers them on, pursues them, adds more."[2]

Rhoda's story is one of several strains comprising *A Woman-Hater*, which is primarily centered around the marriage plots of Harrington Vizard, an English country gentleman, and his half-sister, Zoe. As the novel opens, the pair is traveling on the continent, along with their cousin, Fanny Dover, and Harrington's friend, Edward Severne. Harrington, the misogynist of the title, attends an operatic performance in Hamburg with his companions and is smitten by the main singer, Ina Klosking, to generate one of the main plotlines. Ina, meanwhile, is attempting to track down her errant lover, who has deserted her and left

1. Julia Kristeva, *About Chinese Women*, 154.
2. Hélène Cixous, "Sorties," 84–85.

her bereft. Though his identity is kept secret until late in the novel, Ina's lover is actually Severne, whom she had married long before. Severne, however, is wooing young Zoe in hopes of marrying beauty and wealth, concealing his previous marriage as he schemes, cheats, forges, and lies to improve his impoverished condition. The impressionable Zoe, enamored of Severne, becomes increasingly attached to him, so much so that their marriage seems inevitable. Another suitor appears, however, who is a Vizard neighbor in England and a highly regarded aristocrat, Lord Uxmoor. Though he proposes to Zoe, she refuses his offer and continues to be enthralled by the disreputable Severne.

Eventually, the Vizard party travels to London on the way to the family's ancestral estate in Bartfordshire. While wandering in a Leicester Square garden, Harrington unexpectedly encounters Rhoda Gale, who appears pale and weak. He fears she is on the verge of fainting and offers assistance. Initially resistant, she joins Harrington for a meal and relates her history to him in elaborate detail, describing the many obstacles she had and still confronts in seeking to become a practicing physician. She relates the numerous instances in which she was denied fair treatment in England and Edinburgh because of the opposition of the male medical establishment. Her background, which touches upon nonfictional biographical detail, is a continual account of discrimination and injustice facing women seeking to become physicians. As David Finkelstein states, "Reade's work was one of the first to dramatize the pioneering efforts of Elizabeth Blackwell and Sophia Jex-Blake to breach social and medical antagonism and prejudices, and to redefine women's role in British society."[3] Though Rhoda's medical studies have been completed, she has been unable to obtain the appropriate license to practice, again due to widespread discriminatory actions as well as unfair laws.

Greatly impressed by Rhoda's obvious intelligence and dedication to medicine, Harrington ignores the law and installs Rhoda as a physician in Bartfordshire. There, too, she meets resistance, in this case primarily through the villagers' distrust of a woman physician. Meanwhile, Ina's

3. David Finkelstein, "A Woman Hater and Women Healers: John Blackwood, Charles Reade, and the Victorian Women's Medical Movement," 330. See also Swenson, *Medical Women and Victorian Fiction* (a lengthy study of actual and fictional medical women, including Rhoda Gale), and Susan Wells, *Out of the Dead House: Nineteenth-Century Women Physicians and the Writing of Medicine.*

continual search for Severne brings her to the Vizard home, where she encounters the philanderer. As Ina confronts him before the Vizards, Severne strikes her severely and flees. The badly injured Ina is treated by Rhoda and gradually recovers. Severne, meanwhile, secretly contacts Zoe while she is caring for a sickly aunt in another village and again gains her affections. Though Severne plans a surreptitious marriage to the young woman, he is thwarted when his previous marriage to Ina is revealed. He then turns his attention to Ina, following her from performance to performance, in hopes of enjoying her wealth.

Severne, however, is stricken with a fatal health problem and is nursed by Ina. He conveniently dies, though, freeing Ina for an eventual marriage to the enamored Harrington. While Harrington pursues the grieving Ina, Uxmoor renews his attentions to Zoe. In typical marriage-plot fashion, the worthy suitors win the hearts and hands of their beloveds, and the respective pairs are finally united. In the closing pages of the novel, Rhoda continues her care of the villagers, who have slowly warmed to her as they recognize her concern and Harrington's support. Though the medical establishment resists Rhoda's presence, Harrington and Uxmoor exert sufficient pressure to help Rhoda gain acceptance and respect. Though Rhoda technically is disobeying the law by not having a license, the text emphasizes the injustice and immorality of the legislation and notes encouraging signs of change in Parliament.

Contemporary reviewers gave mixed responses to the novel. The *Academy,* for instance, commented that "[a]ltogether it is a beautiful story, beautifully and powerfully told." The *Athenaeum* huffed that "Mr. Reade is very far indeed from being a novelist of the highest order" but added that "the reading world really ought to feel grateful to any one who takes the least trouble to construct a story, and knows the importance of forming some definite conception of the characters which he wishes to set before his readers, even though his development of the conception may leave something to be desired."[4]

Some reviewers, including Jex-Blake, remarked on the veracity of the novel's treatment of a woman's struggles to become a doctor. Said the *Academy* in discussing the characterization of Rhoda Gale, "It is from her lips that we hear the story, and very accurately told too, of the

4. "New Novels: *A Woman Hater,*" 59; "Novels of the Week: *A Woman Hater,*" 765.

difficulties and hardships that she and her fellow-students endured in the process of their medical studies." The journal added that "Mr. Reade has brought all the influence of his great reputation" to this controversy and "ma[de] his story one which will be read and enjoyed." Jex-Blake stated in an 1893 essay that "the author puts into [Rhoda Gale's] mouth a very carefully compiled narrative of some of the most striking events in the course of the Edinburgh struggle" to gain medical education, which Jex-Blake herself experienced. She added that "in spite of a few minor errors that an outsider could hardly avoid, the chapter [of Rhoda's medical education] thus occupied may take and keep its place in contemporary history in virtue of its great general accuracy." Another commentator on literary treatments of medical women, though asserting that the novel was not "one of Reade's finest works," nevertheless wrote in 1898 that "we would recommend the study of this portion, at least, of the book to the medical woman of to-day who is inclined to accept her privileges with an easy complacency, forgetting the 'great fight of afflictions' through which they were gained for her." Less positively, the *Saturday Review* deemed the account of Rhoda Gale's struggles as "spirited, vigorous, and interesting," yet judged the plotline "simply absurd—an affront to the common sense of the reader." The reviewer added that "[t]he digression about medical women does not fit easily into the rest of the rambling story." The *Athenaeum* said that "[i]t is needless to say that Mr. Reade has a didactic as well as an artistic string to his bow, or nib to his pen," condescendingly observing: "The adventures, successes, and discomfitures of Miss Rhoda Gale, M.D., in her efforts to open the medical career to herself and other ladies, are of course Mr. Reade's opportunity for utilizing the last Blue-book he has read."[5]

FEMININE TYPES

The current status of female evolution is revealed primarily through the characterizations of Zoe and Ina, whose qualities are filtered through the essentialist and periodically misogynist voices of the narrator and

5. "New Novels: *A Woman Hater*," 59; Sophia Jex-Blake, "Medical Women in Fiction," 262; "The Medical Woman in Fiction," 95–96; "A Woman-Hater," 51; "Novels of the Week: *A Woman Hater*," 765.

the titular character. Both women are represented as the pinnacles of two somewhat divergent types of female development—the angel in the house and the apotheosis of feminine accomplishments—though both also reveal unflattering traits typically considered part of "female nature."[6] As the more conventional of the two characters, Zoe quite smoothly conforms to the nineteenth-century standard of idyllic womanhood. In customary Victorian fashion, the text's initial description of Zoe concentrates on her admirable physical attributes, assessing and objectifying her as an assemblage of body parts, reminding us of the similar strategy for presenting *Heart and Science*'s Carmina. The depiction of Zoe, a "young lady of rare and dazzling beauty," proceeds systematically through the catalog of her features, as if detailing a particularly striking specimen of her type:

> Her face was a long but perfect oval, pure forehead, straight nose, with exquisite nostrils; coral lips, and ivory teeth. But what first struck the beholder were her glorious dark eyes, and magnificent eyebrows as black as jet. Her hair was really like a raven's dark purple wing.
> . . . [H]er form and limbs were grand and statuesque for her age; but all was softened down to sweet womanhood by long silken lashes, often lowered, and a gracious face that blushed at a word, blushed little, blushed much, blushed pinky, blushed pink, blushed roseate, blushed rosy. (20)[7]

Ensconced in her expected and customary habitat within a domestic environment, Zoe has positioned her body, "with feminine instinct," upon a couch "that framed her to perfection" as she immerses herself in embroidery work (21). As befits a feminine ideal, Zoe's penchant for blushing attests not only to her "transparent face" but also her pellucid character, with the coursing blood "painting her thoughts upon her countenance" and revealing a mind that lacks even "a grain of . . . subtlety."

6. As Finkelstein observes about several female figures in Reade's text, they "were little more than iconic representations of women as Victorian patriarchal society wished to see them" ("Woman Hater," 342).
7. All page citations come from the P. F. Collier and Son edition of Charles Reade, *A Woman-Hater*.

Subsequent references underscore her conformity to feminine traits. "[G]uileless and inexperienced," Zoe is termed "Angel of goodness!" by the besotted Severne (28). This "high-minded creature" (56) and "peerless creature" (36), with the identical noun choices emphasizing the dismissive estimation of Victorian women, displays the "instinctive delicacy and modesty of a truly virgin soul" (89). As befits an exemplar of femininity, Zoe has internalized the cultural discourses that value subservience, silence, and self-abnegation as well as an acceptable level of self-display. Though "a good girl, and a generous girl," Zoe betrays the "share of vanity" (117) associated with woman, evidenced in her case by an attentiveness to careful dress, effusive compliments, and unstinting adoration. Hesitant to express her opinion, Zoe is even astonished "at her boldness in advancing an opinion on so large a matter" as the tired Victorian truism of female emotionality, blushingly averring that "women have greater hearts to love" (97). Impressed at Lord Uxmoor's manifestation of male friendship on one occasion, Zoe concludes her praise of his selflessness by noting that "[w]e poor, emotional, cowardly girls should sit down and cry" (55). She agrees with her brother's estimation of female deception, telling her cousin Fanny that "girls are artful creatures, especially when they put their heads together," and proceeds to relate "the end of all our cunning" in sharing an anecdote (25). Her presumed intellectual inferiority to the Victorian male is implicitly accepted as a cultural verity through her undiscriminating and shallow choices of conversational topics and her customary airing of frivolous concerns; thus, she immediately accedes to her brother's unflattering perception of "[f]eminine logic" and diminished reasoning capacity by responding, "You are right. . . . Thank you, for thinking for me" (125). Like all women apprised by a conventional Victorian mind, Zoe carries the taint of Eve and timeless treachery, as evidenced by her coiffure of "polished ebon snakes" and her innate ability to bewitch an unsuspecting male, who is left "dazzled, transfixed, at the vision" she presents (35). "[A] mere female in embryo," according to her brother, Zoe has "not yet developed the vices of [her] sex" but, as the adverb indicates, eventually will do so (24).

In effect, Zoe is a product of a misguided process of natural selection validated by Victorian culture, whereby the qualities deemed most suitable for propagating the angel in the house are admired and reinforced.

As feminist novelist and essayist Mona Caird would argue nearly twenty years later in "Phases of Human Development," a two-part essay examining essentialist illogicality, "Varieties are obviously unlikely to occur often in a race, when half its numbers are placed in similar conditions, trained in the same fashion." The unenviable result is the production of "precisely the same set of qualities and instincts—to the discouragement of others—[that] are called forth age after age, and exaggerated as far as possible." Such a process precludes the possibility of human development, for "[i]t is inconceivable that a people can go on progressing while they continue to cripple half their numbers."[8]

Like Zoe, Ina somatically displays the attributes of ideal womanhood, which are similarly delineated as a series of body parts when she first enters the narrative. Appearing "comely, sedate, and womanly" to the narrator at a cursory glance, Ina then is examined in almost microscopic detail, noting both her conformance to and slight deviations from a precise standard of beauty, with the fragmented sentences mirroring the semantic segmentation of her countenance:

> Her forehead high and white, but a little broader than sculptors affect. Her long hair, coiled tight, in a great many smooth snakes, upon her snowy nape, was almost flaxen, yet her eyebrows and long lashes not pale but a reddish brown. Her gray eyes, large and profound; her mouth rather large, beautifully shaped, amiable, and expressive, but full of resolution; her chin a little broad; her neck and hands admirably white and polished. (3)

Again a serpentine reference emerges, as in the depiction of Zoe, to position Ina within the parameters of female essence, revealing her as both strikingly attractive and vaguely menacing. In other regards, too, Ina conforms to the Victorian view of womanhood. Her "female nerves" cause her to weep (18), and she displays "feminine quickness" (42), "innocent vanity" (377), an "angelic" look (379), and "ravishing sweetness" (463). Appropriately associated with feminine orality rather than masculine textuality, Ina manifests "[t]he soul of womanhood" when she sings with her "honey lips" (68) in a "sweet" voice (17), and she speaks

8. Mona Caird, "Phases of Human Development I," 42; Caird, "Phases of Human Development II," 165.

according to the "vague, suggestive way her sex excels in" (486). Like Tess Durbeyfield and other Victorian female characters, Ina is evaluated in terms of an object of art, intimated in the above reference to the sculpting process, as if female essence can be unproblematically captured and represented. Periodically, her "truly feminine features stiffen into marble" to present a loveliness "worthy of epic song" that "rises beyond the wing of prose" (463), like that of a mythological figure whose female essence ostensibly transcends the centuries.

Nevertheless, Ina departs from feminine typicality in significant respects, primarily through a defining quality of depth rather than superficiality, as the reference to her "profound eyes," quoted above in the text's opening description, implies. The quality is so unexpected that the narrator cites as "a peculiarity of this woman" her tendency "nearly always to think—if but for half a moment—before she spoke" (6). Coupled with this proclivity for careful thought is a strict conformance to truth, a tendency the narrator finds equally astonishing in remarking that Ina "say[s] things, whether about herself or others, only because they were the truth," a point immediately reiterated with the observation that her words "were weighty by their extraordinary air of truthfulness." Other references similarly call attention to Ina's depth of character and veracity. "[L]ittle versed in guile," Ina shows "tact and self-possession," revealing her "not an angel, after all"—a superficial domestic paragon, like Zoe—"but a woman whose wits were sharpened by love and suffering" (318). As the narrator admiringly comments on one occasion, Ina's "face seemed slowly to fill with intellectual power" (316), and other characters recognize that she is "as deep as the ocean" (386), even the highly critical Fanny, who admits that Ina is "wiser than any one of us" (407). Somatic markers further attest, in emphatic alliteration, to Ina's noteworthy qualities, for "[d]ress and deportment were all of a piece—decent and deep" (139).

In her career of professional singer, too, Ina departs from the feminine model. As one who has attained enviable success in her profession, Ina functions as a kind of female boundary figure; though her talent rests in music, one of the most highly valued feminine accomplishments, she displays that skill in a public forum rather than within the domestic confines of a drawing room, and she earns a comfortable living through her efforts. One telling sentence foregrounds this curious juxtaposition of feminine and masculine qualities: Ina is "beautiful on the stage," with a "figure rather tall and stately," yet "her face [is] full of power" as she "showed the step and carriage of an artist at home upon the boards" (44). Moreover, she sings in "a heavenly contralto" (46), an intriguing melding of gender attributes in that this musical range encompasses either the lowest of female voices or the highest of male voices. Appearing in the part of "Siebel" when first observed by the Vizard party, Ina is "dressed like a velvet youth" but "look[s] like no earthly boy" (47); indeed, to Harrington, in Ina "shone all the beauties that adorn the body, all the virtues and graces that embellish the soul" as this "paragon glide[d] away, like a goddess" (69).

Despite her seeming departures from ideal femininity, however, Ina never presents an overt threat to conventional notions of womanhood. Repeatedly, references to her professional activities are inextricably aligned with the feminine qualities of comeliness, emotion, affection, and irrationality. Though designated as "not an angel," as I noted, Ina nevertheless is immediately associated with traditional femininity in achieving that very status through her suffering over the unworthy Severne. In fact, her professional career is wholly arranged around the romantic attachment; engagements are accepted or canceled, trips are made or deferred, based on Severne's movements and her attempts to rejoin him. Even his death directs her professional interests, for she retires in widowhood and secludes herself within the parental home. Never does she display an unfeminine self-assertiveness that would threaten male authority, evidenced most notably in her conduct after marriage to Harrington. Requesting a continental honeymoon, Ina "did not stipulate even for that," but "only asked it submissively, as one whose duty it now was to obey, not dictate" (518). Importantly, she is designated an "angel" by the adoring Harrington shortly before their marriage (515), further negating the narrator's earlier disavowal of the applicability of the term.

ESSENTIALIST TRAITS

Both Harrington and the narrator are particularly explicit in presenting not only Ina and Zoe, but all women, in essentialist terms. Patronizing and dismissive, the two voices punctuate the story with references to attributes and inclinations that all women presumably share. By conveying Harrington's views without disputative commentary, the text and its narrator take on an element of veracity and authority, suggesting Harrington's as a natural reading of the characters and their proclivities, despite the narrator's identification of Harrington's misogyny as an "eccentricity" (35). Further conferring authority on Harrington's opinions is the fact that he is a respected representative of the ruling patriarchal structure with appropriate bloodlines, property, and wealth, a "squire, with twelve thousand acres, and a library" (19). Not only is he a valued member of society by virtue of being part of the landed gentry, Harrington also is depicted as a judicious and clever individual with the inclusion of the library in the description of his holdings, a point validated by a subsequent reference to him as one who "really did suck good books as well as cigars" (35).

Like most Victorian observers of their society, the text fails to distinguish between biological attributes and cultural influences in making seemingly authoritative pronouncements, so that even casual comments about feminine propensities and preferences assume the guise of objective analysis as the division between nature and nurture is blurred. With an outlook matching Harrington's condescending attitude toward women, the narrator is assumed to be male, yet that supposition is undercut by the narrator's offhand statement beginning, "When I was a girl; or a boy; I forget which—it is so long ago" (235). The gender ambiguity is important, for it implies that the narrator conveys impressions from the perspective of both male and female, which creates a universalizing and additionally naturalizing effect. Thus, though a reader might react skeptically to the disdainful criticisms of women uttered by the self-avowed misogynist Harrington, the narrator's confirmations of female inferiority and essentialist proclivities confer approbation on the "woman-hater's" commentaries.

A sampling of the narrator's observations conveys the perspectives that an undiscriminating Victorian reader would readily absorb. Relating a conversation between Fanny and Zoe, the narrator notes that the pair were brushing their hair, "a soothing operation" considered "famous for stimulating females to friendly gossip" (51). The cousins speak indirectly of events uppermost in their minds before proceeding to their main concerns, which the narrator summarizes as "preliminary puffs of articulated wind" (52) in an unveiled critique of female intellectual ability. Though the narrator comments that some writers would relate the conversation in detail, this narrator "leave[s] the glory of photographing nullities to the geniuses of the age" and instead will "run to the first words which could, without impiety, be called dialogue" (52). Later, the narrator similarly opines that "most women are a little cat-like" in conversational forays, for "they go away once or twice from the subject nearest their heart, before they turn and pounce on it" (380). A casual and seemingly innocuous comment about women's preference for early dining assumes an underlying essentialist tone with the narrator's explanation that "Nature is strong in them, and they are hungriest when the sun is high" (444). When the Vizard party visits a gambling establishment, Zoe's "female eye" is drawn, "by her nature," to the "pictorial and amusing" roulette table, where "the female understanding sees something it can grasp" (133)—a game wholly dependent on chance rather than skill. In other essentializing gestures, Zoe is dubiously credited with evincing a "marvellous female instinct" (27) and "a woman's broad instinct" (171), a sweeping generalization of womanhood that is more typically uttered by the main character and primary misogynist.

Harrington's disdainful and essentialist attitude toward women surfaces early in the narrative with references to his female companions as "my hen-party" (33) and the disgruntled assessment that "my hens will be sure to cackle *mal-à-propos*" if the "terribly over-petticoated" group accompanies him to the opera (34). Other disparaging remarks about female intelligence abound. Harrington considers women "[i]diots" in all respects except "taking in the men," shortly before the narrator approvingly refers to "the superiority of the male intellect" (86). In a subtle confirmation of the Victorian scientific view that women excel at perception rather than cognition, Harrington avers that "[t]he female eye is naturally swift," able to observe extensively "in *half a moment of time*" (301). Asserting that he "never met a woman" who was just (393), Harrington condemns the "diabolically subtle" deceptions of women, which "seem to vary only on the surface" (67). Moreover, he contends, "there is not a single wild animal so cruel to another wild animal, as a woman is to a woman" (125). "You are cruel to one another by instinct," he informs Zoe, adding that "I appeal to your reason—if you have any." When she demurs to a suggestion, he praises her as one would a dutiful child with the condescending rejoinder, "That is a good girl" (126).

The text's various appraisals of Fanny additionally serve to adumbrate the novel's misogynist and essentialist consciousness. Besides being the quintessential female temptress who wields her gaze "in a way to magnetize a man," Fanny is constructed as innately deceptive in that she was "born artful" (19). The narrator demonstrates this artifice in commenting, for instance, that Fanny spoke to a potential husband by "purr[ing] pretty nothings at his ear, in a soft tone she reserved for males," in comparison to the "loud, and rather high-pitched" tone she adopted for females. A mercenary streak is further insinuated, for Fanny boasts physical attributes that frequently "enable a poor girl to conquer landed estates, with their male incumbrances." In this and other diminutive references to Fanny as a "girl," she appears immature and immaterial, despite being designated as "keen" and "sensible" (19). The girlishness suggests an intellectual deficiency as well, an estimation reiterated when she laments, "Oh, . . . if we are to talk nothing but science, it *will* be a weary world" (284).

WOMEN AS "NATURAL" PHYSICIANS

As the dominant textual voices, then, Harrington and the narrator shape the reader's judgments of female characters, mainly in the constrictive ways female subjectivity is delineated. Not surprisingly, the entry of Rhoda Gale into the novel initially follows a reader's expectations that she, too, will be inserted into a paradigmatic female script. When Harrington first encounters her, faint and fragile from near starvation, he immediately places her within the script of the damsel in distress as he offers her sustenance and assistance in chivalric fashion. Yet she rapidly departs from that narrative pattern, both through her own agency and the altered impressions that Harrington and the narrator express.[9] Condescending and reductive assessments of female subjectivity give way to respect and admiration while apparently opening possibilities of new

9. In a letter to John Blackwood, the publisher of the serial version, Reade referred to Rhoda Gale as "Aesculapia" and termed her experience "a great chapter of human nature and of unjust civilization" (quoted in Malcolm Elwin, *Charles Reade,* 298).

modes for women's development. The initial effect is not only a reshaping of cultural attitudes toward female possibilities, but also a suggestion that Rhoda Gale exemplifies a variant and vital path for evolutionary progression. Nevertheless, the text adheres to its essentialist principles in detailing Rhoda's accomplishments and potentialities, viewing her foray into medicine as a logical consequence of female predilections. In fact, in the final paragraph, the novel proclaims that medicine represents for women "an honorable ambition, and an honorable pursuit, towards which their hearts and instincts are bent by Nature herself" (532). Thus, the novel builds upon essentialist notions but somewhat reconfigures them to position the female physician as a natural evolutionary product.

In terms of intellectual abilities, Rhoda certainly is adjudged more than capable for entering the medical profession. As she informs Harrington, she is "well qualified by genuine gifts, by study from my infancy, by zeal, quick senses, and cultivated judgment"—so much so that "leading London physicians . . . would cut an indifferent figure in modern science" in comparison (183). Though Rhoda is herself making this declaration, and biased self-interest would be readily suspected, neither the narrator nor Harrington ever disputes her claim to scientific prowess; rather, the text is sprinkled with their references to her decided intellectual abilities. As Harrington tells his half-sister, Rhoda is "more learned, more scientific, more eloquent, . . . than I ever saw, or even read of,—a woman of *genius*" (233). "[F]ull of fire and intelligence," as the narrator readily comments (252), Rhoda is "[b]right and keen as steel, quick and spirited, yet controlled by judgment" (279), and "she shone with intelligence" (332). Even Severne, who views Rhoda as a dangerous nemesis, considers her "a new species" and a "new woman" (279).

The novelistic assumption that women are innately and uniquely suited for medicine is reinforced by frequent references to the maternal role in nurturing Rhoda's capabilities. Identifying her mother as "an ideal woman" (184) who was "valued by men of intellect" (185), Rhoda credits her with an early and sustained training to hone the daughter's keen understanding and prodigious memory. The mother "milked jurists, physicians, and theologians, and historians" of their learning, Rhoda recalls, with her predicate accentuating the maternal connection to the instillment of knowledge. Through the mother's "sharp training," school became "child's play" to Rhoda, who garnered numerous scholarly prizes (185). Furthermore, the mother "corrected the special blots of the female character" in the process, Rhoda asserts, and "made me, as far as she could, a—what shall I say?—a kind of little intellectual gymnast, fit to begin any study" (186). Rhoda is so advanced in her studies that she is allowed to select her own books and subjects once she masters, in a scathing criticism of female education, "what little they teach in schools." As both child and adult, Rhoda's "heart glowed with love of knowledge" (202).

Yet the novel emphasizes that Rhoda represents a female anomaly in her intellectual gifts and refuses to accord women, in general, with a cognitive ability equal to that of men. In this respect the text mirrors cultural discourses, related in my introductory chapter, that position the male as an intellectual superior, with only rare female exceptions to that standard. To reinforce the notion, the novel designates Rhoda herself as the character to identify female mental deficiencies. Although she claims that "the picked female is immeasurably more superior to the average male," she extends the comparison to the average male and female, surmising that "the intellect of the average male is to the average female as ten to six" (203). In the final sentence of the novel, the narrator reiterates the point of female inferiority in assessing medical study as a means for women to advance "towards mental equality with men" (533).

Woman's innate capacity for medical study is attributed, in part, to the scientific supposition noted earlier that the female is more perceptive than the male, though she trails him in more complex mental activities. The feminine attentiveness to detail becomes in *A Woman-Hater* a quality that can be refined into a remarkable ability to make perspicacious and pertinent observations, thereby enhancing medical aptitude and vital diagnostic skills. Again, maternal influence performs a crucial role, in this case encouraging such observational prowess from girlhood. Rhoda comments that her mother "taught me three rarities—attention, observation, and accuracy" (184). As Rhoda continues to relate her past to Harrington, she repeatedly returns to the critical importance of observational acuity and attentiveness to detail in preparing her for a medical vocation—"a noble science, a practical science, and a subtle science," as she terms it (188). "Medicine is a thing one can do," she explains, a field "where I thought my powers of study and observation might help me to be keen at reading symptoms, and do good."

Rhoda's account of her transformation from observant girl to medical proficient follows a series of developmental steps, with each leading systematically and smoothly to the next. Demonstrating an early affinity for scientific study, devolving from her mother's tutelage of the necessary skills for its pursuit, Rhoda in girlhood turned to natural history, so successfully that her collection of bird eggs continues to be showcased in a museum. After exposure to lectures and treatises by learned scientists, Rhoda "pried into every living thing" as she realized that "the humblest spot in nature becomes extraordinary the moment extraordinary observation is applied" (187). From her fascination with natural history she was led, "in due course," to investigating "the wonders of the human body" (188). "[F]rom that," Rhoda adds, "I was led on to surgery and medicine."

Throughout the novel, Rhoda is further credited with exceptional observational ability, in part through repeated references to her use of a microscope, an inclination that first appeared in childhood. After a visit to the Vizard estate shortly after her arrival in Bartfordshire, Rhoda pens a note to Harrington, eagerly asking if the word "Micro" she saw on a wooden case referred to the prized instrument and pleading that he lend it to her (290). Subsequent microscopic studies enable Rhoda to detect bacterial anomalies and other health risks, while her attentiveness to detail allows her to describe in minute fashion the precise requirements for constructing a well necessary for improving public health. "Why, this is Detail made woman," Harrington responds to her elaborate directions before agreeing to the project (333). Once the digging of the well is under way, Rhoda finds "[t]he various strata and their fossil deposits . . . an endless study" that "kept her microscope employed" (359). With her "Argus eye" (334), Rhoda is admiringly termed a "too observant lady" (340) by her patron, Harrington, who muses that "[t]he female eye is naturally swift" (301), a point the narrator similarly makes in calling Rhoda "the quick-sighted doctress" (392). Rhoda herself alludes to the crucial role of observation in explaining her approach to medicine. Maintaining it is "not so easy to cure diseases as people think," she asserts that "a part of medicine is to prevent [disease]," which necessitates the removal of "predisposing causes"; to detect them, she notes, one "must have eyes, and use them" (326). Moreover, in the novel's final chapter, a summary of Rhoda's activities is prefaced with the phrase that "Doctress Gale is still all eyes, and notices everything" as she continues to practice medicine (526). No less of an authority than Darwin attested to the importance of observation in his own scientific work, as nineteenth-century physician Elizabeth Blackwell remarked: "This necessity for making the most painstaking observation of facts . . . is well-illustrated in the life of Darwin."[10]

The novelistic supposition that women are innately suited to pursue a medical vocation is additionally stressed through Rhoda's self-identification as a physiognomist (341) who seeks to be "keen at reading symptoms" (188). In the Victorian scientific vocabulary, a physiognomist discerns character and mental abilities through observation of the body in general and the face in particular. In John Caspar Lavater's landmark eighteenth-century treatise on physiognomy, the key requirements of a practitioner include "accuracy of sensation, capable of receiving the most minute outward impressions, and easily transmitting them faithfully to memory." Of particular interest for assessing Rhoda, Lavater asserts that the physiognomist's "eye, in particular, must be excellent, clear, acute, rapid, and firm." Indeed, Lavater continues, "[p]recision in observation is the very soul of physiognomy," and "[t]he physiognomist must possess a most delicate, swift, certain, most extensive spirit of observation."[11]

Though Lavater's text invariably adopts the customary masculine pronoun in analyzing physiognomy, the practice could be equated with the conventionally feminine propensity of reading the body. Fictional and nonfictional tomes alike, of course, have traditionally attributed to women an inseverable (and unenviable) connection to the body, which suggests that the ability to interpret somatic indicators—the core of the physiognomic enterprise—rests on a gendered trait. As *A Woman-Hater* surmises in identifying a gender fluidity in Severne's character, "he watched faces like a woman" (280). Rhoda's physiognomic aptitude is periodically cited, especially in her interpretation of Severne himself. Thus, for instance, Rhoda "bent her eyes on him with that prodigious

10. Blackwell, *Essays in Medical Sociology,* 2:14–15. Blackwell proceeds to quote Darwin's letter to a friend in which he stated, "I have been hard at work for the last month in dissecting a little animal about the size of a pin's head, from the Chronos Archipelago, and I could spend another month and daily see more beautiful structure" (2:15).
11. John Caspar Lavater, *Essays on Physiognomy,* 64.

keenness she could throw into those steel-gray orbs, when her mind put on its full power of observation" (281), and soon thereafter she again "eyed him with steady and composed curiosity, as a zoologist studying a new specimen and all its little movements" (282). The implication that reading the body is a feminine predilection is indirectly reinforced by the narrative voice, which describes Rhoda as a "keen witch" (281) while she deftly scrutinizes Severne's features. Although a link between femininity and physiognomy would presumably undercut the scientific pretensions of the practice, in *A Woman-Hater* the connection is presented as a causal relationship: the feminized adeptness for detecting and deciphering the language of the body uniquely qualifies a woman for scientific endeavors.

The medical value of reading the body emerges convincingly in Rhoda's assessment of the health problems of Bartfordshire villagers. It is through careful observation of "putty-faced children" (329) that Rhoda concludes the local water supply is harmful, a hypothesis she is able to test, again through her observational acumen, with microscopic study. Similarly, her keen observation leads her to identify a "muck-heap" (334) as "a hotbed of malaria" (335). Disguised by blooming roses, the scene conceals "a foul, unwholesome den" in which offal fosters disease. On another occasion, Rhoda's observational prowess causes her to probe the reason that local youths have undeveloped calves, which she identifies as "a sure sign of a deteriorating species" (337). This discovery leads her, in turn, to other significant conclusions about the villagers' injudicious diets and the ramifications for future generations (338). "The race has declined," she concludes, since only the men of the previous generation displayed needed strength. Again her observational powers come into play, since "the stalwart race that filled the little village . . . left proofs of their wholesome food on the tombstones," which Rhoda carefully read to determine that "far more people reached eighty-five" in the past.

Even the gendered accomplishment of drawing participates in the nurturance of the feminine proclivity for medicine. Rhoda particularly designates the drawing skills learned in girlhood as "useful in scientific pursuits" (186), which she in later life turns to practical application in sketching bacteria and other medically significant phenomena. In assessing the health problems of Bartfordshire residents, for example, Rhoda sketches the "animalcules" detected microscopically to arrive at a prescient diagnosis (330). Yet on no occasion does Rhoda praise feminine drawing for its own sake; it gains value only through scientific functionality.

The "natural" association of women to medical practice emerges, too, in the minority cultural assessment that female physicians are best suited for treatment of female patients, especially in regard to "private" female complaints. As Rhoda explains, "would-be doctresses look *mainly to attending women*" (208), a practice greeted enthusiastically by those patients. Females "thanked God for [women physicians] openly," Rhoda recalls in textually emphatic upper case as she relates her history to Harrington (218), and they even expressed gratitude in a more public forum by writing to journals pleading for "female students . . . to come between them and the brutal curiosity of the male students" whose behavior is termed "offensive" and causing "agonies of shame" (219). The preference of female patients for physicians of their own sex gains additional cultural value in promoting the prized trait of modesty by protecting a female patient from intrusive male eyes.

Contemporary writings also remarked on the value of preserving modesty through the presence of women physicians. As Frances Power Cobbe argued a few years after *A Woman-Hater* was published, "No doctor can be dull enough to ignore the fact that the feelings of a woman with a crowd of curious young students round her bed of agony must be almost worse than death." So traumatic is the experience to a woman, Cobbe contended, that it "must lessen her chances of recovery if any such there be." Physician Sophia Jex-Blake also argued the point in recalling her interactions with women who avoided medical treatment because of a marked sense of modesty. Jex-Blake repeatedly heard some female patients explain that the reason they did not seek early care for certain health problems was that they could not consult a man about the problem, while other patients noted their pleasure in finally being able to consult with a woman practitioner. Education advocate Emily Davies stressed that female physicians would be ideal caregivers for both women and children. "[A]ll diseases to which women and children are liable would naturally come within the province of the female physician," Davies wrote, "and surely that is a domain wide enough, without encroaching upon the sphere of men." She added, "[L]adies who have had time to think, are almost unanimous in declaring that if they could secure the attendance of equally well-educated women . . . they would give them the preference."[12]

Some Victorian observers, though contesting the notion that women physicians could ever achieve equality with their male counterparts, nevertheless saw value in women ministering to other women and their children. Said one obviously male contributor to *Blackwood's* in 1874: "If it would not emasculate the female sex too much, we would suggest that they would have much more chance of attaining medical diplomas if, instead of asserting identical claims with men, to study in the same dissecting and lecture rooms, and an identical right to practise, they would limit themselves to claiming women and children as their appropriate patients." The essayist added that women "should recognise in practice, as it appears that they do in theory, that there is sex in mind, as well as sex in education" and "give up the equality . . . theory, both as regards aims, *status*, and rights, and substitute the theory of appropriateness."[13]

In a related vein, a widespread supposition that women physicians wrongly seek to rid themselves of modesty is countered in *A Woman-Hater* through Rhoda's commentary on the responsibilities and behavior of female nurses. "Nurses are not, as a class, unfeminine," she stresses, despite the fact that "all that is most appalling, disgusting, horrible, and *unsexing* in the art of healing is monopolized by them" (207). In 1862, one essayist made an analogous declaration in praising nurses, yet the writer saw a dramatic distinction between women serving as nurses or as physicians. "We reverence and bless the nurse who applies an emollient," the essayist remarked, but "very different, indeed, would be our feelings if we saw a bare-armed fury striding into our chamber with a bistoury in her hand to perform a surgical operation." Jex-Blake, however, pointed to the logical flaw in such views, using the example of famed and revered Crimean War nurse Florence Nightingale. Jex-Blake spoke of the "curious inconsistency" of the broad admiration accorded Nightingale for courageous endeavors to help patients. Nightingale and her disciples

12. Frances Power Cobbe, "The Medical Profession and Its Morality," 311; Sophia Jex-Blake, *Medical Women: A Thesis and a History,* 44; Davies, *Thoughts on Some Questions,* 23–24.
13. "Sex in Mind and Education: A Commentary," 748.

escaped accusations that they lacked "feminine delicacy in their going among the foulest sights and most painful scenes to succour, not their own sex, but the other." Nevertheless, Jex-Blake pointed out, "many people yet profess to be shocked when other women desire to fit themselves to take the medical care of those of their sisters who would gladly welcome their aid." The physician added, "It is indeed hard to see any reason of delicacy, at least, which can be adduced in favour of women as nurses, and against them as physicians."[14]

Other Victorian commentators also disputed the presumption that becoming a physician would jeopardize "womanliness." As Millicent Garrett Fawcett, suffragist and sister of physician Elizabeth Garrett Anderson, would maintain in 1891, "[m]ake [a woman] a doctor, put her through the mental discipline and the physical toil of the profession; . . . [s]he remains womanly to her finger-tips, and a good doctor in proportion as the truly womanly qualities in her are strongly developed. . . . It is not too much to say that a woman can never hope to be a good doctor unless she is truly and really a womanly woman."[15]

A Woman-Hater also seeks to link medical practice to femininity as a logical extension of the gendered predilection for domestic talent. As the novel observes, women should act the part of "viceroy" in overseeing "little domestic matters" that help ensure the preservation of health (336). Rhoda puts theory into praxis in her care of the convalescing Ina as Rhoda "cooked," "nursed," "lighted fires," and "aired her bed" to promote the singer's recovery (475). "Women are good advisers in such things," Rhoda comments in identifying a vital domestic capacity that a male physician is ostensibly unable to fulfill (336). "The male physician," she continues, "relies on drugs" inappropriately; consequently, "[m]edical women are wanted to moderate that delusion," for they can "prevent disease by domestic vigilance, and cure it by well-selected esculents and pure air." Such an approach, she avers, "will cure fifty for one that medicine can." She points to the case of an elderly man, "nearly *exsanguis*"; there exists "not a drug in creation that could do him an atom of good," but "[n]ourishing food may" (355). Furthermore, "drugs kill ever so many," while her approach "never killed a creature" (336). As Cobbe noted, "we may say in our day as safely as Voltaire did in his time,

14. "The Rights of Woman," 197; Jex-Blake, *Medical Women,* 40–41.
15. Fawcett, "Education of Women," 674.

that a doctor is a man who pours drugs of which he knows little into stomachs of which he knows less."[16]

To reinforce the importance of a woman's domestic abilities for the practice of medicine, the admirable Lord Uxmoor turns to Rhoda for assistance in his endeavors to promote the health of his workers as he prepares to embark for a lengthy stay on the continent. The masculine sphere of public work blends with the feminine realm of domestic perspicacity as the peer visits Rhoda "upon business" in hopes that she will further his activities, invoking the feminine quality of sympathy as well as domestic ability in urging his cause (448). "Men . . . are always making oversights in matters of domestic comfort," he tells her, whereas Rhoda is "full of ideas." Public and private spheres continue to merge through Uxmoor's terminology, as he maintains that Rhoda would make an ideal "viceroy" whom he would invest "with full power" so that she could act as she wished.

The novel's judgment that Rhoda's approach to medical care far exceeds that of the typical male physician is conveyed less overtly as well. Harrington's desire to install Rhoda as Bartfordshire practitioner is initiated because of a dearth of proper care for the villagers, which male physicians of the area presumably have ignored; none has identified the root causes of the villagers' health problems, as Rhoda does. Of all the characters in the novel, only Rhoda is allowed to speak at great length in her own voice, unmediated by narratorial interjections and judgments. Moreover, no male physician receives more than an offhand reference; thus, there is no model male physician who overshadows Rhoda or acts as a foil to point to deficiencies in a woman doctor. Instead, Rhoda functions as an unfailed Lydgate: progressive, incorruptible, and dedicated.

Rhoda displays the most enviable qualities of Lydgate in several respects. Like him, she battles ineffective approaches to medical care, a firmly entrenched medical profession determined to protect its own fiefdom, and a superstitious dread of change or innovation. In this regard, Rhoda resembles other medical heroes of Reade's novels, such as Dr. Sampson in the 1863 *Hard Cash* or Dr. Amboyne in the 1870 *Put Yourself in His Place*, who also value preventive care and castigate overprescription. Dr. Sampson is particularly harsh in his judgment of fellow

16. See also Swenson for commentary on Rhoda's "domestic vigilance" (*Medical Women and Victorian Fiction*, 97); Cobbe, "Medical Profession," 299.

physicians, whom he describes in his curious dialect as "fools and lyres" as well as "assassins." He terms his "lairned Profession" as "a rascally one": "It is like a barrel of beer," he says, and answers his own question as to "What rises to the top?" in vivid capital letters as "the scum." Along similar lines, Dr. Amboyne remarks that "[w]e doctors are dissembling dogs" who "have still something to learn in curing diseases." The issue of overprescription is also addressed in the 1871 *A Terrible Temptation*: "the system which prescribes drugs, drugs, drugs, at every visit, and in every case, and does not give a severe selection of esculents the first place, but only the second or third, must be rotten at the core."[17] Yet there is a suggestion that Rhoda exceeds these worthy physicians in intent and effectiveness, as if she is taking medical practice to its next level of expertise and progression. Unlike her fictional counterparts, Rhoda makes a positive difference on a broad scale rather than merely affecting a few or even a single individual. It is as if she represents the subsequent stage of evolutionary development as a medical practitioner, able to effect change in varied and significant ways.

In contrast to the mature Lydgate, as well as the male physicians Cobbe would castigate for avaricious self-aggrandizement, Rhoda's perceived responsibility is to tend to the poor (326). In a veiled criticism of male practitioners, Rhoda implies that expediency motivates their care of wealthy patients accustomed to the excessive (and enriching) prescribing habits of the profession. "Physicians are obliged to send the rich to the chemist," she says, "or else the fools would think they were slighted" (355). She continues in an acerbic and ironic tone that a physician "need not be so nice with the poor" but instead "can prescribe to do them good." Even one of the initially resistant villagers recognizes Rhoda's appropriate motive in appraising her as "a young lady that leaves the pomps and vanities" and "gives her mind to bettering the condishing of poor folk" (327). Yet an essentialist connection obtains in this regard as well as others I have traced. Since an economically comfortable woman would feel compelled to visit and minister to the local poor in Lady Bountiful fashion, Rhoda's similar activities would seem merely an extension of that perceived duty. Rhoda's concern for the poor meshes

17. Charles Reade, *Hard Cash*, 57, 271, 58; Reade, *Put Yourself in His Place*, 79; Reade, *A Terrible Temptation*, 280.

smoothly with the Victorian perception that women are the sympathetic and philanthropic sex.

Physician Elizabeth Blackwell and other contemporaries also considered medical practice an appropriate realm for women because of their perceived status as moral authorities in Victorian culture. Blackwell enumerated the qualities that particularly suited women for such a role: "the subordination of self to the welfare of others; the recognition of the claim which helplessness and ignorance make upon the stronger and more intelligent; . . . [and] pity and sympathy." Women bear "the weighty responsibility of becoming more and more the moral guides in life's journey," Blackwell added. "[T]he legitimate study" of medicine, Blackwell believed, "requires the preservation in full force of those beneficient moral qualities—tenderness, sympathy, guardianship—which form an indispensable spiritual element of maternity." Thus, Blackwell contended that "[t]he true physician must possess the essential qualities of maternity," for "[t]he sick are as helpless in [a physician's] hands as the infant."[18]

Nineteenth-century observers also drew the connection between gendered qualities and effective medical ministration to the poor. Fawcett asserted, for instance, that London's female physicians "show their poor patients womanly sympathy, gentleness, and patience, womanly insight and thoughtfulness in little things." Blackwell analogously saw treatment of the poor dependent on the feminine qualities of "pity" and "patience," arguing that "[t]he attitude of the student and doctor to the sick poor is a real test of the true physician."[19]

The presumption that medicine represents a "natural" female function gains additional credence when one turns to Jex-Blake's writings and her tracing of medical women throughout history. Though Rhoda herself does not make the argument that Victorian female physicians are simply following in their maternal ancestors' footprints, the fact that Rhoda's fictional history is, in part, based on Jex-Blake's own experiences provides an important link. The latter's musings on the subject built upon Victorian preconceptions in underscoring the nurturing capabilities of females through the centuries. From ancient times, Jex-Blake

18. Blackwell, *Essays in Medical Sociology,* 2:9, 10, 12.
19. Millicent Garrett Fawcett, "The Emancipation of Women," 674; Blackwell, *Essays in Medical Sociology,* 1:13.

wrote, women applied various treatments to ease the suffering of others, and that practice served as "the germ of the future profession of medicine." Jex-Blake adumbrated the domestic abilities of women to provide additional support for her gender-based argument. Women's quotidian activities in aiding a hurt child, assisting an ailing individual living in an isolated countryside, or the like brought her to conclude "that women are *naturally* inclined and fitted for medical practice." In effect, Jex-Blake suggests, medical practice merely represents the expansion of the domestic sphere.[20]

With all of the presumed "evidence" that *A Woman-Hater*, like several Victorian essayists, musters to trace an essentialist link between women and medicine, the novel must turn to other grounds in discerning the reason for their virtual exclusion from the profession. Blatant self-interest on the part of male practitioners is wholly blamed for the female ostracism, as Rhoda's own history demonstrates. The medical profession is merely a type of union, the novel argues, with "an overpowering interest to exclude qualified women," just as other unions seek to protect their own (196). The novel appeals to the British sense of justice and fairness in assailing the exclusionary practices, asserting that women not only were "robbed . . . of their old common-law rights," but the "trades-union . . . thrust them out of their new statutory rights." The issue takes on even greater importance as the narrator asserts that "it matters greatly to *mankind* whether the whole race of women are to be allowed to study medicine, and practise it" or if they can "be debarred" and "outlawed . . . in defiance of British liberty" (194).

A Woman-Hater was not alone in comparing the medical profession to a union; Cobbe would make the same claim in "The Medical Profession and Its Morality." After noting that "[t]he pecuniary prizes within reach of a successful surgeon or physician are enormous," Cobbe attributed the exclusion of women to avarice. "Never, indeed, has there been a more absurd public manifestation of trades-unionism," she argued, "than this effort to keep ladies out of the lucrative profession of physicians" and instead "crowd them into the ill-paid one of nurses." Earlier, Cobbe warned that "doctors are daily assuming authority which [is], at first, perhaps, legitimate and beneficial, [but] has a prevailing

20. Jex-Blake, *Medical Women*, 5, 6.

tendency to become meddling and despotic." She added that "in every department of public and private life the doctors are acquiring power and influence, and coming to the front."[21]

"UNWOMANLY" WOMAN

A Woman-Hater's insistence that women are innately and uniquely qualified for the medical profession at first glance seems to be undercut, however, by the representation of Rhoda herself as a masculine individual. To the womanizer Severne, for instance, Rhoda is "an extraordinary woman, but too masculine for his taste," who should recognize that "her true line"—and most appropriate—is to become a governess (242). To the highly feminine Zoe, Rhoda lacks womanly attractions, boasting "not one beautiful feature in her whole face"; instead, Rhoda has a "large" mouth, "ivory" rather than "pearl" teeth, and an "ordinary" chin (251). To Zoe as well as Fanny, Rhoda is "an irrelevant zealot, who talked neither love nor dress, nor anything that reaches the [feminine] soul" (343). To a villager, Rhoda is "not a young lady" in appearance but wears "plain boots . . . and a felt hat like a boy" (296). In fact, Rhoda looks like "the parish had dressed her for ten shillings, and got a pot of beer out on't" (296–97).

As Rhoda's determined ally and respectful friend, Harrington offers the most useful assessment of her femininity, for his apparent bias in her favor positions him as her strongest advocate and the likeliest character to praise her virtues. Though effusively complimentary of her intellectual talents and vocational ambition, Harrington views Rhoda as a masculine anomaly, with only brief references to feminine traits.[22] After hearing Rhoda's history, for example, Harrington concludes that she appeared "a very brave little fellow, damnably ill used"; he "forgave the

21. Cobbe, "Medical Profession," 301, 323, 297, 299.

22. As Elton E. Smith remarks, "the qualities woman-hater Vizard admires in Dr. Gale are those of an attractive and deserving boy" (*Charles Reade*, 132–33). See also Finkelstein's discussion of Rhoda as "a sexually ambiguous individual" ("Woman Hater," 345–46). Swenson comments that "Reade is careful not to 'unsex' his heroine entirely, compensating for her 'masculine' traits with a feminine sensibility." Swenson adds that the novel's "androgynous doctor remains ambiguously strange and frightening" (*Medical Women and Victorian Fiction*, 99).

poor girl her petticoats" and "lost sight of them" (247). Rhoda "speak[s] out like a man," he comments (337), and at one point he chastises her for a perceived attempt "to play the woman," which he designates as "an abominable breach of faith" for this "third grace, a virago" of "solidified vinegar" (290). In these assessments, Harrington mimics not only the scientific but also the religious discourses circulating in Victorian culture that considered an extensive education as causing the "unsexing" of women. Christianity, Rhoda mentions, designates the "[w]oman's sphere [as] the hearth" and fears the sex would be unsexed by study, with her "brain four ounces lighter than a man's" and her inability "to cope with long study and practical science" (205). "In short," Rhoda adds, a woman "was too good, and too stupid, for medicine."

In other respects as well, Rhoda's actions suggest "unwomanly" behavior. She muses that she would readily don a "boy's clothes" and pose "as a common sailor" to visit her mother (252), for instance, and at one point positions herself "not like a woman, but a brave boy" seeking to conceal tears (254). Her reaction to an exquisite garden is most unfeminine, for her exclamation "Oh, what a garden!" is uttered not in response to its beauties but to its scientific offerings (342). "Come along," she instructs Zoe and Fanny, "and I will tell you their names and properties." As the villager noted, Rhoda's dress is customarily plain and unfeminine, chosen for its utility rather than attractiveness. Unlike Zoe and Fanny, Rhoda never speaks of improving her clothing or physical attributes but instead keeps her comments focused on medical concerns. In fact, Rhoda rhetorically separates herself from other women, opining that "[t]hey are such geese at times, every one of them," as she appraises "a woman's impulse" (510).

Moreover, Rhoda repeatedly attacks the traditionally feminine accomplishment of music, revealing a distaste so intense that it borders on obsession. Rhoda "hated music like poison" (404), and she proclaims on more than one occasion that women "are, by nature, the medical and *unmusical* sex" (226, my emphasis), as if the two proclivities exist in total opposition. Rhoda's dislike of music can be traced to maternal influence, and the fact that the mother has been presented as a highly admirable figure gives credence to Rhoda's negative reaction. In girlhood, Rhoda's mother insisted that "[m]usic extracts what little brains a girl has" and consequently refused to allow Rhoda to "waste a single minute over music" (185). Rhoda's vitriolic assessment of music seems odd, though, in light of the fact that the only other impressive female character in the novel is the professional singer Ina, of whom Rhoda becomes extraordinarily fond. This apparent inconsistency can be explained through the novel's Lamarckian and Darwinian perspectives, however, as I shall later consider.

Rhoda's affection for Ina leads as well to another apparent evidentiary proof of the physician's "unwomanliness." Unlike the feminine icon Zoe, for instance, whose emotional attachment to the unsavory Severne is typical of female affection in Victorian fiction, Rhoda "was not of an amorous temperament" (388); she avers, like a detached scientist, that love is "a fever of the mind" (191), which "disturbs the judgment, and perverts the conscience" (192). Tellingly, a lack of interest in a male mate makes her "all the more open to female attachments" (388). The bond Rhoda forges with Ina—and, to a lesser extent, with Zoe—carries a distinct homoerotic component.[23] Even though Victorian female friendships were frequently depicted in effusive and amatory language, the depth of Rhoda's fondness for Ina seems, at first glance, too pronounced to represent a typical sororal reaction. Indeed, Rhoda shifts affection to Ina after a brief but unrequited interest in Zoe; Rhoda, the narrator asserts, "was in love with Zoe" (336).

Rhoda's amatory bond with Ina commences with the singer's need for medical attention, which obliquely forges a connection between a woman's practice of medicine and an unnatural affectional preference, which had remained mostly dormant in interactions with Zoe. As Rhoda cares for the ailing Ina, the physician's attraction becomes increasingly apparent, proceeding from a general humanitarian reaction that "[m]y own heart bleeds for her" (368) to a jealous fascination that causes her to act "almost like a male lover defending the object of his affection" (388). "I dote on her," Rhoda tells Harrington. She gazes upon the recovering Ina like a lover assessing his beloved's physical attractions: "How beautiful she is with her sweet lips parted, and her white teeth peeping, and her upper and lower lashes wedded! and how graceful!" (462). Rhoda insists she loves Ina "better than any man can love her" (408),

23. Critical commentary has also pointed to the homoerotic elements of the novel; see, for example, Swenson, *Medical Women and Victorian Fiction*, 99–101; Finkelstein, "Woman Hater," 345–46; and Smith, *Charles Reade*, 133.

demonstrating affection by such actions as "enfolding her delicately" as the physician "laid a pair of wet eyes softly on her shoulder" (404). Eventually, Rhoda spirits the patient away to promote the singer's recuperation, tending to her like a devoted spouse and sleeping with her in a tender embrace (475). After a healthy Ina departs, Rhoda pens "loveletters twice a week" (486) and happily rejoins the singer upon the latter's request. Though the women "communed till two o'clock in the morning," the narrator relegates the details of their reunion to the interstices of the text with the comment that "the limits of my tale forbid me to repeat what passed," as if inappropriate for the Victorian reader (490). Shortly thereafter, when the pair again separates, Rhoda laments that "I must give up loving women," for "they throw me over the moment a man comes, if it happens to be the right one" (510). When Ina fails to correspond, Rhoda reacts like a spurned lover in commenting that Ina wrote "[n]ot a line, the monster!" (511).

Yet Rhoda's fervent attraction to Ina must be assessed within the context of other female bonds in the novel. Both Zoe and Ina, the two feminine models, utter extravagant expressions of affection for women while wielding the sexual power of a forceful gaze. When Zoe first looks intently upon Ina, performing as Siebel, she claims that Ina "fixed [her eyes] on me, and they magnetized me, and drew me to her" (46). "Now, if I was a man," Zoe continues, "I should love that woman, and make her love me." Subsequently, Zoe "rapturously" identifies Ina as "*my* Siebel" (100), and she labors to arrange a meeting with the entrancing singer. Ina, on her part, returns the interest. While performing as Siebel, Ina notices the lovely Zoe, whom she deems "such a beautiful creature, with black hair and eyes!" (45). Zoe's "glorious eyes," Ina continues, "speak to mine, and inspire me," causing Ina to "drink sunbeams at her." As the performance ends, Zoe flings a bouquet to the singer, who "fixed her eyes on Zoe, and then put her hand to her heart with a most touching gesture, that said, 'Most of all I value your bouquet and your praise'" (49). When Zoe informs her half-brother that she intends to call upon Ina and meet her in person, the young woman exclaims, "I am sure of my welcome. How often must I tell you that we have mesmerized each other, that lady and I; and are only waiting an opportunity to rush into each other's arms!" (112). Long after the two meet, Ina recalls their first encounter as she again fixes her gaze on Zoe. "Let me look at you," Ina says (376). "Ah! you are beautiful. When I saw you at the theatre you fascinated me!"

Ina's reaction to Rhoda is even more effusive. Once under Rhoda's medical care, Ina returns the intense displays of affection that the physician makes. Ina comments, for example, that she will "sing for love" before finally gathering Rhoda "to her bosom" (382). When Rhoda gently chastises her as a "naughty patient," Ina responds with the appellations, "[s]weet physician" and "loving nurse," and she punctuates later comments to her caretaker with similar phrases of endearment. Rhoda subsequently remarks that Ina "is beginning to love me" (388), and their mutual feeling is evidenced by the women's departure from the Vizard estate to coexist in solitude while the patient regains her health. In their new quarters, "these two friends slept together in each other's arms" (475). After the pair has separated and reunited, Ina "enveloped Rhoda in her arms, and rested a hot cheek against hers" (488). Ina then "dismissed her dresser, at Rhoda's request, and Rhoda filled that office" so that, the narrator ambiguously comments, "they could talk freely" (489).

Despite these avowals of affection on the part of Ina as well as Zoe, the homoerotic element is channeled into heterosexual relationships. Zoe's exclamations of regard for Ina occur as she is being wooed by Severne, whose amatory interest Zoe returns; Ina's interest in Zoe arises as the singer is herself endeavoring to rejoin Severne, her secretly errant husband. Because neither woman ultimately achieves success with the loathsome Severne, the homoerotic encounters seem to suggest his inappropriateness as a mate. Since the women are expressing desire for each other, the text implies that Severne cannot function as an adequate object of desire for either; consequently, the women's mutual affection interrupts a textual move toward closure that so frequently in Victorian fiction comes through a satisfying heterosexual union. In a sense, the homoerotic bond disrupts textual momentum toward closure, suspending the narrative to allow events to take place that will enable the proper marriages of Zoe with Lord Uxmoor and Ina with Harrington.

Rhoda's overt affection for Ina can be attributed to a similar textual motivation but with a slightly different twist. Though Rhoda enacts the role of jealous lover, she seeks to protect Ina from questionable attachments. Suspecting Ina's relationship with Severne and fearing that the smitten Harrington will entangle himself in a murky situation, Rhoda explains her fierce protectiveness of the convalescing singer to the squire:

> She is not to love any man again, who will not marry her. I won't let her. I'll kill her first, I love her so; a rogue she shan't marry, and I can't let you marry her, because her connection with that Severne is mysterious. She seems the soul of virtue, but I could not let *you* marry her until things are clearer. (388)

Despite Rhoda's extreme affection for Ina, it is not the singer's heterosexual relationships that Rhoda enviously guards against, but an inappropriate match—a crucial concern in the novelistic economy.

EVOLUTIONARY LINK

Since marriage (or death) tends to be the common fate for a Victorian female character, whether a feminine icon or transgressive rebel, the fact that Rhoda not only does not marry but never even reveals a glimmer of romantic interest in a male character raises an interesting question: why does the novel not match her with a suitable male partner with whom she could bear children and pass along her vast knowledge to the next generation? After all, despite Rhoda's masculine propensities, the novel has labored to depict her as an admirable individual marked by the worthy traits of intelligence, honor, dedication, humanity, and loyalty. Yet, as Rhoda emphasizes, "[f]alling in love is not my business" (341). The explanation lies within the complex web of Victorian gender and scientific discourses, whereby Rhoda can be viewed as a transitional form in an evolutionary process that borrows from both Jean-Baptiste Lamarck and Darwin in a curious melding of divergent approaches.

As my analysis of Rhoda thus far has indicated, the physician displays both masculine and feminine qualities. The result is an awkward, imperfect blending of masculinity and femininity, reflected in part by Harrington's persistent references to Rhoda as a "virago," a term that would be employed so frequently later in the century to connote the unruly New Woman and invoke a powerful, masculinized anomaly. Harrington attests to the admixture of gender qualities—masculine authority and feminine manipulation—in his protégé when he informs a visitor wishing to converse with the convalescing Ina that "as we are all under the orders of her physician, and that physician is a woman, and a bit of a vixen, you must allow me to go and consult her first" (411).[24]

Somewhat surprisingly, in light of the emphasis on masculinity that will follow, Rhoda's feminine side is accentuated in her initial depiction. That description focuses on fragility and modesty in almost every phrase describing her encounter with Harrington as she is in the throes of hunger, with only an occasional hint of unwomanly resistance:

> He looked at her,—a tall, slim, young lady, black merino, by no means new, clean cuffs and collar, leaning against the chair for support, and yet sacrificing herself to conventional propriety, and even withstanding him with a pretty little air of defiance that was pitiable, her pallor and the weakness of her body considered.
> . . . She looked him up and down very keenly, and at last, with a slight expression of feminine approval, the first she had vouchsafed him. Then she folded her arms, and leveled her little nose at him like a bayonet. (180)

Furthermore, she fears to relate her history because "I am afraid I could not tell it to you without crying" (182), a feminine inclination to which she surrenders upon other emotional occasions in the novel. "[A] daughter of Eve," Rhoda is characterized in essentialist terms through "her insidious questions, her artful statements, her cat-like retreats and cat-like returns" (303), and Harrington designates her as woman in commenting, "Who can resist this fatal sex?" (333). Rhoda is prone to blushing (328)—a female tendency, as Darwin pointed out, and one strongly associated with the feminine Zoe.[25] She even "looked beautiful for the moment" as "her face was transfigured" when excited about improving the villagers' diet (338). So emotional does she become moments thereafter that she appears on the verge of fainting (339), like a distraught Victorian heroine. When Ina is struck by the blackguard

24. Swenson comments that Reade's novel "reveals a distinct unease about Rhoda: ambiguity about the New Woman," whom Rhoda anticipates, "is expressed as moral and sexual ambiguity about Rhoda Gale" (*Medical Women and Victorian Fiction*, 98–99).
25. In *The Expression of the Emotions in Man and Animals*, Darwin devoted an entire chapter to blushing, commenting that "[w]omen blush much more than men" (310).

Severne, Rhoda's nerves "shook, for a moment" (372), which recalls the scientific estimations that a woman's nervous system is more delicate and easily disrupted than a man's. Despite her professional function, Rhoda is designated by the narrator more frequently as "Miss Gale" than as a physician, suggesting her primary identification as a woman rather than a practitioner.

Also, as Kristine Swenson has commented, Rhoda depends on the robust patriarchal figures of Harrington and Lord Uxmoor for her opportunity to practice medicine.[26] Without their avid support and standing in the community, Rhoda would meet irresistible pressures that would preclude her from actively entering the profession. To one villager, for example, Rhoda is "a young 'oman a prowling about this here parish, as don't belong to *hus*" (323), adding that "I don't want no women-folk to come here a-doctoring o' me, that's sartin" (324). As Zoe advises the elderly woman declaiming against "she-doctoresses," it is through Harrington's "invitation" that Rhoda is tending to the villagers (326). "She has his authority," Zoe explains, yet suggests that Rhoda's ability to practice is totally subject to his desires, for her brother "wishes to *try* one [female physician]" (326). Similarly, the medical establishment's efforts to exclude Rhoda from the local infirmary crumble through male intervention, which arises after "she went almost crying to Vizard," who "exploded with wrath" and, along with Lord Uxmoor, threatened to withdraw necessary financial support (526).

Yet, as the novel has demonstrated so insistently, Rhoda is by no means a model of womanhood, especially since her masculine qualities tend to overshadow her feminine traits. In that regard, Rhoda does resemble the "unsexed" individual that Victorian scientists warned would result from extensive education. Being "unsexed" implies an inability to reproduce, for the term innately suggests that an entity lacks sexual potency. If Rhoda is effectually asexual, but many of her attributes are considered worthy of reproduction, how can this problematic situation be resolved within the marriage-plot economy of the novel?

One solution is to assess Rhoda as a kind of necessary mutation, but too extreme of an oddity in Victorian culture to survive through future generations in current form. Instead, Rhoda acts as a crucial

---

26. Swenson, *Medical Women and Victorian Fiction*, 96–97.

shaping influence on other characters, who are altered in significant ways through her unique perspectives and actions in a kind of Lamarckian process of alteration. Preceding Darwin, Lamarck argued that intentionality could bring forth evolutionary change, a point that Darwin disputed but that Victorians nevertheless found enticing, as scholarship has noted. Under the Lamarckian scenario, the womanly ideal, Ina, and the physician's advocate, Harrington, provide the vehicles for producing a reconfigured conception of gender possibilities in their own eventual offspring—following the customary Victorian progression from marriage to breeding—by passing their altered perceptions to a new generation. We have already witnessed the many ways in which Ina epitomizes positive qualities of womanhood, but Harrington may, at first glance, seem a more curious exemplar of manhood. His misogyny, however, is connected solely to the feminine attributes selected out in Darwinian fashion by Victorian society that reinforce fragility, superficiality, and frivolity as noteworthy qualities, the type of misguided approach that Mona Caird cautioned against in her writings on human development. As Severne comments in a rare moment of insight, Harrington "despises the whole sex—in theory; and he is very hard upon ordinary women, . . . [b]ut, when he meets a remarkable woman, he catches fire" (244). Although Severne is alluding to Harrington's romantic interest in Ina, the same response holds true for his interactions with the remarkable Rhoda. His misogynistic leanings tend to be cast aside during his many encounters with and discussions about her, suggesting a discerning sense of character and admirable abilities that allow him to recognize Rhoda's worth and potential. Once the misogynistic aspect of his personality is bracketed off, Harrington's many "manly" traits are apparent: loyalty, generosity, intelligence, protectiveness, assertiveness, and judiciousness, to name merely a representative sample. As a respected member of the landed gentry—wealthy, paternal, and socially conscious—Harrington occupies an enviable position in the class structure, too. Coupled with his positive personality traits, his social status works to position him as a Victorian masculine ideal, a suitable counterpart to the admirable Ina.

With all of her enviable qualities, Ina in some respects could seem to represent a pinnacle of female development to the Victorian mind, as I have suggested. Nevertheless, with the introduction of Rhoda to the text, the reader is exposed to a host of other positive traits that offer possibilities for proceeding to the next stage of evolutionary growth. In that scenario, the near-perfect "womanliness" of an Ina can be combined with the extraordinary intelligence of a Rhoda to produce an acutely incisive yet wholly feminine individual. Applied to the specific medical concerns of the novel, this melding of characteristics would presumably create the ideal woman physician; such a figure would build upon the "innate" qualities that, as the novel has argued, uniquely suit women for medical practice without sacrificing what are perceived as the best aspects of essentialized womanhood.

In this evolutionary schemata, Rhoda's strong aversion to music functions is an important response because it serves as a general commentary on femininity. This traditional female accomplishment, like other gender-imbued practices, gains value only when it becomes a means to a more important end. As the narrator remarks, Rhoda "despised music on its own merits, but she despised nothing that could be pressed into the service of medicine" (392). If that statement is extrapolated, conventional feminine behaviors as a whole gain value only when they are considered intermediary steps leading to a higher level of female evolution. Ina, as a professional singer, has carried the feminized faculty of musicality to its utmost limits; for the female of the human species to reach the next evolutionary stage, women must move beyond the constraints on their vast potentialities that Victorian culture has established.

The homoerotic relationship between Ina and Rhoda also participates in this evolutionary process. As I have commented, Ina adopts affectionate phrases in addressing Rhoda, but it is important to consider that these terms almost entirely focus on Rhoda's capacity as a physician. Also, Ina's marked fondness for Rhoda emerges only after the singer comes under Rhoda's medical care, suggesting that Ina's admiration is inextricably linked to her companion's medical skills. A kind of metonymic Lamarckian relationship obtains here; through the physician's proximity, Ina is herself altered as a genuine respect and regard for Rhoda's talents emerges and expands. In a sense, Ina has been "modified"; the modifications she has experienced ostensibly can then be transmitted to her offspring, who would presumably display a more advanced view than that of the previous generation in recognizing and validating a woman's desire to become a physician. As Elizabeth Blackwell stated, "We see as a positive fact that mental or moral qualities quite as much as physical peculiarities, tend to reproduce themselves in children."[27]

Since the novel does not confer on Rhoda the ability to produce off-spring, she can alter the course of female development only through her influence on those women who can. Intriguingly, the "very sprightly and commanding" Rhoda—an adjectival phrase suggesting masculine assertiveness—is compared to Diana, the virginal goddess who also invokes masculine connotations through a proclivity for hunting, while a "pale" and delicate Ina is compared to Juno, the goddess of marriage (457). Through Rhoda's homoerotic response to Ina, then, the unfeminine physician effectually bonds with a "true woman" who will serve as the evolutionary vehicle for the next level of female development. To a lesser extent, a similar process unfolds through Rhoda's effect on Zoe. Though Zoe initially considers Rhoda an oddity because the latter shows no interest in fashion, romance, and other feminine pursuits, Zoe's perceptions change dramatically, to such an extent that Zoe "became devoted to her" (502). Like Ina, Zoe will presumably bear children, which again bodes well for the next generation; Zoe's husband, the "manly" Lord Uxmoor (38), is, like Harrington, an admirable figure who similarly values Rhoda's talents as a physician.

The evolutionary strain emerges in more general terms as well through the novel's assessment of women's role in human development as a whole. In its plea for admission of women to the practice of medicine, *A Woman-Hater* argues that "[t]he good effect on the whole mind of woman would be incalculable":

> Great prizes of study and genius offered to the able few have always a salutary and wonderful operation on the many who never gain them. It would be great and glad tidings to our whole female youth to say, "You *need* not be frivolous idlers; . . . you need not waste three hours of the short working day in dressing and undressing, and combing your hair. You need not throw away the very seed-time of life . . . on your three 'C's'—croquet, crochet, and coquetry. . . ."
>
> I say that this prize, and frequent intercourse with those superior women who have won it, would leave the whole sex with higher views of life than enter their heads at present; would raise their self-

27. Blackwell, *Essays in Medical Sociology,* 1:201.

respect, and set thousands of them to study the great and noble things that are in medicine, and connected with it, instead of child-ish things. (531)

Indeed, the novel's final words reinforce the notion that improving women's intellectual opportunities through medical study would benefit the human species in its entirety:[28]

> . . . [I]t will give the larger half of the nation an honorable am-bition, and an honorable pursuit, towards which their hearts and instincts are bent by Nature herself; it will tend to elevate this whole sex, and its young children, male as well as female, and so will ad-vance the civilization of the world, which in ages past, in our day, and in all time, hath, and doth, and will keep step exactly with the progress of women towards mental equality with men. (532–33)

Elizabeth Blackwell made the same point in arguing that "the progress of the race demands that the intellectual horizons be enlarged, and the understanding strengthened by the observation and reasoning which will give increased efficiency to those moral qualities" that women in-nately possess. According to Blackwell, "The intellectual training re-quired for the physician is admirably adapted to supply deficiencies in the ordinary experience of women."[29] Rhoda's own experience attests to the notion that women would be improved through medical study, as she recalls her student days. "There was not an anti-student or downright flirt amongst us," she tells Harrington. "[A]nd, indeed, I have observed that an earnest love of study and science controls the amorous frivolity of women even more than men's" (209).

The novel's contention that the advancement of the human species depends to a large extent on improving the condition of women rever-berates with some contemporary scientific discourses as well. Even one reactionary zoologist, W. K. Brooks, traced the connection. "The study

28. Blackwell also cited "the great value that enthusiasm for natural science would be to woman, value to the individual life, to the home life, and to society" (ibid., 2:208–9). She noted that "[i]nterest in natural objects, careful, comprehensive observation of them, enthusiasm for unselfish and impersonal ends, are the main principles of scientific study—principles that would enter with invigorating force into the mental development of every girl, that would regenerate the life of women" (2:207).

29. Ibid., 2:12, 14.

of the growth of civilization shows that human advancement has been accompanied by a slow but constant improvement in the condition of women, as compared with men, and that it may be very accurately measured by this standard," Brooks wrote shortly after *A Woman-Hater* was published. "Judging from the past," he continued, "we may be sure that one of the paths for the future progress of the race lies in this improvement, and the position of women must therefore be regarded as a most important social problem."[30]

In calling for the encouragement, nurturance, and acceptance of female physicians, *A Woman-Hater* trod revolutionary ground at a time when female pioneers were entrenched in the battle to become physicians. With the talented and dedicated Rhoda Gale, the novel offered a seemingly new and exciting script for the Victorian woman, moving beyond the standard possibilities of marriage and maternity. Indeed, an 1886 essay titled "Aesculapia Victrix" traced the astounding change in the situation of women seeking to enter the medical profession in the previous decade. "Little more than ten years ago," wrote Robert Wilson, "the mere suggestion that a woman might be encouraged to practice medicine simply horrified decent people. . . . Now, however, this foolish prejudice scarcely exists." He added, "That women *are* practicing medicine with much popular acceptance and success both in private practice and in dispensaries and hospitals proves the reality of the need or demand for their services."[31]

As the century moved to its final year, the *Spectator* enthused about women's accomplishments in scientific study and predicted broader acceptance in future generations. In assessing the situation thirty years earlier, "when women first made their demand for more thorough education," the *Spectator* recalled the presumption that women "would never do anything in mathematics or science." Instead, "[t]he whole educational history of that period shows that women have a distinct proclivity towards science and mathematics." Despite such a pronouncement, the *Spectator* piece revealed the essentialist perspective that continued to inform scientific views of women. "The truth is, we believe, that women, so far from being incapable of studying the exact sciences, have a natural

30. Brooks, "Condition of Women I," 145.
31. Robert Wilson, "Aesculapia Victrix," 18–19, 27.

capacity for comprehending them," the essay said. Women's "defect," the *Spectator* continued, "is not want of the power of rigid thinking, but deficiency of imagination as well as of creative force." Nonetheless, women's "ratiocinative faculties are admirable, and they can learn anything which requires only logical deduction from accepted facts." That is, "[t]hey can think along a groove, so to speak, better than men."[32]

A Woman-Hater leaves the reader with a disturbing message that essentialist qualities, derived from centuries of preconceptions of a female "nature," enable women to fulfill the role of caring physician. In validating essentialism while opening a virtually uncharted vocational path, *A Woman-Hater* forecloses cultural change even while apparently promoting it. In the final analysis, then, *A Woman-Hater* undermines its feminist pretensions and reifies unsettling perceptions of femininity.

32. "Women and Science," 409, 410.

Afterword

Prince Albert once said that "facts are 'objective' and belong to everybody," but as the preceding chapters have shown, such a conclusion must be viewed skeptically when we consider Victorian perceptions of science and gender in late-century literature.[1] The texts I have analyzed in this study serve as especially illustrative examples of the ways in which science could be manipulated, in a far from "objective" manner, to reinforce gender assumptions. Nevertheless, it is instructive to glance at other literary offerings of the time that sought both to reify and contest gender suppositions, though few other texts feature female characters as centrally concerned with science. My study has focused mainly on literary writings appearing in the 1870s and 1880s, but a glimpse at other texts not only in those decades but also in the 1890s offers a helpful perspective.

Surprisingly, even in the latter part of the 1870s, several years after *The Descent of Man* appeared, gendered science received fairly limited literary attention, as did science itself. In comparison to the plethora of nonfiction essays and books on science, we might expect more literary treatment of the topic. Along with the 1876 *Daniel Deronda* and 1879 *The Egoist* mentioned in my introductory chapter, one of the relatively few scientifically attuned literary examples is Hardy's 1878 *The Return of the Native*, with its Egdon Heath seemingly existing since far back in the recesses of time, as if "it had waited . . . unmoved, during so many centuries, through the crises of so many things." The heath, with its terrain displaying "[e]ver since the beginning of vegetation . . . the same

1. Prince Albert, "Science and the State," 52.

215

antique brown dress," revealed "an ancient permanence which the sea cannot claim" and "remained as the very finger-touches of the last geological change" had worked upon it.[2] Yet the novel's scientific aspects evoke Darwin's *Origin of Species* rather than *Descent* with Hardy's narrative repeatedly reminding its readers of the vast time scale behind earthly formations. Olive Schreiner's *From Man to Man,* initiated in the 1870s but not appearing in finished form for half a century, does touch upon gender and science with protagonist Rebekah's fascination with geological and botanical study; yet the linkage does not constitute an overriding aspect of the narrative.[3]

In the 1880s, a few novels featuring medical women appeared, now buried in obscurity. As noted in my second chapter, a few of Constance Naden's contemporaries found Darwinian ideas intriguing but tended to focus on broader issues of human and animal development. When science was coupled with gender, as in Naden's oeuvre, the results could be dismaying. May Kendall, though she wrote several poems based upon evolutionary ideas without expressly addressing gender, as did her contemporary Mary Robinson, took issue in "Woman's Future" with the essentialist presumptions typical of *Descent.* With reference to a seemingly monolithic "they," the poem disputes the contention that "[o]ur intellects, bound by a limit decisive, / To the level of Homer's may never arise." Instead, citing "the falsehood, the base innuendo," the speaker proclaims that "[o]ur talents shall rise in a mighty crescendo, / We trust Evolution to make us amends!" Proceeding to assail women's tendency to bow before social pressures and follow traditional feminine pursuits, the speaker urges women to reach their full potential and "rouse to a lifework—do something worth doing!" Mathilde Blind's 1889 *The Ascent of Man,* replete with evolutionary language reflecting *Origin,* briefly addresses *Descent*'s gender aspects in invoking the process of sexual selection as life forms began to develop. Males in the animal kingdom were "[p]roudly displaying in the sun / With antics strange and looks elate, / The vigour of their mighty thews / Or charm of million-coloured

2. Thomas Hardy, *The Return of the Native,* 10, 12.

3. As Henkin comments, Rebekah is "a sincere student of botany and geology" who seeks spare moments for pursuing these interests. "There amid her fossils and botanical specimens, debating with herself, she spins out her lengthy thoughts on the survival of the fittest which are duly recorded in her notebooks" (*Darwinism in the English Novel,* 217).

hues." Darwin's claims, made in more prosaic terms, were summarized by Blind: rival males sought to "win the prize / Of those impassive female eyes."[4]

The most familiar of scientifically attuned novels of the 1880s, *The Strange Case of Dr. Jekyll and Mr. Hyde,* made a statement on science and gender through omission with an almost complete exclusion of women, as scholarship has remarked. It is as if, by avoiding virtually all female presence in the domain of science, the 1886 narrative is suggesting that women are neither necessary nor desirable participants within it. One could even surmise that the menacing Mr. Hyde is a manifestation of the feminine, a monstrous presence that prevents Dr. Jekyll from surviving and flourishing. In H. Rider Haggard's most significant novels, the 1885 *King Solomon's Mines* and 1887 *She,* also notable in critical commentary for their depiction of exclusionary male spaces, the connection between gender and science arises briefly through the horrific devolutionary figures of the evil Gagool and the aggressive Ayesha. Gagool, a "wizened monkey-like figure," who "crept on all fours" and displays the mannerisms of a serpent, is, in brief, "very terrible." Ayesha assumes similar simian form in her death throes, as she shrinks into a wrinkled baboonlike creature with talonlike appendages that is "hideous—ah, too hideous for words." Both women, of course, pose dangers to the male protagonists who populate the novels, and they must be destroyed.[5]

When we turn to the 1890s, the intersections between science and gender are frequently treated most intriguingly in novels penned by women. Their interest perhaps could be attributed not only to the cultural anxieties of the late century and continuing nervousness over the Woman Question, but also to the fact that female authors, simply by virtue of their own personal experience as women, were more attuned than their male counterparts to the gender implications of scientific conclusions. Nevertheless, the gender ramifications of evolutionary and historical time are disturbingly evident in Hardy's 1891 *Tess of the D'Urber-*

4. May Kendall, "Woman's Future"; Mathilde Blind, *The Ascent of Man,* 11, 12.

5. As Janice Doane and Devon Hodges state, "many descriptions of Hyde's physical characteristics are congruent with cultural descriptions of femininity" ("Demonic Disturbances of Sexual Identity: The Strange Case of Dr. Jekyll and Mr/s Hyde," 69). Doane and Hodges also point to Julia Kristeva's notion of abjection and a "concern for separating the sexes" (73). H. Rider Haggard, *King Solomon's Mines* (147, 148), and Haggard, *She* (293, 294).

villes and 1895 *Jude the Obscure*, for example, though the narratives also apply their Darwinian precepts to humanity as a whole.[6]

Three female-authored 1890s novels that carry important observations about gender and science are especially noteworthy: Mona Caird's *The Daughters of Danaus* and Sarah Grand's *The Heavenly Twins* and *The Beth Book*. Caird's 1894 novel, like her two-part nonfiction essay titled "Phases of Human Development" published the same year, assails Victorian society's validation of mediocre female characteristics that are reinforced at the expense of productive variations being allowed to flourish and prevail. As the main character, Hadria, laments, "It is cunning, shallow, heartless women, who really fare best in our society. . . . *That is the sort of 'woman's nature' that our conditions are busy selecting.*" Grand's enormously successful *Heavenly Twins*, published the same year as Caird's novel, made a similar argument in decrying the presumption that women were physiologically destined to be intellectually inferior. Instead, the novel emphasizes, cultural conditions and preconceptions were responsible for the perceived lack of cognitive ability. A few years later, in the 1897 *The Beth Book*, Grand would argue in the characterization of the eponymous protagonist that women's intellectual abilities not only matched but also could exceed those of men.[7]

As in previous years, fiction on medical women also appeared, written by both men and women.[8] Although other novels of the 1890s also reveal perceptions of gender and science, only rarely are women treated in a positive way, perhaps attributable in part to male authorship. Like *Dr. Jekyll and Mr. Hyde*, H. G. Wells's 1896 *The Island of Dr. Moreau* excludes female presence from the realm of science, at least in terms of human presence. As scholarship has discussed, the novel's excruciating experimentation upon a female puma can be read as an attack upon the New Woman, and the island's hazardous terrain takes on a decidedly feminine cast.[9] Bram Stoker's 1897 *Dracula* analogously makes scientific

6. I explore this topic, with primary focus on *Tess*, in my volume *Time Is of the Essence: Temporality, Gender, and the New Woman*.
7. Mona Caird, *The Daughters of Danaus*, 347. *Time Is of the Essence* examines these novels in detail, with gendered science among the study's concerns.
8. For discussion of such novels, see Swenson, *Medical Women and Victorian Fiction*.
9. As Elaine Showalter comments in *Sexual Anarchy: Gender and Culture at the Fin de Siècle*, the puma serves as "a kind of New Woman figure, or shrieking sister, who indeed reacts to the torture 'with a shriek almost like that of an angry virago'" (179).

endeavor the province of men while women function as objects to be acted upon. Lucy Westenra's harrowing demise as her "undead" form is repeatedly stabbed under the direction of Dr. Van Helsing is obviously the most dramatic example, but Mina Harker, too, becomes an object of medical scrutiny.

All of the post-*Descent* literary writings that I have investigated in the preceding chapters offer a cautionary tale that is highly significant today. It is tempting for us, as individuals considering Victorian culture from the vantage point of the early twenty-first century, to see our own approach to science as immeasurably more astute, rigorous, and verifiable. More than a hundred years after the Victorian period came to a close, however, the marginalization of women by and from science, albeit less intensely, continues.[10] The comforting belief that our culture is a far more enlightened one than that of our Victorian predecessors is, at least in regard to women and science, a rather illusory one. As perceptive feminist observers of our era have amply demonstrated, cultural verities still affect scientific approaches and conclusions, and women still are being represented by the discipline in troubling ways. Though the absurdity of many Victorian scientific truisms—the belief that the mental ability of males dramatically exceeds that of females, for instance—is readily recognized, of course, more subtle preconceptions remain to inform scientific methodologies, practices, and outcomes. A careful evaluation of the myriad ways in which conceptions of gendered science shaped late Victorian literature is crucial not only for our comprehension of the nineteenth century, but for our own time as well.

10. See also Malane on the current situation (*Sex in Mind*, 203–5).

Bibliography

Adams, J. F. A. "Is Botany a Suitable Study for Young Men?" *Science* 9 (February 4, 1887): 116–17.

Albert, Prince. "Science and the State." In *Victorian Science: A Self-Portrait from the Presidential Addresses of the British Association for the Advancement of Science,* ed. George Basalla, William Coleman, and Robert H. Kargon, 45–59. Garden City: Anchor, 1970.

Allan, J. McGrigor. "Influence of Sex on Mind: Cranial Contour." *Knowledge* 1 (November 25, 1881): 78–79.

———. "Influence of Sex on Mind III: Historical Evidence." *Knowledge* 1 (January 13, 1882): 230–31.

———. "On the Real Differences in the Minds of Men and Women." *Journal of the Anthropological Society of London* 7 (1869): cxcv–ccxix.

Allen, Grant. "Plain Words on the Woman Question." *Fortnightly Review* 52 (1889): 448–58.

———. "Woman's Place in Nature." *Forum* 7 (1889): 258–63.

Barloon, Jim. "Star-Crossed Love: The Gravity of Science in Hardy's *Two on a Tower.*" *Victorian Newsletter* 94 (fall 1998): 27–32.

Barreca, Regina, ed. *Desire and Imagination: Classic Essays in Sexuality.* New York: Meridian, 1995.

Bayley, John. "The Love Story in *Two on a Tower.*" *Thomas Hardy Annual* 1 (1982): 60–70.

Becker, Lydia E. "Is There Any Specific Distinction between Male and Female Intellect?" 1868. In *The Englishwoman's Review of Social and Industrial Questions: 1868–1869,* 483–91. New York: Garland, 1985.

———. "On the Study of Science by Women." *Contemporary Review* 10 (1869): 386–404.

Beer, Gillian. *Darwin's Plots*. London: Ark, 1985.

Birkett, Dea. *Spinsters Abroad: Victorian Lady Travelers*. Oxford: Basil Blackwell, 1989.

Blackwell, Antoinette Brown. "Comparative Mental Power Physiologically Considered." *Victoria* 28 (1870): 405–16.

———. *The Sexes throughout Nature*. New York: G. P. Putnam's Sons, 1875.

Blackwell, Elizabeth. *Essays in Medical Sociology*. 2 vols. New York: Arno, 1972.

Blind, Mathilde. *The Ascent of Man*. London: T. Fisher Unwin, 1899.

Brockway, Lucile H. *Science and Colonial Expansion: The Role of the British Royal Botanic Gardens*. New York: Academic, 1979.

Brooks, W. K. "The Condition of Women from a Zoological Point of View I." *Popular Science Monthly* 15 (1879): 145–55.

———. "The Condition of Women from a Zoological Point of View II." *Popular Science Monthly* 15 (1879): 347–56.

Burstyn, Joan N. "Education and Sex: The Medical Case against Higher Education for Women in England, 1870–1900." *Proceedings of the American Philosophical Society* 117, no. 2 (1973): 79–89.

Burton, Antoinette. *Burdens of History: British Feminists, Indian Women, and Imperial Culture, 1865–1915*. Chapel Hill: University of North Carolina Press, 1994.

Butler, Judith. "Performative Acts and Gender Constitution: An Essay in Phenomenology and Feminist Theory." In *Performing Feminisms: Feminist Critical Theory and Theatre*, ed. Sue-Ellen Case, 270–82. Baltimore: Johns Hopkins University Press, 1990.

Caird, Mona. *The Daughters of Danaus*. 1894. New York: Feminist Press, 1989.

———. "Phases of Human Development I." *Westminster Review* 141 (1894): 37–51.

———. "Phases of Human Development II." *Westminster Review* 141 (1894): 162–79.

Caldwell, Janis McLarren. *Literature and Medicine in Nineteenth-Century Britain: From Mary Shelley to George Eliot*. Cambridge: Cambridge University Press, 2004.

Campbell, Harry. *Differences in the Nervous Organisation of Man and Woman: Physiological and Pathological*. London: H. K. Lewis, 1891.

Carpenter, W. B. "Man the Interpreter of Nature." In *Victorian Science: A Self-Portrait from the Presidential Addresses of the British Association for the Advancement of Science,* ed. George Basalla, William Coleman, and Robert H. Kargon, 411–35. Garden City: Anchor, 1970.

Carter, Robert Brudenell. *On the Pathology and Treatment of Hysteria.* In *Embodied Selves: An Anthology of Psychological Texts, 1830–1890,* ed. Jenny Bourne Taylor and Sally Shuttleworth, 190–93. Oxford: Clarendon, 1998.

Chapple, J. A.V. *Science and Literature in the Nineteenth Century.* Houndmills, England: Macmillan, 1986.

Cixous, Hélène. "Sorties." In *The Newly Born Woman,* by Hélène Cixous and Catherine Clément, trans. Betsy Wing, 63–132. Minneapolis: University of Minnesota Press, 1986.

Clouston, T. S. "Female Education from a Medical Point of View." *Popular Science Monthly* 24 (1883–1884): 214–28.

Cobbe, Frances Power. "The Ethics of Zoophily: A Reply." *Contemporary Review* 68 (1895): 497–508.

———. "The Little Health of Ladies." *Contemporary Review* 31 (1878): 276–96.

———. "The Medical Profession and Its Morality." *Modern Review* 2 (1881): 296–326.

Collins, Wilkie. *Heart and Science,* ed. Steve Farmer. 1883. Peterborough, Ont.: Broadview, 1996.

———. *Jezebel's Daughter.* 1880. New York: Peter Fenelon Collier, n.d.

Conolly, John. Entry in *Cyclopaedia of Practical Medicine.* In *Embodied Selves: An Anthology of Psychological Texts, 1830–1890,* ed. Jenny Bourne Taylor and Sally Shuttleworth, 184–87. Oxford: Clarendon, 1998.

Curran, Stuart. Introduction to *The Poems of Charlotte Smith,* ed. Stuart Curran. New York: Oxford University Press, 1993.

Dale, R. W. "Constance Naden." *Contemporary Review* 59 (1891): 508–22.

Darwin, Charles. *The Autobiography of Charles Darwin, 1809–1882.* New York: Norton, 1958.

———. *The Descent of Man, and Selection in Relation to Sex.* New York: Hurst, n.d.

————. *The Expression of the Emotions in Man and Animals*. Chicago: University of Chicago Press, 1965.

Davies, Emily. *Thoughts on Some Questions Relating to Women, 1860– 1908*. Cambridge: Bowes and Bowes, 1910.

Delauney, G. "Equality and Inequality in Sex." *Popular Science Monthly* 20 (1881–1882): 184–92.

Dickens, Charles. *Bleak House*. 1853. London: Penguin, 1985.

————. *The Pickwick Papers*. 1836–1837. Harmondsworth, England: Penguin, 1985.

Dickins, Molly. "Marianne North." *Cornhill* 1031 (1962): 319–29.

Distant, W. L. "On the Mental Differences between the Sexes." *Journal of the Anthropological Institute of Great Britain and Ireland* 4 (1874): 78–87.

Doane, Janice, and Devon Hodges. "Demonic Disturbances of Sexual Identity: The Strange Case of Dr. Jekyll and Mr/s Hyde." *Novel* 23, no. 1 (1989): 63–74.

Dutta, Shanta. *Ambivalence in Hardy: A Study of His Attitude to Women*. Houndmills, England: St. Martin's, 2000.

"Earlier Recollections of Marianne North." Review of *Some Further Recollections of a Happy Life*, by Marianne North. *Nature* 48 (July 27, 1893): 291–92.

Eliot, George. *Middlemarch*. 1871–1872. London: Penguin, 1994.

Ellis, Havelock. "Thomas Hardy's Novels." *Westminster Review*, April 1883. In *The Critical Heritage*, ed. R. G. Cox, 103–32. New York: Barnes and Noble, 1970.

————. *Women and Marriage: Or, Evolution in Sex*. London: William Reeves, 1888.

Elwin, Malcolm. *Charles Reade*. New York: Russell and Russell, 1969.

Farmer, Steve. Introduction to *Heart and Science*, by Wilkie Collins. Peterborough, Ont.: Broadview, 1996.

Fawcett, Millicent Garrett. "The Education of Women of the Middle and Upper Classes." *Macmillan's* 17 (1868): 511–17.

————. "The Emancipation of Women." *Fortnightly Review* 56 (1891): 681–85.

"Female Poaching on Male Preserves." *Westminster Review* 129 (1888): 290–97.

Ferguson, Christine. "Decadence as Scientific Fulfillment." *PMLA* 117, no. 3 (2002): 465–78.

Finkelstein, David. "A Woman Hater and Women Healers: John Blackwood, Charles Reade, and the Victorian Women's Medical Movement." *Victorian Periodicals Review* 28 (1995): 330–52.

Fjagesund, Peter. "Thomas Hardy's *Two on a Tower:* The Failure of a Symbol." *Thomas Hardy Journal* 14, no. 1 (1998): 85–93.

Frawley, Maria H. *A Wider Range: Travel Writing by Women in Victorian England.* Rutherford, N.J.: Fairleigh Dickinson University Press, 1994.

Frick, Patricia. "The Fallen Angels of Wilkie Collins." *International Journal of Women's Studies* 7 (1984): 343–51.

Furst, Lilian R., ed. *Medical Progress and Social Reality: A Reader in Nineteenth-Century Medicine and Literature.* New York: State University of New York Press, 2000.

Galton, Francis. *Hereditary Genius: An Inquiry into Its Laws and Consequences.* 1869. London: Macmillan, 1914.

Gamble, Eliza Burt. *The Evolution of Woman: An Inquiry into the Dogma of Her Inferiority to Man.* New York: G. P. Putnam's Sons, 1894.

Gardener, Helen. "Sex in Brain-Weight." *Popular Science Monthly* 31 (1887): 266–67.

Garrett Anderson, Elizabeth. "Sex in Mind and Education: A Reply." *Fortnightly Review* 21 (1874): 582–94.

Gates, Barbara T. *Kindred Nature: Victorian and Edwardian Women Embrace the Living World.* Chicago: University of Chicago Press, 1998.

Gates, Barbara T., ed. *In Nature's Name: An Anthology of Women's Writing and Illustration, 1780–1930.* Chicago: University of Chicago Press, 2002.

Geddes, Patrick, and J. Arthur Thomson. *The Evolution of Sex.* New York: Charles Scribner's Sons, 1889.

Gilbert, Sandra, and Susan Gubar. *No Man's Land: The Place of the Woman Writer in the Twentieth Century.* Vol. 2: *Sexchanges.* New Haven: Yale University Press, 1989.

Gladstone, W. E. "British Poetry of the Nineteenth Century." *Speaker,* January 11, 1890, 34–35.

Grand, Sarah. *The Heavenly Twins.* 1893. Ann Arbor: University of Michigan Press, 1992.

Grosz, Elizabeth. *Volatile Bodies: Toward a Corporeal Feminism.* Bloomington: Indiana University Press, 1994.

Haggard, H. Rider. *King Solomon's Mines.* 1885. Oxford: Oxford University Press, 1991.

———. *She.* 1887. Oxford: Oxford University Press, 1991.

Hardaker, Miss M. A. "Science and the Woman Question." *Popular Science Monthly* 20 (1882): 577–84.

Hardy, Thomas. *The Return of the Native.* 1878. London: Penguin, 1999.

———. *Two on a Tower.* 1882. Oxford: Oxford University Press, 1993.

Harper, Lila Marz. *Solitary Travelers: Nineteenth-Century Women's Travel Narratives and the Scientific Vocation.* Madison, N.J.: Fairleigh Dickinson University Press, 2001.

Harrison, Frederic. "The Emancipation of Women." *Fortnightly Review* 56 (1891): 437–52.

Hemsley, W. Botting. "The Marianne North Gallery of Paintings of 'Plants and Their Homes,' Royal Gardens, Kew." *Nature,* June 15, 1882, 155–56.

Henkin, Leo J. *Darwinism in the English Novel, 1860–1910: The Impact of Evolution on Victorian Fiction.* New York: Russell and Russell, 1963.

"The Higher Education of Women." *Westminster Review* 129 (1888): 152–62.

Hughes, William R. *Constance Naden: A Memoir.* London: Bickers and Son, 1890.

Huxley, Thomas H. *Science and Education Essays.* New York: Greenwood, 1968.

Ingham, Patricia. *Thomas Hardy.* Atlantic Highlands, N.J.: Humanities Press International, 1990.

Irigaray, Luce. *The Irigaray Reader.* Ed. Margaret Whitford. Oxford: Blackwell, 1992.

———. *This Sex Which Is Not One.* Trans. Catherine Porter and Carolyn Burke. Ithaca: Cornell University Press, 1985.

James, William. *The Principles of Psychology.* 1890. 2 vols. New York: Dover, 1950.

Jekel, Pamela L. *Thomas Hardy's Heroines: A Chorus of Priorities.* Troy: Whitson, 1986.

Jex-Blake, Sophia. *Medical Women: A Thesis and a History.* 1886. New York: Source, 1970.

———. "Medical Women in Fiction." *Nineteenth Century* 33 (1893): 261–72.

———. "Sex in Education." *Examiner,* May 2, 1874, 457.

Keiller, Alexander. "What May Be the Dangers of Educational Overwork for Both Sexes. . . ." In *Free and Ennobled: Source Readings in the Development of Victorian Feminism,* ed. Carol Bauer and Lawrence Ritt, 250–52. Oxford: Pergamon, 1979.

Kendall, May. "Woman's Future." In *British Women Poets of the 19th Century,* ed. Margaret Randolph Higonnet, 508. New York: Meridian, 1996.

Kenealy, Arabella. "The Talent of Motherhood." *National Review* 16 (1890): 446–559.

Kent, Christopher. "Probability, Reality, and Sensation in the Novels of Wilkie Collins." In *Wilkie Collins to the Forefront: Some Reassessments,* ed. Nelson Smith and R. C. Terry, 53–74. New York: AMS, 1995.

Kristeva, Julia. *About Chinese Women.* In *The Kristeva Reader,* ed. Toril Moi, 138–59. New York: Columbia University Press, 1986.

———. *Powers of Horror.* Trans. Leon S. Roudiez. New York: Columbia University Press, 1982.

———. *Revolution in Poetic Language.* Trans. Margaret Waller. New York: Columbia University Press, 1984.

Lansbury, Coral. *The Old Brown Dog: Women, Workers, and Vivisection in Edwardian England.* Madison: University of Wisconsin Press, 1985.

Lavater, John Caspar. *Essays on Physiognomy.* 18th ed. Trans. Thomas Holcroft. London: Ward, Lock, n.d.

Laycock, Thomas. "A Treatise on the Nervous Diseases of Women." 1840. In *Embodied Selves: An Anthology of Psychological Texts, 1830–1890,* ed. Jenny Bourne Taylor and Sally Shuttleworth, 188–90. Oxford: Clarendon, 1998.

Lee, Vernon. "Vivisection: An Evolutionist to Evolutionists." *Contemporary Review* 41 (1882): 788–811.

Lees-Milne, Alvide. "Marianne North." *Journal of the Royal Horticultural Society* 89 (1964): 231–40.

Leighton, Angela. "Constance Naden." In *Victorian Women Poets: An Anthology,* ed. Angela Leighton and Margaret Reynolds, 558–59. Oxford: Blackwell, 1995.

Levine, George. *Darwin and the Novelists: Patterns of Science in Victorian Fiction.* Chicago: University of Chicago Press, 1991.

Linton, Eliza Lynn. "The Higher Education of Woman." *Fortnightly Review* 46 (1886): 498–510.

Lombroso, Cesare. *The Man of Genius.* London: Walter Scott, 1891.

Lonoff, Sue. *Wilkie Collins and His Victorian Readers: A Study in the Rhetoric of Authorship.* New York: AMS, 1982.

Malane, Rachel. *Sex in Mind: The Gendered Brain in Nineteenth-Century Literature and Mental Sciences.* New York: Peter Lang, 2005.

Maudsley, Henry. "Sex in Mind and in Education." *Fortnightly Review* 21 (1874): 466–83.

McKerlie, Helen. "The Lower Education of Women." *Contemporary Review* 51 (1887): 112–19.

"The Medical Woman in Fiction." *Blackwood's* 164 (1898): 94–109.

Meredith, George. *The Egoist.* 1879. Oxford: Oxford University Press, 1992.

Middleton, Dorothy. *Victorian Lady Travellers.* New York: Dutton, 1965.

Mill, John Stuart. *The Subjection of Women.* 1869. Mineola, N.Y.: Dover, 1997.

Mills, Sara. *Discourses of Difference: An Analysis of Women's Travel Writing and Colonialism.* London: Routledge, 1991.

———. "Knowledge, Gender, and Empire." In *Writing Women and Space: Colonial and Postcolonial Geographies,* ed. Alison Blunt and Gillian Rose, 29–50. New York: Guilford, 1994.

"Miss Marianne North." *Athenaeum* 3280 (September 6, 1890): 319.

Moon, Brenda E. "Marianne North's *Recollections of a Happy Life:* How They Came to Be Written and Published." *Journal of the Society for the Bibliography of Natural History* 8 (1978): 497–505.

Moore, James R. "The Erotics of Evolution: Constance Naden and Hylo-Idealism." In *One Culture: Essays in Science and Literature,* ed. George Levine, 225–57. Madison: University of Wisconsin Press, 1987.

Morgan, Susan. Introduction to *Recollections of a Happy Life,* by Marianne North. Charlottesville: University Press of Virginia, 1993.

————. *Place Matters: Gendered Geography in Victorian Women's Travel Books about Southeast Asia.* New Brunswick: Rutgers, 1996.

Mosedale, Susan Sleeth. "Science Corrupted: Victorian Biologists Consider 'The Woman Question.'" *Journal of the History of Biology* 11 (1978): 1–55.

"Mr. Wilkie Collins's New Novel." Review of *Heart and Science,* by Wilkie Collins. *Pall Mall Budget* (1883). Appendix A. *Heart and Science,* 331–33. Peterborough, Ont.: Broadview, 1996.

Murphy, Patricia. *Time Is of the Essence: Temporality, Gender, and the New Woman.* New York: State University of New York Press, 2001.

Naden, Constance. *The Complete Poetical Works of Constance Naden.* Ed. Robert Lewins. London: Bickers and Son, 1894.

"New Novels: *A Woman Hater.*" Review of *A Woman-Hater,* by Charles Reade. *Academy* 12 (July 21, 1877): 59.

"New Novels: *Heart and Science.*" Review of *Heart and Science,* by Wilkie Collins. *Academy* 23 (April 28, 1883): 289–90.

North, Marianne. *Recollections of a Happy Life.* Ed. Susan Morgan. Vol. 1. Charlottesville: University of Virginia Press, 1993.

————. *Recollections of a Happy Life.* Vol. 2. London: Macmillan, 1892.

————. *Some Further Recollections of a Happy Life.* London: Macmillan, 1893.

"Novels of the Quarter: *Heart and Science.*" Review of *Heart and Science,* by Wilkie Collins. *British Quarterly Review* 78 (1883): 231–32.

"Novels of the Week: *A Woman Hater.*" Review of *A Woman-Hater,* by Charles Reade. *Athenaeum* 2590 (June 16, 1877): 765.

"Novels of the Week: *Two on a Tower.*" Review of *Two on a Tower,* by Thomas Hardy. *Athenaeum* 2873 (November 18, 1882): 658.

O'Fallon, Kathleen. "Breaking the Laws about Ladies: Wilkie Collins' Questioning of Gender Roles." In *Wilkie Collins to the Forefront: Some Reassessments,* ed. Nelson Smith and R. C. Terry, 227–39. New York: AMS, 1995.

O'Neill, Philip. *Wilkie Collins: Women, Property, and Propriety.* Totowa: Barnes and Noble, 1988.

O'Toole, Tess. *Genealogy and Fiction in Hardy: Family Lineage and Narrative Lines.* New York: St. Martin's, 1997.

Pearson, Karl. *The Ethic of Freethought.* 2d ed. London: Adam and Charles Black, 1901.

Pike, Luke Owen. "Woman and Political Power." *Popular Science Monthly* 1 (1872): 82–94.

Pionke, Albert D. " 'A Sweet *"Quod Erat Demonstrandum!"* ' The Poetics of Parody in Constance Naden's 'Scientific Wooing.' " *CEA Magazine* (Middle Atlantic Group 2002) 15: 3–11.

Pitha, J. Jakub. "Constance Naden." *Dictionary of Literary Biography.* Vol. 199. Ed. William B. Thesing, 211–15. Detroit: Gale, 1999.

Ponsonby, Laura. *Marianne North at Kew Gardens.* London: Stationery Office, 1996.

Pratt, Mary Louise. *Imperial Eyes: Travel Writing and Transculturation.* London: Routledge, 1992.

"The President's Address." *British Medical Journal,* August 14, 1886, 338–39.

Preston, S. Tolver. "Evolution and Female Education." *Nature* 22 (1880): 485–86.

"The Probable Retrogression of Women." *Saturday Review,* July 1, 1871, 10–11.

Quilter, Harry. Review of *Two on a Tower,* by Thomas Hardy. *Spectator,* February 3, 1883. In *The Critical Heritage,* ed. R. G. Cox, 101–3. New York: Barnes and Noble, 1970.

Reade, Charles. *Hard Cash.* 1863. London: Collins, n.d.

———. *Put Yourself in His Place.* 1870. New York: Colonial, n.d.

———. *A Terrible Temptation.* 1871. New York: Colonial, n.d.

———. *A Woman-Hater.* 1877. New York: P. F. Collier and Son, n.d.

Reierstad, Keith. "Innocent Indecency: The Questionable Heroines of Wilkie Collins' Sensation Novels." *Victorians Institute Journal* 9 (1980): 57–69.

Review of *Heart and Science,* by Wilkie Collins. *Athenaeum,* April 28, 1883. In *Wilkie Collins: The Critical Heritage,* ed. Norman Page, 214–15. London: Routledge and Kegan Paul, 1974.

Review of *Jezebel's Daughter,* by Wilkie Collins. *Spectator,* May 15, 1880. In *Wilkie Collins: The Critical Heritage,* ed. Norman Page, 207–10. London: Routledge and Kegan Paul, 1974.

Review of *Recollections of a Happy Life,* by Marianne North. *Athenaeum* 3357 (February 27, 1892): 269–70.

Review of *Some Further Recollections of a Happy Life,* by Marianne North. *Athenaeum* 3425 (June 17, 1893): 755–56.

Review of *Two on a Tower*, by Thomas Hardy. *Saturday Review* 54 (November 18, 1882): 674–75.

Richardson, Benjamin Ward. "Woman's Work in Creation." *Longman's* 8 (1886): 604–19.

"The Rights of Woman." *Blackwood's* 92 (1862): 183–201.

Ritchie, David G. *Darwinism and Politics.* London: Swan Sonnenschein, 1889.

Romanes, George J. "Mental Differences between Men and Women." *Nineteenth Century* 21 (1887): 654–72.

Rowold, Katharina, ed. *Gender and Science: Late Nineteenth-Century Debates on the Female Mind and Body.* Bristol: Thoemmes, 1996.

Russett, Cynthia Eagle. *Sexual Science: The Victorian Construction of Womanhood.* Cambridge: Harvard University Press, 1989.

Schiebinger, Londa. *The Mind Has No Sex? Women in the Origins of Modern Science.* Cambridge: Harvard University Press, 1989.

Schweik, Robert. "The Influence of Religion, Science, and Philosophy on Hardy's Writings." In *The Cambridge Companion to Thomas Hardy,* ed. Dale Kramer, 54–72. Cambridge: Cambridge University Press, 1999.

"Sex in Education." *Saturday Review* 37 (1874): 584–86.

"Sex in Mind and Education: A Commentary." *Blackwood's* 115 (1874): 736–49.

Sheffield, Suzanne Le-May. *Revealing New Worlds: Three Victorian Women Naturalists.* London: Routledge, 2001.

Showalter, Elaine. *Sexual Anarchy: Gender and Culture at the Fin de Siècle.* New York: Viking, 1990.

Shteir, Ann B. *Cultivating Women, Cultivating Science.* Baltimore: Johns Hopkins University Press, 1996.

Simcox, Edith. "The Capacity of Woman." *Nineteenth Century* 22 (1887): 391–402.

"Some Personal and Press Opinions on the Works of Constance Naden" (Watts and Co.). In *The Complete Poetical Works of Constance Naden,* ed. Robert Lewins. London: Bickers and Son, 1894.

Smith, Elton E. *Charles Reade.* Boston: Twayne, 1976.

Sparks, Tabitha. "Surgical Injury and Narrative Cure in Wilkie Collins's *Poor Miss Finch* and *Heart and Science.*" *Journal of Narrative Theory* 32, no. 1 (2002): 1–31.

Spencer, Herbert. *The Principles of Psychology.* New York: D. Appleton, 1895.

———. *The Principles of Sociology.* New York: D. Appleton, 1896.

———. "Psychology of the Sexes." *Popular Science Monthly* 4 (1873–1874): 30–38.

Stevenson, Catherine Barnes. *Victorian Women Travel Writers in Africa.* Boston: Twayne, 1982.

Strobel, Margaret. *European Women and the Second British Empire.* Bloomington: Indiana University Press, 1991.

Sumner, Rosemary. "The Experimental and the Absurd in *Two on a Tower.*" *Thomas Hardy Annual* 1 (1982): 71–81.

Swenson, Kristine. *Medical Women and Victorian Fiction.* Columbia: University of Missouri Press, 2005.

Sylvia, Richard D. "Hardy's Feminism: Apollonian Myth and *Two on a Tower.*" *Thomas Hardy Journal* 12, no. 2 (1996): 48–59.

Taylor, Jenny Bourne. *In the Secret Theatre of Home: Wilkie Collins, Sensation Narrative, and Nineteenth-Century Psychology.* London: Routledge, 1988.

Taylor, Jenny Bourne, and Sally Shuttleworth, eds. *Embodied Selves: An Anthology of Psychological Texts, 1830–1890.* Oxford: Clarendon, 1998.

Taylor, Richard H. *The Neglected Hardy: Thomas Hardy's Lesser Novels.* London: Macmillan, 1982.

Thain, Marion. " 'Scientific Wooing': Constance Naden's Marriage of Science and Poetry." *Victorian Poetry* 41, no. 1 (2003): 151–69.

"Theories and Practice of Modern Fiction." Review of *Heart and Science,* by Wilkie Collins. *Fortnightly Review* 40 (1883): 880.

Tilden, William A. "Part III." In William R. Hughes, *Constance Naden: A Memoir,* 67–70. London: Bickers and Son, 1890.

"The Travels of a Painter of Flowers." Review of *Recollections of a Happy Life,* by Marianne North. *Nature* 45 (April 28, 1892): 602–3.

Wallington, Emma. "The Physical and Intellectual Capacities of Woman Equal to Those of Man," followed by "Discussion." *Anthropologia* 1 (1874): 552–65.

Ward, Lester F. "Our Better Halves." *Forum* 6 (November 1888): 266–75.

Wells, Susan. *Out of the Dead House: Nineteenth-Century Women Physicians and the Writing of Medicine.* Madison: University of Wisconsin Press, 2001.

Wiesenthal, C. S. "From Charcot to Plato: The History of Hysteria in *Heart and Science.*" In *Wilkie Collins to the Forefront: Some Reassessments,* ed. Nelson Smith and R. C. Terry, 257–68. New York: AMS, 1995.

Wilson, Robert. "Aesculapia Victrix." *Fortnightly Review* 45 (1886): 18–33.

"A Woman-Hater." Review of *A Woman-Hater,* by Charles Reade. *Saturday Review* 44 (July 14, 1877): 50–51.

"Women and Science." *Spectator* 82 (March 25, 1899): 409–10.

Index

James, William, 24, 26
Jane Eyre (C. Brontë), 5
Jekel, Pamela L., 93*n*12
Jex-Blake, Sophia, 32, 178, 179–80, 194, 195–96, 199–200
Jezebel's Daughter (Collins), 136–39
Jude the Obscure (Hardy), 218

Keiller, Alexander, 35
Kendall, May, 45, 216
Kenealy, Arabella, 39
Kent, Christopher, 119*n*10
Kew Gardens, 141, 157, 158, 161
Kingsley, Mary, 161
King Solomon's Mines (Haggard), 217
Kristeva, Julia, 8, 46–47, 72–73, 176–77, 217*n*5

Lamarck, Jean Baptiste, 206, 209, 210
Lansbury, Coral, 123
Lapworth, Charles, 42–43
Lavater, John Caspar, 192
Laycock, Thomas, 133
Lee, Vernon, 122
Lees-Milne, Alvide, 141*n*2
Leighton, Angela, 45
Levine, George, 5
Lewins, Robert, 42
Linton, Eliza Lynn, 36
Lombroso, Cesare, 28
Lonoff, Sue, 125*n*17
Lyell, Charles, 162

Madness, 5, 133–36, 138–39
Malane, Rachel, 10*n*10, 81*n*7, 91*n*11, 101*n*16, 110*n*6, 113*n*8, 129*n*19, 133*n*22, 219*n*10
Mary Barton (Gaskell), 5
Maudsley, Henry, 13, 20, 21, 27, 29–31, 32, 33
McKerlie, Helen, 39
Mental abilities of women, 10, 36, 41, 42, 45, 48, 60, 63, 65, 66, 69, 71, 111, 130–31, 164, 182, 186, 188, 189, 190, 212, 214; compared to children's, 3, 13, 21, 25, 55, 70, 125–26, 127; compared to "lower" races, 3, 21, 24, 25; compared to men's, 3, 10, 11–32, 36, 37, 38, 48,

56, 61, 62, 64, 130–31, 186, 190, 212, 214, 218; environment vs. biology, 18–20, 29, 186. *See also* Development, arrest of; Women, inferiority of
Middlemarch (Eliot), 5, 6
Middleton, Dorothy, 151
Mill, John Stuart, 18, 20, 29
Mills, Sara, 144, 148, 161*n*26, 171*n*36
Mimicry, 46, 60, 65, 71, 79, 108, 147
Moon, Brenda E., 141*n*2, 149*n*14
Moore, James R., 42*n*1
Morgan, Susan, 144, 145, 156*n*22, 157*n*23, 164, 166, 167, 168, 171*n*36
Mosedale, Susan Sleeth, 10*n*10

Naden, Constance, 8, 41, 216; others' perceptions of, 42–43; scientific background of, 42–43
—works: "Evolutional Erotics," 47, 52, 57, 60, 61, 62; "The Lady Doctor," 66–69; "Lament of the Cork-Cell," 44*n*4; "Love *versus* Learning," 62–65; "Natural Selection," 52–55, 65; "The New Orthodoxy," 57–62; "Poet and Botanist," 61; "Scientific Wooing," 47–52, 54, 55, 63, 64, 68; "Solomon Redivivus," 55–57, 65; "The Story of Clarice," 69–71
Natural selection, 52–55, 182–83
Nervous systems, 20–21, 133, 208
Nightingale, Florence, 195–96
North, Marianne: education of, 147; family of, 141, 146. *See also Recollections of a Happy Life*

O'Fallon, Kathleen, 110*n*5
O'Neill, Philip, 125*n*17
O'Toole, Tess, 94*n*13

Pair of Blue Eyes, A (Hardy), 6
Pearson, Karl, 38
Perception. *See* Intuition and perception
Performance, 91–92, 114, 148, 177
Physician: flawed male, 6, 107, 108, 119–24, 129–30, 131, 132–33, 196–98, 200; as male ideal, 129–32, 197–98; as profession for women,

9–10, 33, 66–69, 176, 178, 179–80, 188–201, 208, 210, 211–12, 213
Physiognomy, 85, 192–93
Pickwick Papers, The (Dickens), 4, 108
Pike, Luke Owen, 11, 17, 26
Pionke, Albert D., 49n9
Pitha, J. Jakub, 45
Ponsonby, Laura, 152, 158
Pratt, Mary Louise, 143, 166, 167
Preston, S. Tolver, 37

Reade, Charles. *See A Woman-Hater*
Recollections of a Happy Life (North): construction of artist in, 149–60, 169; construction of scientist in, 160–68, 169; gardens in, 155–58; paintings described in, 152–55; race and otherness in, 145–46, 164–69; reviews of, 141–42, 149; separation from womanhood in, 168–75; and Victorian travel writing, 142–49, 165, 169, 171; work in, 149–51, 155–56, 157, 158, 159
Reierstad, Keith, 137
Reproduction, 6, 15, 16, 26–27, 37, 38, 66. *See also* Development, arrest of
Return of the Native, The (Hardy), 215–16
Richardson, Benjamin Ward, 36, 38–40
Ritchie, David G., 19, 56
Robinson, Mary, 45, 216
Romanes, George J., 12, 20, 22, 23–24
Rowold, Katharina, 4n3, 30n44
Russett, Cynthia Eagle, 10n10, 21

Schiebinger, Londa, 155
Schweik, Robert, 96
Sexual selection, 6, 7, 26, 50, 53–54
She (Haggard), 78n6, 217
Sheffield, Suzanne Le-May, 151n15, 152n16, 153, 164n34
Showalter, Elaine, 218n9
Shteir, Ann B., 162–63, 168n34
Shuttleworth, Sally, 4n3
Simcox, Edith, 19
Skey, F. C., 134
Smith, Charlotte, 44
Smith, Elton, 210n22, 203n23
Somerville, Mary, 81

Sparks, Tabitha, 113n8
Spencer, Herbert, 15, 20, 23, 26, 34–35, 42, 57, 66, 164
Stevenson, Catherine Barnes, 143, 148, 149
Strange Case of Dr. Jekyll and Mr. Hyde, The (Stevenson), 217, 218
Strobel, Margaret, 171n36
Sumner, Rosemary, 93n12
Swenson, Kristine, 178n3, 197n16, 201n22, 203n23, 207n24, 208, 218n8
Sylvia, Richard D., 93n12, 101n16, 102, 103n18
Symonds, Catherine, 141, 149

Tancred (Disraeli), 5
Taylor, Jenny Bourne, 4n3, 118, 137
Taylor, Richard H., 96n15
Tennyson, Alfred, 7
Tess of the D'Urbervilles (Hardy), 217–18
Thain, Marion, 45n5
Thomson, J. Arthur, 12, 23, 26
Travel writing, 142–49, 165, 169, 171
Trollope, Anthony, 5
Two on a Tower (Hardy), 9, 106; blurring of gendered boundaries in, 72–73, 79–80, 81, 93–105; emotionality vs. rationality in, 78, 81–83, 85; female menace to science in, 74–75, 81, 87–93, 104–5; gendered imagery in, 76–80, 85–86, 88, 92, 93, 97–100, 102, 104–5; personal vs. public interests in, 80–86, 88; reviews of, 73; sexuality in, 78, 81, 87, 92, 93, 100, 102

Unsexing, 38–39, 66, 68, 119, 201–6, 208

Vivisection, 115, 120, 121–24, 132
Vogt, Carl, 21

Wallace, Alfred Russel, 160
Wallington, Emma, 17, 19
Ward, Lester F., 30
Water Babies (C. Kingsley), 5
Wells, Susan, 178n3
Wiesenthal, C. S., 129, 129n19, 131, 133n22